COCAINE

COCAINE

White Gold Rush in Peru

Edmundo Morales

The University of Arizona Press / Tucson

The University of Arizona Press

Copyright © 1989
The Arizona Board of Regents
All Rights Reserved

This book was set in 10/13 Linotron 202 Galliard.
∞ This book is printed on acid-free, archival-quality paper.
Manufactured in the United States of America.
97 95 93 91 90   5 4 3 2 1
Library of Congress Cataloging-in-Publication Data

Morales, Edmundo, 1943–
Cocaine : white gold rush in Peru / Edmundo Morales.
p.   cm.
Bibliography: p.
Includes index.
ISBN 0-8165-1066-0 (alk. paper)
1. Cocaine industry–Peru.
2. Narcotics, Control of–United States.
I. Title.
HV5840.P46M67   1990   88-30303
363.4'5'0985–dc19   CIP

British Library Cataloguing in Publication data are available.

To my sons
Angel and Edmundo, Jr.

There are terrible people who, instead of solving a problem,
bungle it and make it more difficult for all who come after.
Whoever can't hit the nail on the head should, please, not hit at all.

Friedrich Nietzsche

Contents

Acknowledgments

By the nature of this work, I was dependent upon a great many people who assisted me in the different stages of this study. There were those who interested me in a set of problems and allowed themselves to be studied, oriented me towards appropriate concepts and methods, took their time and imagination to challenge and constructively to criticize my ideas, provided funding, assisted in the data collection, and finally made suggestions on the presentation of the data. The result of this rather complex and long experience and interaction is a piece of research bearing only my name, which could not have been accomplished without the generosity of many. Unfortunately, I can only mention a few of many obligations I incurred during the research and the writing periods of this book.

I owe my deepest appreciation to Frances F. Harris for her continued editorial assistance. In the long and tedious writing stage, Fran's role was crucial. She spent numerous hours clipping my drafts and helping me reorganize my concepts. Fran also shared the excitement and the frustration of the review period. In that sense and in this society, Fran is a rare kind of person to find. No word can describe my friendship with Fran and her family. The least I can say here is that this is also Fran's book.

I would like also to acknowledge my debts to several distinguished scholars, especially Eric R. Wolf for honoring me with his friendship and William Kornblum for providing continuous advice and assistance during and after my graduate training and for standing by his graduates in an upstream battle. I have also benefitted greatly from the knowledgeable and objective comments of Ray Henkel of Arizona State University and from Peter White of *National Geographic*.

Although my research was not tied to any funding source, I am thankful to Bruce D. Johnson, director of the Behavioral Sciences Training in Drug Abuse Research, and to Douglas S. Lipton, director of Research for Narcotic and Drug Research, Inc., for giving me the opportunity to gain more experience in drug research.

My friends and colleagues Mary Cuadrado, Abu Abdul-Quader, Gregory Falkin, Douglas Goldsmith, Bruce Stepherson, Mitchell Kaplan, and Harry Sanabria critiqued and cheered my project. Herman Joseph of the New York State Division of Substance Abuse Services (DSAS) and Charles D. Kaplan of Erasmus University at Rotterdam, Holland, helped me expose the results of my research at international conferences and professional meetings. Ken Robertson, Praimattie Singh, Charles Hwang, and Andrea Kale graciously and disinterestedly contributed their knowledge of computer software.

Other professionals and people also contributed to this work with their own personal expertise. To Peter J. Harris, Wayne Geist, and Emily Stroh go my thanks for their friendship, advice, and patience during my stay at CUNY Graduate School, and to Barbara Trapido my gratitude for drawing the map of Peru. In Peru, Dalmacio Rodríguez, Circución Pari, Lucio Prieto, Julio Segura, the late Laveriano Segura, Carlos Ponce, Ignacio Cervantes, Esther León, Gregorio Calixto, Rubén Chavez, Mercedes Cruz, Amadeo Julca, Eleuterio Mauricio, Edwin Arevalo, Julio Carbajal, Corsino Lescano, Esther de Flores, Catalina de Amuy, my fellow peasants in Paras, and many of my relatives made my stay an enjoyable and invaluable learning experience. My friends, acquaintances, and many other subjects who asked me not to mention their names in the book let me unveil their everyday plights and convey their message to the world; the essence of their message is not distorted, only rephrased. Last but not least, my thanks go to the two most important persons in my life: to my wife Norma for her moral and material support during my graduate studies, and to my mother, Felícitas Bayona. I also wish to thank my brother Edinson Quijano for his dedicated attentions during my numerous field trips to Peru.

Because of the critical analysis of a complex and political subject such as cocaine presented in this work, some of my friends and colleagues will probably take pride in my position, while others whose livelihood may reside in the status quo of drug research will desert me. It is my responsibility to accept either reaction. Needless to say, accountability for the contents of this book rests exclusively on my shoulders.

Note on Equivalents

Unit	U.S. Equivalent
1 hectare	2.47 acres
1 kilometer	0.62 mile
1 kilogram	2.2 pounds
1 arroba	25 pounds

At the time of initial research in 1981, U.S. $1 was worth 500 soles; at the time this book was written, $1 was worth 10,000 soles. In 1985 the Peruvian government changed the national currency from soles to intis. Each inti is worth 1,000 soles.

Introduction

Often known as "white gold," cocaine and its derivatives have become the drugs of the 1980s. In Peru the new cocaine economy has displaced the old Andean coca trade. Much of what passes for information about the vast illegal industry is distorted, if not false. The governments of the United States and Peru have not taken into account the realities of this huge underground economy in their efforts to eradicate coca production. As a result they have failed to solve the international drug problem, and they will continue to fail until the objectives in cocaine control are defined in an entirely new way.

Bolivia, Colombia, and Peru are the source of 95 percent of the cocaine smuggled into the United States.[1] While in industrial societies cocaine is a social evil, in the Andes of Peru, coca and cocaine preparation and traffic are part of the traditional ecological exchange as well as an important source of cash. The infiltration of an underground economy into the indigenous people's lifestyle has brought about a new type of economic dependence. Unlike the indirect relationship created by formal economic ties between Third World countries and the international metropolis, the cash/commodity/labor relationship in cocaine trafficking is direct. The illegal circulation of "coca dollars" supports local economies, feeds inflation, and causes changes—such as cocaine smoking—in the social behavior of the indigenous.

Tingo María, like the other small towns of the Upper Huallaga valley, deep in the humid, mountainous jungles of eastern Peru, is an easy place to buy small appliances. Unlike stores in the rest of the country, the shops in the Upper Huallaga also sell watches, fifths of Scotch, and imported jeans and canned food for about the same prices paid in New

York City. The Upper Huallaga, in fact, is the only area on the eastern slopes of the Andes where some small towns boast car dealerships. Showrooms for Nissan, Honda, and Toyota stand alongside one another. An old, barefoot Indian man walked into one of the showrooms recently, carrying a large sack on his back. He looked around a moment, spotted a little blue pickup, and asked the price. The dealer named a sum, the equivalent (in 1980) in Peruvian soles of about U.S. $10,000. Fine, the old man said. He would take it. He opened his sack, took out a heap of crumpled bills and counted out the money. The dealer handed him the keys, and the sale was over. The heavily forested Upper Huallaga is awash in cocaine money.

Though most finished cocaine comes from Colombia, more than half of the coca paste that feeds the factories there comes from the vast jungle slopes shared by Bolivia and Peru. Peru alone produces a total of about 170,000 metric tons of coca every year, enough to make 400 metric tons of cocaine hydrochloride.[2] Coca farming is nothing new. Andeans have chewed coca leaves from the jungles for centuries to raise their spirits and ward off hunger and fatigue.[3] It was only in the last twenty years, as cocaine became the drug of choice among the young and comfortable of western Europe and the United States, that coca farming went from a cultural artifact to the best-paying industry in Peru. International organized crime came to the jungle, adapting the traditional culture of coca to its own purposes, and creating an underground economy of unemployed migrants, peasants, officials, and criminals that now reaches from the jungle throughout the rest of the country, contributing to a culture of shakedowns, payoffs, and cynicism.

Most crops raised on the mountain slopes require a great deal of care and money. The nutrient-poor soil of the jungle must be continually fertilized and seeds must be purchased (often every year, since many food crops are grown from hybrid seeds whose plants do not produce seeds of their own). Coca, by contrast, is a hardy shrub that requires only a small investment. Having evolved to grow in jungle conditions, it needs little or no fertilizer; because the plant is plentiful, its seeds are easily obtained. Once a coca field is planted, it will yield four to five crops a year for thirty to forty years, needing little in return but seasonal weeding.

For centuries, coca has been cultivated in the jungle slopes and transported up to the mountain highlands, where the leaves are chewed with a bit of powdered lime or ash. Archaeologists have found evidence from as early as 1800 B.C. that the inhabitants of villages on the Peruvian coast were chewing coca leaves grown in the rain forests.[4] Sculpture from several different periods in Indian history depict men with the tell-tale bulge in their cheeks. The Spanish conquistadors, with their propensity for exploitation, recognized that coca chewing increased the vigor and morale of Indian workers in the mines while lowering their appetites, so they did nothing to discourage chewing.[5]

That economy persists to this day. In the highlands of Peru, the caravan of burros bearing coca from the jungle, to be bartered for corn, potatoes, or meat, is still a common sight. In modern times, the Peruvian government, recognizing the cultural significance of coca chewing for the highland populations, has permitted the plant's cultivation and has used a separate bureau, the Estanco de la Coca, now Empresa Nacional de la Coca, to supervise the trade.

Change first came to this ancient social system in the 1950s, when the Peruvian government initiated a program to encourage migration from the overcrowded coastal cities to the scarcely peopled forests along the eastern slopes of the Andes. Most of the colonization took place in the province of Leoncio Prado, of which Tingo María, located in the heart of the coca belt at 1,250 meters above sea level, is the capital.[6] The government-sponsored plantations of tea, coffee, and tobacco did not yield anything close to the returns that the new colonists expected, so they quickly turned their lands to the traditional and easy crop—coca. It was a good time to cultivate the plant. The boom in cocaine use had begun in industrialized countries, so growing numbers of cocaine-processing hideouts in the forests stood ready to absorb the increased production of coca. The town of Tingo María soon became a mecca of unrefined cocaine (coca paste) traffic, and nearby towns emerged as strategic locations for turning the leaves into the paste that results from the chemical extraction of their alkaloids. An ancient social system for the exchange of labor and food, based on the trade of coca, has been infiltrated and altered by the international underworld, who now use the peasants' traditions of coca raising as agents of production and trafficking. In the same day that an unskilled laborer in the capital earns about $1, a peasant carting a bale of dried coca leaves, the lowest-paid worker in the underground industry, can easily earn about $3 plus meals and drinks. It is hardly surprising that migrants began making the trek to the jungle from the highlands of the Andes and from the coastal cities. Indeed, the population density of the Peruvian jungle has grown from one person per square kilometer in 1961 to ten people per square kilometer in 1981.[7] The prosperity of the region creates expectations that cannot be met by any other more modest source of income. Like cocaine itself, the money of the jungle is addictive.

The ongoing struggle in the jungle is between the Peruvian government and the U.S.-sponsored international agencies that want to restrict coca production—the people's main economic activity—and those who have made that activity a smoothly running subsidiary of international organized crime. The conflicts between the authorities and organized crime determine the social structure in which hundreds of thousands of Peruvians, who have come to the jungle simply to make a decent wage, must live.

The underground network is a rigid hierarchy. At the top of the pyramid is the boss of the operation, who is its link to international organizations. He is always known as a *colocho*—a nickname used in the jungle to denote a Colombian but which, in the cocaine subculture, simply means someone associated with the processing and trafficking that are centered in Colombia.[8] (Some colochos are Mexicans, some Cubans, and some Central Americans.) The outside boss will generally supervise several local gangs scattered throughout the jungle; to those who live in the jungle, the boss is a shadowy figure, known only by his code name. Other groups structured around their participation in the illicit economy are the pick-up men; local bosses, or patrones; runners, or collectors of coca paste; and the local and interstate burros or mules. From the big boss to the delivery men, the members of this hierarchy live by a code of loyalty, silence, and quick punishment for those who do not cooperate.

Of course, not everyone who makes his way to the jungle goes with the intent of signing up for the underworld. Many of the jobs created by the cocaine industry are perfectly legal. Indeed, the cocaine boom benefits every sector of the national economy, not to mention Japanese car manufacturers and Scotch whiskey distillers. But the ones who benefit the most economically from the cocaine trade are those charged with fighting it, which grossly distorts their social function as enforcers of the law and agents of control. The various forces of social control, linked to local and national middle-class groups, monitor the roads and routes of traffic, and so have the most opportunities to find drugs and to make deals with those carrying them.

Peru's five agencies of control are the Guardia Civil (the regular police); the Guardia Republicana del Peru (GRP), or the National Guard; the Policía de Investigaciones del Perú (PIP), the Peruvian equivalent of the U.S. Federal Bureau of Investigation; the Unidad Movil de Patrullaje Rural (UMOPAR), the agency charged exclusively with controlling the coca trade in the mountainous forests; and the Sinchis, a special antisubversive unit that combats the Maoist Shining Path guerrillas (the name derives from Sinchi, a legendary Inca warrior from the days before the Spanish conquest).

The five enforcement agencies, each of which has responsibility for particular aspects of the broad problem, do not coordinate their actions, which causes endless confusion and inefficiency. Police control posts make routine checks of all passengers entering the jungle on *colectivos*, the minibuses that are the area's only mode of public transportation. One or two agents will board a colectivo, ask passengers for their national identity cards, and search their bags. On a bus leaving the jungle, they will often look at the hands of all the peasants and young men, looking for sulphuric acid burns as evidence of their having worked in the coca pits. If they find burns, they search the suspect thoroughly, looking for the money he must have earned. Though the peasants are the most common victims of this shakedown, anybody carrying money or valuables is a suspect of cocaine trafficking or currency violations. When the police want to take in more sizeable sums than are available in the shakedowns, they follow petty traffickers until they have enough evidence to arrest them.

The "white gold rush" is so pervasive that bribes and payoffs are the rule rather than the exception. Everyone in the system tries to make the most of everyone else's situation, and it is always safest to assume the worst about the other party. In the general environment of crime, there is little room for doubt. It is those who have nothing to pay who bear the brunt of police actions. There is no doubt that hundreds of peasants are manufacturing and distributing cocaine. But the majority of the hundreds of thousands of people working in the jungle are mere wage earners. They are the scapegoats of the system, comprising the vast majority of the arrest statistics collected in Lima and cited as evidence of national progress against the cocaine trade.

The United States sponsors two types of programs to eliminate cocaine production by eradicating the coca leaf, but these are no more successful than Peruvian law enforcement efforts. In 1981, the U.S. Agency for International Development (AID) and the Peruvian government launched a five-year program aimed at encouraging the farmers of the prime coca-growing area, Upper Huallaga, to replace their coca with rice, cacao, corn, palm trees, and other crops, or with cattle. The Peruvian government supplied $8.5 million for the project; AID provided $15 million in loans and $3 million in grants. The program's headquarters are in a town where the production of both coca and cocaine is heavy. Here peasants spend day after day waiting in line to apply for short-term loans whose annual interest rate, thanks to Peru's economic troubles, is 106 percent. One of the many requirements for such a loan is signing an affidavit clearly stating that the loan money will never, under any circumstances, be used to plant coca. Certainly, many of those who have obtained the money will plant palm trees or raise cattle as a front for their coca growing, but only the easily raised, abundant four to five crops a year of coca bring enough money to support life and pay back the loan.

The other program for eliminating cocaine production centers on destroying the crop itself. This project is financed by the U.S. State Department's Bureau of International Narcotics Matters, which also sponsors enforcement efforts. The program, Reduction and Control of Coca Planting in the Upper Huallaga (known by its Spanish acronym CORAH) began in May 1983. Its central office is in Tingo María, and it employs three professionals, a clerical staff, and 780 "pullers," who, theoretically, tear out some forty to fifty hectares of coca a day. Those farmers who have a license to plant coca from the Peruvian Ministry of

Agriculture are paid for the loss of their plants at the rate of $300 for every hectare uprooted. Those who have planted it illegally are neither notified nor compensated. Working as a "puller" is not the safest way to earn a living in Peru. Though UMOPAR protects the pullers while they work, hordes of armed peasants have been known to attack CORAH projects.

Historically, coca growing has been an important, if not a predominant, economic activity in Peru. Regardless of the legal status or social effects of coca growing, it is a way of surviving to which hundreds of thousands of poor, landless, and unemployed people have turned. To them, it is simply the industry with the most opportunities, no different from the country's fishing boom of the early 1960s or the gold and silver mines of the Spanish Empire. In the 1980s the jungle holds the brightest attractions. Participating in the cocaine economy is the goal of the great majority of people in the Andes. Compared to the cash yields of the coca and cocaine industries, the millions invested in eradication programs is minimal. More importantly, the programs do not address the fundamental problem: What economic force will replace coca? Without a plan for alternative economic development, coca will continue to thrive, and the forces of both government authority and the criminal underworld will keep on exploiting the farmers and cocaine entrepreneurs for their own gain.

The purpose of this study is to suggest alternative means of making a living for impoverished populations that currently support the cocaine black market as a means of supporting themselves. This study analyzes the social, cultural, economic, and political meaning of the cocaine industry.

The Appendix discusses the methodological aspect of ethnographic research in drug production. The issues of the validity of the researcher's covert and overt roles and infiltrating the underground world are addressed.[9] Chapter One provides a brief description of the people and the traditional use of the coca leaf. "The Frontier" provides statistics on the physical setting, land areas, migration and the demographics of coca agriculture. It examines and criticizes social and economic policies, as well as international aid geared to economic development that led to an irrational land distribution in the forests. Failure of land reform to satisfy the material needs of highland populations is seen as a major factor contributing to the emergence of the current underground industry.

"Coca Culture and Economy" deals with the historical and ecological interchange between the highland peoples and coca-leaf-producing areas and discusses migration, coca agriculture, and the beginnings of the black-market economy supported by Indians and peasants. Though the agricultural economic base remains dependent on nature and established methods of cultivation and harvest, the traditional need for coca and the modern need for cash induces the people to supply coca growers and cocaine producers with necessary labor.

The final three chapters deal specifically with production, distribution, control, and eradication of coca and cocaine. "The Cocaine Economy" documents the process of making coca paste (extraction of alkaloid cocaine from the coca leaves) and cocaine hydrochloride from the smuggling of chemicals to the manufacturing of cocaine. Proportions and amounts of materials, including coca leaves, are provided, as well as accurate calculations of production costs of high-quality cocaine. The study reveals the social structure involved in the production and distribution of cocaine, often using original, firsthand accounts.

The efforts to control production of coca and drug traffic have brought into the scene the direct participation of the United States. "Politics of Control and Eradication" evaluates the role of foreign aid and political pressure vis-á-vis the internal resistance and group interests in the national society. Investment in coca-leaf eradication is minimal and ineffective. High interest rates and bureaucratic red tape to be dealt with in distributing money provided through foreign aid force coca-leaf farmers to turn to illegal loans and aids.

Discussion of the subject should not be limited to ethnographic accounts of the processes, but must critically explore the social and political implications of the international underground economy in Peru. A concluding chapter, based on the findings of the study, deals with national and international policy implications. The latter are analyzed critically in relation to economic development, migration spurred by the lack of opportunities in the countryside, and the function of the United States in drug control and reduction (not eradication), as well as in foreign-aid policy.

Andeans, Coca Leaf, and Tradition

In writing about Peru, terms such as "Indian" and "peasant" are categories for the country's inhabitants that have been widely accepted in academic circles, as well as in the lay world, often with the assumption that "Indian" is the native of the Andes. The peasant is conceived of as the rustic or the rural countryman whose function within a larger social system is to produce rent for a dominant group of rulers.[1] Thus, all Andean indigenous populations are lumped into a generic category of Peruvian Indians. However, Indians can be defined as groups of native people related by common descent and ethnic characteristics. A Peruvian Indian would then be the ethnic stock that has more or less maintained physical traits and social, religious, and linguistic traditions transmitted from older generations. In this sense, there are no pure Indians in Peru. In fact, most "Indians" are mestizos absorbed by the Andean traditional culture.

Mestizo is a Spanish word for miscegenation between the native American (Indio) and persons of Spanish descent. Today, the definition of mestizo is much more complex than it was four centuries ago. The native people have mixed with almost every race, religion, and nationality that came to Latin America: Blacks, Asians, Arabs, Jews, Italians, Anglo-Saxons, and so forth. The mestizo is the Latin American who is the result of the combination of different ethnic groups bearing Spanish values, which can be divided into Andean mestizos and coastal mestizos. The majority of Andean mestizos still keep some kind of language identity with their past cultures, whereas the mestizos from the coast identify themselves more with the Spanish culture than with Peruvian native culture.

Andean people are mixtures of mestizos and Europeans who have adapted to traditional life. The term Indian has been used as an umbrella category to designate rural populations, especially of the highlands. New terms such as *cholo, serrano, campesino* are used to describe the highland people. *Cholo* and *serrano* are generally adjectival pejorative terms ascribed to rural people by urban mestizos and Europeans.

> Throughout the past century and a half in Peru, people have said "Indian" when they meant "rural proletariat." They said "mestizo" when they meant the small farmer, the artisan, the industrial laborer, or the member of other low-income groups not attached to the land.[2]

Up until 1864 the baptismal certificates divided the inhabitants of Peru, especially in the highlands, into two clearly defined groups: *casta* and *indio*, the former meaning "of Spanish descent" and the latter, "aboriginal of the Andes." On the left margin (for census and tax purposes), as well as in the text of the baptismal registration, the priest made a notation of the ethnic origin of each child christened.

As a surviving social structure of the Inca empire, Peru is made up of traditional communities, whose social organization, in many ways, still defies the influence of the modern Western world. The traditional community presents three clear characteristics: agrarian, social, and economic. From the agrarian point of view, the traditional community is an indissoluble unit where man is an agent of both continuity and change. Socially, the community has governmental and legislative systems based on free election of its individual members or *comuneros* and on a rigorous scheme of norms and sanctions imposed by tradition. From an economic standpoint, Indian communities are indivisible work units with socialist and collectivist characteristics, that is, units whose members have equal access to communal property.[3]

During the time of the Inca empire, and probably during the colonial period, the Indian community was also a biosocial and economic entity bound together by land, tradition, and customs, and made up of families with ties of common descent and land. In the contemporary

The definitions of Indian and mestizo are based more on the degree of the Andean people's exposure to Western culture than to any substantive ethnic differences.

community, as a result of migration and of violence imposed upon the aboriginal culture, blood relationship has disappeared. Community is no longer based on kinship ties. Once the consanguinity (*ayllu*) disappeared, the ancient society became simply a social and economic institution structured around the use of common land. The ayllu was a social institution of organized groups of extended families within a defined territory (*marca*) with endogenous and patrilocal features.[4]

Up until the late sixties, traditional communities in the countryside fell under the generic name of Indian communities. The military government redefined peasant communities as "communities that before land reform, in June 1969 constituted Indian communities." Thus the new communities consist of juridical individuals with private rights established in national civil codes; they are not comparable to associations, companies, or foundations, for they are not mere legal organizations. Rather, "they consist of individuals whose organizations are based on the ayllu and are recognized in Peruvian as well as some other countries' national legislations."[5]

Although some highland groups still show ethnic and cultural characteristics that link most of the Andean populations to the past *Tahuantinsuyo*, both the tribal and the traditional native communities that existed formerly as political and social organizations have now practically disappeared in Peru. Extermination of the Indian community may have been due to external political factors which were critical for the existence and support of new ethnic and social groups, namely, the colonial social system in which land became a market commodity and the dispossessed Indian was appended to the colonial estate.[6]

Castro Pozo argues that, of all the changes in the traditional society, the household and the extended family are the social elements which have conceded most to European civilization.[7] Nonetheless, during the last two decades, transformation of the Andean society and culture at large is more evident, and its western direction is inevitable. These changes may be the result of conscious and unconscious policies of land distribution and population control in the country at large. The most recent land policy reform was put forth by the military revolutionary government in 1968. However, the reform that was designed to create equal distribution of land further impoverished the peasantry due to topographic variations, low temperature, drought, especially on the western Andes, lack of capital investment and technical support, and marketing obstacles.[8] The highland agricultural frontier did not work, causing Indian and peasant populations to search for other sources of subsistence.

The publicized land reform may seem to present the countryside as homogeneous groups of peasants with equal access to land resources. Yet, in reality, Peruvian peasants are grouped in gradations based on unequal distribution of land, creating conflict and polarity in communities. To undertake an analysis of the situation of highland peasants, it is necessary briefly to survey the categories that existed in feudal times as a basis of comparison with the social changes of the last two decades, that is, the role the peasant has played in the feudal (*hacienda*) system, his relationship to the land, and his new material needs.

In the highlands, as well as in the rest of the nation's countryside, the feudal social system was based on land distribution. Social organization was more or less the same throughout Peru. All feudal class and status denominations fell under the generic category of *yanaconaje*. *Yanacunas* were subjects who served noblemen and government officials. The Spanish maintained the term on the coast and gave a variety of names to the highland populations that fell under this category.[9]

The feudal society in the countryside was divided into four categories: the tenant farmer, or *locatario*, and his family; the subtenant; the *pampero* (field laborer); and the *agregado* (adjunct to the subtenant). The tenant farmer leased the hacienda from the landowner for a fixed number of years. He lived in the administrative quarters (*casa hacienda*) with his family and his staff. The tenant's lifestyle was patterned after the standards of the city or town from which he came. Maintenance of the tenant's household was left to the peasants and their families who were bound in servitude on the estate. The tenant was respected and feared. The peasant always addressed the tenant humbly, calling him *Papa* (master) rather than by his name. The tenant had power to act as the supreme judge; his decisions could not be appealed. Defiance or disobedience led to misfortune and punishment. He could whip the guilty and mediate in family problems. Some elderly peasants give accounts of punishments that caused death.

The subtenant was the peasant who subleased land from the tenant farmer. The right to lease the land passed from generation to generation. Upon the death of the father, it was the eldest son's duty to register his name as the new head of the family. He would pay a yearly rent to the tenant farmer. As part of the contract established by tradition, the subtenant had to work a number of days during each event in the agricultural cycle.[10] Every adult male from the subtenant's household had to report to the fields as part of the labor force.

The pampero was a person granted the usufruct of land by the tenant farmer towards whom he and his family contracted a number of labor obligations similar to the bondage that existed in the colonial period. The pampero paid rent for land he held with his labor.[11] Because of his full-year labor attachment to the hacienda, oftentimes the pampero could not till his own land. He had to earn his livelihood working for the subtenant who paid him in kind. Other adult members of the pampero's family performed menial work at the casa hacienda for one week every year (*pongo*) and in some cases whenever requested. Furthermore, the pampero's children were also required to serve in the hacienda quarters when requested to do so by the tenant farmer. Unmarried girls were assigned to housekeeping positions (*mita*) or to serve hacienda employees. Since most pampero families produced limited crops, the various kinds of services furnished to the hacienda provided a needed source of food.

The agregado was a family who was part of the extended household of the subtenant. The agregado included two different groups: the subtenant's married children and some families who had migrated to the hacienda from other communities. The latter group lived in a state of complete vassalage and had three labor obligations. First, the tenant farmer counted them as part of the subtenant's labor force; second, the tenant farmer imposed upon them a direct labor tribute for living on the property of the hacienda; and third, they had a labor debt to their immediate lord, the subtenant, for the rest of their lives. The social structure as well as the division of labor in the family and between the groups, though under different names, have remained about the same. Changes in the modern world, albeit significant, are not substantive in nature.

Each member in the household is assigned a specific task according to sex and age. Children and the elderly usually help in the preparation of food, collection of wood for fuel, herding household animals, and so forth. Women and children also take part in agricultural work: sowing seeds behind the plow, weeding, and the work of harvesting some crops such as *quinua* (*Chenopodium quinua*, a grain), broad beans, legumes, and so forth, which is done almost exclusively by them. They also are involved in other, though limited, work within the community, such as temporary and seasonal labor in some neighboring areas. During the Inca period, labor was organized by importance. Land reserved to the Inti (Sun God) was worked first. Next, communal labor was done on the land of the handicapped, the widows, and the elderly. Individual plots were tilled only after work on the land of those who could not keep their land productive themselves was finished. The last collective labor, which was carried out as a festive event, was on Inca land. At such times, the Indians wore their best dresses ornamented with feathers and gold and silver jewelry. They composed and sang praises to their lords with special music because they were working on land reserved for their god and their king.[12]

Today, the Andean people practice four different types of labor: *rantín* (traditional labor exchange), festive labor, in-kind payment, and wage labor. *Rantín*, or mutual aid labor, may come from *rantikuy*, which in Quechua means "to buy." Rantín could be translated as the purchase or exchange of the labor of two entities (humans or animals) of comparable strength. The process of mutual exchange of labor is called *rantinpanakuy*, an oral agreement or contract binding two individuals to one type of labor. This ends only when the party who benefited first performs the same kind of work for the labor creditor. Rantín is a social bond that links peasants of the same stratum, and a manifestation of good relations with friends, relatives, and neighbors. In some instances, the labor debt can be paid with a different type of work than that originally agreed upon, if requested by the creditor, but it may be paid only in labor. However, a rantín agreement using animal labor can be broken without creating any conflict between undersigners.

When animal labor is exchanged, the owner can request payment in comparable strength, in kind, or in cash. Some animal labor could also be exchanged for human labor. This type of labor exchange is more evident in the town mestizo-peasant relationship. The indigene always has some spiritual and social ties to local middle-class people such as the traditional *compadrazgo* (coparenthood). The countryman's labor spent in the mestizo's work set could be returned in two ways. The mestizo may help the peasant in some minor bureaucratic procedures, or he may pay his labor debt with the labor of his servants or his animals. Probably the most interesting form of traditional labor in the Andes is *faena*. Faena is a work festival that has been practiced in the Andes for many centuries. Under the Inca rule, there were different labor tributes which the Indians had to perform in the fields that were dedicated to the gods, as well as in the government fields. The latter had to be tilled before the familial and communal land.[13] This collective labor was called *minka*. After the conquest, the Catholic church also adopted this labor practice. The church demanded a religious labor tribute on land reserved for its maintenance. This labor practice was imposed as late as the 1960s. Currently, faena as a traditional social custom still remains in the form of free labor service from one individual to another, performed in exchange for food, drink, coca, and music. Under different names, faena is practiced to benefit larger groups such as the community. In Ayacucho, south central Peru, for example, the peasants use this kind of collective labor, which is called *yarqa aspiy*, to clean communal irrigation canals.[14]

When communal work is to be performed, the *varayoq*, or traditional political authority, is responsible for scheduling and notifying the rest of the population. The varayoq goes to a section in the community from which he can call out his fellow peasants. As the community requires mostly male labor, the announcer urges every male adult to show up to work with his own, appropriate tool at a date and place set by the leader. In towns and small populations with no traditional leadership, it is the mayor's obligation to carry out the details of the collective work. Announcements are made by means of loud speakers, written notices, and house-to-house personal visits.

In agriculture, faena is free, voluntary group labor for the benefit of one person, the host. The sponsor of the festival plans the event many weeks before the actual day of faena. He prepares *chicha*, a traditional beverage made out of germinated corn (*jora*). He also buys alcohol, coca, and cigarettes. After contracting the *maestro* (musician), who will act as foreman or supervisor for the day, the sponsor spreads word of the upcoming festival in the community. When the day of work arrives, many volunteers show up early in the morning, bringing with them their own tools. A *cajero* (musician) plays his drum and his flute, inviting more volunteers. *Yahuapa*, a heavy breakfast generally consisting of two courses, is served. Yahuapa in faena usually consists of *uman caldo*, soup made of the head and tripe of lamb, and *llushtu pichu*, unhusked corn or wheat stewed with dried pork or fresh lamb meat. Chicha and coca follow the yahuapa. The volunteers chew the coca leaves for about half an hour before they go to the field.

As the musician starts beating his drum and playing his *pincullo* (flute), everyone goes out to the field to start the faena. During work, the musician stops playing in order to give his workers brief breaks, to which the owner never objects. Coca, chicha, and alcohol are given out either at the workers' request or at the owner's will. Provision of these treats is far more important than the food itself. Failure to satisfy the volunteers with their favorite pastimes and foods would create discontent and unfavorable conditions for future recruitment. The host slaughters at least two sheep and unhusks about two arrobas of corn or wheat to feed approximately fifteen volunteers. The total cost of a decent faena is about $30, an expense affordable only by peasants who are well-off. Thus, if recruitment were motivated by wages, the cost would fall to less than one-third the cost of the faena, but not many laborers would volunteer.

At the end of the day, the owner and his helpers dance, waving their tools around the land if the faena is in plowing or weeding, and around the threshing floor if the faena is to collect the wheat crop. The last round of the dance is done with the owner on the shoulders of one of the helpers. Supper (*merienda*) is then served. The musician's wife always attends supper, and it is the host's obligation to provide food for her. When night comes, everyone, including the musician, drinks and chews coca at the faena sponsor's expense.

Festive labor, as a psychological predisposition for the exploitation of the peasantry in the Andes, did not end with the land reform of 1969. In the 1980s, it was still practiced in some cooperatives that were organized by the military government in the 1970s. In the cooperatives, festive labor is called to benefit the state-controlled organization. Such exploitation totally contradicts the aim of land reform laws synthesized in the slogan: "Peasant, from now on, you will not nourish the landlord with your work." Large landowners in the highlands also gain from

Peruvian Andeans still use an age-old harvesting technique. Here wheat is separated from chaff by running pack animals for many hours.

this unique labor supply. While for the indigenous peasant faena is a status symbol, for the landed it is a source of cheap mass labor. The landed rich usually buy coca wholesale and, in most cases, make their own alcohol (*aguardiente*) from sugar cane. Some landowners are old established families and the rest of the population around their land, at some point in time, probably were serfs. The Indian and the peasant's historical tie is still manifested in free labor supply to the dominant class.

Besides the labor described above, there is in the highland communities work paid in kind—that is, the laborer may choose to be paid in crops and other goods in an exchange of labor. One day's work is paid with one *selmin* (half an arroba) of grain or one *jacu* (approximately 10 kilos) of potatoes. Considering the current market price for crops paid as wages, and depending on the quality of crops, labor paid in kind can become far more expensive than wages paid in money. Ten kilos of potatoes are equivalent to about $1.00, and 5.75 kilos of wheat are worth about $.75. But a peasant supplies labor only based on the knowledge that he will be paid in kind, and the owner's need for labor makes him meet the conditions set by both tradition and circumstances. The fact that peasants sell their labor for food points to the shortage of food supply among the poor. Land size, quality of soil, and lack of appropriate technology do not match the needs of the increasing population. Exchange of labor for crops is also applied to specialized labor, such as weaving and construction work.

Although there is not an active cash economy in most isolated Andean villages, money is still needed to buy some commodities supplied from the outside, commodities that the local *bodegueros* (small shopkeepers) will not exchange for grains. If there is nothing to sell in the market or the traveling merchants do not bring commodities wanted in the villages, the only source of cash is wages earned working on small private landholdings and in neighboring communities and towns. Peasants travel as long as one day looking for jobs. Some haciendas, because of their own year-round supply of water and good soil, produce two crops each year. Hacienda owners exploit their land with wage and collective festive labor and recruit workers from surrounding areas.

Peasants and Indians work in the neighboring towns and haciendas for local minimum wages of about twenty-five cents per day plus lunch and drinks. If a worker comes from a distant community, breakfast generally consisting of *mazamorra* (a kind of pap) or egg-drop soup is also served by the employer. Wages vary, depending on the supply and demand of labor and food. Employers prefer to pay in wages, whereas the peasants would rather be paid in kind. Some peasants also have to work in order to supplement feed for their cattle and sheep that graze on the property of neighboring *hacendados* (landholders).[15]

Another type of work is a combination of exchange, wage, and communal labor. This kind of labor is, theoretically, oriented to benefit the indigenous people living in the highlands of Peru. Work for food (*trabajo-alimento*) is actually a modernization program where labor is paid for with food donated by Catholic relief services such as the Cooperative for American Relief Everywhere (CARE) and other charitable organizations. Caritas is the national nonprofit entity which distributes the donations of food to churches, communities, schools, and so forth. The formal procedure necessary to obtain surplus food sent from the United States, Australia, and some European countries is the presentation of a project which would benefit large populations. Construction of roads, schools, hospitals, or medical posts, and so forth, constitute funding priorities.

After evaluating each project presented, Caritas sends food provisions until the project is finished, which may take many months, or even years. The food given to the peasant is a full payment for piecework labor not exceeding five days. For the sixteen kilos of food received, the contracted person is assigned a specific task calculated to take five days, but generally, the workers either help one another or work longer hours to complete their assignments before the expected date. The work-for-food modernization programs are making the rural and urban poor more and more dependent on international food relief. Obviously, when the projects are completed the stock of food supply to pay for modernization programs is used up. As agriculture is neglected, some dependent peasants must migrate to obtain more food. Most, if not all, work-for-food programs support cosmetic development projects (discussed in chapter 5), such as health and education infrastructures, rather than agricultural development projects.[16]

In theory, the social feudal system bequeathed from the colonial period has disappeared. After the land reform of 1969, social terms such as "pampero," "agregado," "tenant farmer," and "hacendado" have experienced spurious changes. Peasants and Indians whose lives were conditioned by the feudal system of land distribution are more impoverished than ever before. The mass of poor rural populations has become wage seekers, servants, and migrant agricultural workers. As many ex-feudal subjects argue, "In the old system at least food was secure." Although the landed class controlled the Indian's fate and the system did not grant the serfs the freedom of choice, the landless and the poor peasants knew that hunger would knock on their doors only if they were not willing to accept their social inheritance: hard labor.

As described in the preceding sections, the traditional culture is still characterized as follows: 1) technology/ecology is used to facilitate both human adaptation and production and reproduction of resources; 2) in the social organization of labor, the extended family, the hamlet, the village, and the community are the units of production; 3) reciprocal economic obligations function along blood and land-use bonds; 4)

0/2/2 9653

codes and conventions define Andean behavior and its relation to nature.[17] One universal ingredient that is present in all of the foregoing is the use of the coca leaf.

Coca Chewing: Tradition or Social Control

This section discusses the implications of coca chewing as a natural, social practice and its possible use as a social normative artifice imposed on the Andean society; that is, before becoming a widespread social habit, coca chewing may have been encouraged as another method for controlling the populace that Western culture used to gain precedence in the New World. I do not intend, however, to touch on the medical and biological aspect of coca chewing.

In general, as a characterization of the Andean world view, coca chewing is essentially identified with work situations, rituals, and religious practices. Almost every average male Indian, peasant or rustic mestizo in the highlands of the Andes chews approximately one ounce of coca per day. The day laborer (*peón*) and the muleteer (*arriero*), and the construction contractor purchase the amount of coca required to complete their work for the day. The coca leaves may be carried by hand or stashed in plastic bags, in cloth or hide pouches (*cuca pikshas*),[18] or, at times, just in the pockets. The *ishku puru* or *poporo* (Colombia) is made out of a small dry gourd, and it is used to keep the lime or the *llipta* and is part of a man's apparel.[19] The *caleador* is generally a small piece of wire used to add lime to the coca quid in the mouth.

As a rule, at the outset of the day the peasant sits at the workplace and samples his first chewing. A handful of coca leaves is taken from the pouch or pocket. When the rations of coca are handed to the worker or the travel companion, the proper way to receive the leaves is with both palms, on the poncho or any material placed on the lap. The expert chewer puts the leaves either on one or both palms, depending ón the amount of coca available for one chewing.

The leaves bought from stores are always mashed and crumbled because of the shipping methods and storage conditions. The leaves are delicately separated and the stems discarded. Before actually taking the leaves into the mouth, the coca chewer places the leaves on his palms,

Peruvians have been chewing coca for almost 4,000 years. A Chavin stone nailhead (above) and a Mochica statue (right) represent coca chewers from the highlands and the coast respectively.

puts his two hands together, resting the fingers of one hand on the fingers of the other, and makes a slot between the two thumbs. The slot formed by the two thumbs is put to the mouth; this is what they call *pukuy* (to blow or breathe). Actually, this step of the ritual involves a supplication, a prayer to God, to the patron saint, or to the ancestors, rather than to coca itself. The words are mumbled through the slot and as close as possible to the leaves in such a way that only the chewer knows the words he is uttering.

The dry coca leaves are chewed briefly to help drench them with saliva and then the quid is placed in the mouth between the gums and the interior wall of either side of the face. *Ishku* (lime) or llipta is added to the chewing by inserting the caleador in the wet leaves without touching the gums or the teeth. When the quid is in its final position in the mouth, depending on each chewer's taste, more lime or llipta may be added to the quid. The use of ishku or llipta is the most decisive stage in the coca-chewing habit.[20] The green alkaloid fluid is swallowed until the quid runs out of alkaloids. More coca leaves and lime can then be added to the quid. Every renewal of the coca quid involves going through all the rituals and complying with the etiquette prescribed by tradition.

The wage laborer, the peón, and the muleteer take as many breaks at the workplace, in the field, or during long trips as are required to relieve the body of fatigue. Although the actual chewing seems to be the same, both the first chewing and renewal of the coca quid are done for different reasons, depending on the type of labor or the occasion. Thus, for example, when the peasant wants to work long hours, he mumbles to his coca by saying, "Mama coca, use your powers to tie up the sun and make a long day." Long hours, however, refer more to intense labor than to the length of time spent in the workplace. Daylight in the highlands is short, so work usually stops by sunset (at about 6:00 P.M., if not earlier).

In the Andes coca is considered to be the medium between man and the supernatural, as well as the expression and maintenance of social relations.[21] Because of its virtues and powers, Andeans have given mythological or religious explanations for the origins of the plant.

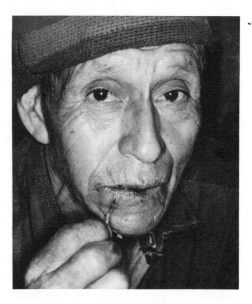

Peasants in the highlands of Peru chew coca as a pastime or to ward off hunger and thirst.

For example, in the northeast, where the Incas came after Europeans had already settled in some parts of America, there is a legend that the coca plant sprang from the grave of a beautiful Indian woman who had been dismembered and buried in punishment for prostitution.[22] Nancy Lois Richards reports that in some parts of Cuzco the belief is that the Virgin Mary chewed coca to quench her thirst in the desert when fleeing to Egypt.[23] The latter is a clear indication of the merger between native beliefs and the Catholic faith in the Andes.

The invading culture, through its official religion, may have fabricated many beliefs about coca to facilitate its use as a mechanism of social control. No scientific evidence exists to prove that the Incas considered coca to be a sacred leaf. The Quechua term "mama" does not mean god or sacred. Rather, the Indian and the peasant apply the word "mama" to any object or being they consider to be of value to them. "Mama" may mean beautiful, beloved, or useful. The alleged fact that the Incas worshiped the sun and called the moon "Mama Killa or Quilla" should not be enough reason to argue that "mama coca" has ever had a sacred meaning in the Andean culture.

In the colonial era, Latin Americans of European extraction hated the natives, but there was no prolonged bloody warfare as that experienced by the North American natives in the seventeenth century. Thus the colonial chroniclers, as well as early historians, were all of Spanish origin and may have had a biased view in recording their accounts. In addition to their social bias, they may not have fully understood the rapidly changing society. While their texts are invaluable today, the colonial documents probably do not reflect the true picture of a period totally dominated by religion and Aristotelian philosophy. The recorders may have written down only government success stories, rather than objective facts.

The accidental discovery of America was economically motivated. Implementation of policies benefitted the conquerors exclusively, and their aim was to support the most unproductive and lavish kingdoms of Europe. The Catholic church played an important role in the emergence of the Spanish empire. Catechizing the new American subjects obviously meant adjusting the church to the culture of the majority; coca may have been instrumental in this historic pursuit. Despite the fact that the use of coca and the attendant idolatry were considered at odds to the tenets of the new official and universal religion, subtle and deceptive manipulations of both native and European beliefs proved much more powerful weapons than the gunpowder that had been brought to America for the purpose of conquering the natives. The use of coca by the Indians in devotion to idols was appended to traditional Catholic belief. Should the conquerors have fully enforced eradication of coca and extirpation of idolatries, they would have been true proselytizers of Catholicism. But the Spanish Catholics lacked the radical concept of life and religion common among the Puritans.

One of the biggest changes wrought by Spanish colonization may have involved the fusion of the Catholic faith with the native belief systems. However, the Spaniards did not face the same political difficulties that the Incas had faced in subduing the tribes dispersed along the central and the eastern Andes, especially the *Antis*. To the conquistadors, for example, coca was not an issue but a weapon to be used to dominate and exploit the Indian; the Incas, on the other hand, reserved the use of coca for the nobility and may have feuded over the status and use of coca with other groups who may have looked at coca leaves in other ways. The Spaniards maximized the cultural use and stimulant effects of coca in Potosí and other mines in the Andes.[24] Moreover, the Catholic church tolerated the habit of coca chewing during religious celebrations, and still does among traditional populations.

In the central Andes of Peru, especially in some communities in the department of Junín, there is a religious ceremonial folkloric practice called the *toril*. On the eve of the patron saint's day, the person who holds the ceremonial office hosts the community either in his house, in a public building, or in a rented salon. Refreshments, liquor, food, music, and coca leaves are provided by the religious official in charge of the festivities. Coca leaves and llipta are placed on a long table. The guests come to the ceremonial table as many times as they want coca leaves or llipta to keep their quids active.

Direct taxes to sustain the Catholic church, such as *diezmo* and *primicia*, were imposed upon Indian populations in addition to the forced labor in the mines.[25] To use Karl Marx's concept of religion as a vehicle of mass alienation, one may conclude that the Andean Indian was drugged using his own tenets. The Latin American version of the Virgin Mary was imposed as the model of the ideal woman and as the symbol of chastity. The use of patron saints narrowed the Indian's mind, thus limiting his ability to reason and compare his situation. The cuca piksha and ishku puru were adopted as part of the patron saint's attire to ease the collection of tribute. The patron saint, draped in his field attire, was presented in procession around the church's field during agricultural labor performed in the fields that were dedicated to the church or the local parish. Some priests provided the peasants with coca, while others just gave the church's classic blessing.

The coca leaf also has a dominant role in the equilibrium or biological homeostasis in the Andes of Peru. Concepts of good health, illness, and death are always tied to the traditional use of the coca leaf. The cause for a disruption in the body's harmony is usually attributed to supernatural forces. Loss of health has two initial manifestations: *alé* (cold) and *aché* (hot). Thus, excessive exposure of the body to heat or cold, or intake of food classified as warm or cold, are the major causes of sickness. The advent of these natural external forces is avoided or controlled. The first attempts to restore health are always limited to the use of medicine available in the natural ecology.

No health service exists locally in the villages, and if it did there would be resistance to accepting modern medical help available in distant centers. Diagnosis, prognosis, and treatment, therefore, are in the exclusive province of traditional doctors and witches. If recovery of health with the traditional medical help available in the household is not achieved, the patient is normally taken to a general practitioner who is a folk doctor (*entendido*) or, in some extreme cases, to the closest specialist. Then, if the patient's condition does not improve, consultation with a shaman or a witch is necessary.

The coca leaf is always the medium in traditional medicine. Before giving medicine to the ill, folk doctors and witches chew coca or have someone chew it for them to avoid error in the diagnosis of the illness and treatment of the patient. Coca's supernatural powers may tell the provider not to make his or her ordinary diagnosis of the illness, but to treat the patient with other more sophisticated methods, such as the guinea pig x-ray method* or the Tuesday or Friday midnight witchcraft session. Many times errors in diagnosing the illness or using wrong methods of treatment can cause further complications for the patient. I was a witness to such a circumstance concerning a young mother-to-be named Juanita.

Juanita was chosen for marriage at the age of twelve, and she had her first child before she was thirteen. She agreed to my photographing her labor and delivery. Since I needed additional film, adequate for the photographic session, I left the village for three days. When I came back, she had already delivered a baby girl and was suffering from the pain of not being able to deliver her placenta (*madres*). The local folk doctor's (*curandera*) prescription was to chop the young tips of *hierba santa* and make a beverage to give to Juanita. To make sure that her prescription was correct, the curandera had another peasant chew coca. The coca chewer's prediction was emphatic: "It will work."

I asked everyone to let me talk to the girl in private. My diagnosis was a simple gas colic, but to avoid confrontation with the local medical know-how, I pretended to go along with the group's decision. I asked them to let me give Juanita a simple analgesic or aspirin (although I actually gave her two anti-gas tablets) and waited for about forty-five minutes before giving Juanita the beverage. I made Juanita change her bed position every five minutes. Soon the gas colic was over and Juanita was relieved. In light of my success, I asked them to put off their prescription until the next morning, arguing that the administration of two different medicines might have a negative effect. The patient delivered her placenta at midnight and they asked me to pick the name for the baby girl; Juanita was saved.[26] Obviously, this isolated case did not affect their faith in the traditional health practice.

Another clear illustration of the traditional use of the coca leaf is the *pago* practice in the southeast Andes, especially in Cuzco. *Pago* consists of offerings of food presented to the *Pacha Mama* (Mother Earth).

---

*This folk medicine practice involves rubbing a live guinea pig over a patient's body either to diagnose illness or to draw it from the patient's body into the guinea pig, after which the organs of the pig are examined and the diagnosis completed or a cure pronounced.

Among others, some of the contents of the pago are dried pig and llama fetus, quinua, store-bought crackers, chocolates, and candies. Pagos are available at the traditional health stands. The pago package's contents do not include coca leaves. In 1987, the smallest pago package sold for about $.90, and the larger size for about $1.80. The pago could be conceived of as both tribute to nature in the form of thanksgiving and as a ceremonial religious medium between man and the superpower, whatever that may be. Pago may also be offerings given to the spirits of the ancestors or to the memory of the community's forefathers.[27]

When used in traditional medicine, the pago is supplied along with coca leaves to the folk doctor by the patient himself or his relative. In addition to the pago and the coca leaves, a personal gift is presented to the curandero. The gift offered, usually translated as *cariño*, at times may be an in-kind payment for the curandero's services. Patients usually find out their folk doctor's personal tastes. Alcohol, wine, brandy, and cigarettes are the most commonly preferred gifts.

In the summer of 1987, I visited a traditional curandero who allegedly had been seen by the American actress Shirley MacLaine. Don Benito is one of the many gifted traditional curanderos (*altomisayoc*) in the town of Huasao, Cuzco, who uses coca leaves in his curing sessions. The setting where Don Benito works is a typical one-room house attached to an extended-family housing cluster. His treatments are long and tedious and in some cases may require several sessions.

The coca leaves brought by the patient or the patient's relative are placed on a piece of cloth on the floor or on a rustic table. A fistful of leaves is separated for its use in diagnosing the illness, after which the altomisayoc selects the leaves he rates adequate for the traditional medical ceremony. Only the best leaves are used in the healing sessions. The curandero picks the intact leaves one by one and places them in piles of three leaves each. The piles of three undamaged leaves are called *kintus*. The number of kintus is limited by the quality of the coca leaves. The curandero, the patient, the assistant, and anyone participating in the healing session are expected to chew coca, drink alcohol or wine, and smoke cigarettes. A description of one case will illustrate the relationship between the altomisayoc and the patient.

A native couple of Cuzco with an average education had relocated in Puerto Maldonado, a town in the southern Amazon lowlands, for purposes of employment (the husband was a government employee). The couple had made many fruitless visits to specialists in Lima with their six-year-old son. Since medical science was unable to treat the child's problem, the parents placed their final hope in a means of cure in which they had never before believed. They chose Don Benito of Huasao as their curandero. The child's speech problems were diagnosed as being caused by *viento*, or cold wind. The father's reaction to Don Benito's diagnosis was that he, indeed, used to take his son for late afternoon motorcycle rides for which he was now sorry. The father felt angry at himself for having wasted money and time seeing speech specialists in Lima. The child was brought to Don Benito at about 7:30 in the morning and the visit lasted almost all day.

Only someone who believes in traditional medicine is allowed in the room. If the patient is a minor, the nearest relative or guardian may sit in for the patient in the traditional doctor's "treatment room." Once the leaves are arranged in kintus, the assistant, or the person representing the patient, bunches the patient's clothes, giving them the shape of a human body. Invocations and prayers in Quechua are mumbled. Then, the pago package and the kintu piles are burned by placing them on wood charcoal. The patient's clothes are exposed to the smoke by holding them over the burning pago and the kintus. Both the folk doctor and the patient expect that wearing the smoked clothes will restore good health. The child's speech problems, diagnosed as having been caused by cold wind (*frío*), are expected to disappear.

Here the question is not whether the coca kintus will actually cure the child's speech problems; here the important thing is the role of coca in the social, cultural, and traditional belief system of average Andean people. In actual fact, as revealed in conversations held with the father of the child, the speech difficulties which the youngster was experiencing could be attributed to the sudden change of environment and the socialization with non-Quechua-speaking children that conflicted with the child's mother tongue.

Witchcraft (*brujería*) and divination rely heavily on the use of coca. The practice of witchery is limited to certain individuals who are thought to have special psychic powers. Witches (*brujos/as*) can discover

Don Benito of Huasao, a *curandero,* known for his *pago* practice in Cuzco. His patients range from local peasants to middle-class professionals.

hidden secrets, cure the ill, and even cast spells that can cause death. Divination, on the other hand, is a gift that every good coca chewer earns through experience. This is not to say that witches do not practice divination, but that witches are consulted, or their services hired, only in extreme cases. Generally, in either case, the consulting person or the patient supplies his or her own coca leaves. Divination practiced by non-witch coca chewers may best be described as "knowledgeable expert advice."

Frequently, peasants appeal to good coca chewers for revelation when they are not sure of their decisions, when they have particular doubts, or when they want to prevent unexpected surprises. The client takes his or her coca to the chewer and asks him: "Please chew these coca leaves for me."[28] Divination chewing differs from the customary chewing ritual in that the first attempt of divination occurs before actually chewing the leaves. After mumbling the plea, the chewer examines the shapes and patterns that the leaves form on his palms. In chewing the leaves, every now and then he pulls the fibrous tissue of the leaf (veins) from his mouth and reconfirms his first prediction. The veins of the leaf may take the form of a cross (death or illness), or other forms which interpreted mean an infidelity, loss of a lawsuit, and so forth. Sometimes, in the middle of the chewing, the chewer says that the quid is tasting too bitter, this as a means of alerting the client to the bad news.

In addition to diagnosing, treating, and fortune-telling through coca, witches can cast spells and reverse or undo other witches' spells. In the belief that curses cause social and biological disequilibrium, people run to brujos for help. Coca tells the witch exactly where the ritual object representing the victim is buried or concealed.[29] At times, when police investigations of systematic burglaries are unsuccessful, peasants appeal to their brujos. For instance, when a village patron saint's jewelry disappeared mysteriously, the priest of a nearby town suggested that the villagers consider the recovery of the sacred jewelry by using the services of a witch.

Finally, in everyday life coca is used to mediate between man and the environment, and to appease the anger of the spirits of the ancestors living in the hills and mountains. To the peasant, the spirits of the ancient (*ahuilus*) protect the fauna and the flora. Before gathering timber for fuel or hunting deer, *vizcacha* (Lepus viscacia, a kind of rabbit), wild guinea pigs, or wild ducks, coca is offered to the ahuilus, or *apus*. This is what in some areas is called ahuilu, or *apu shogay*. The shogay consists of placing coca leaves in caves or rocks in exchange for food. The peasant chewer generally offers his quid, whereas the nonchewer gives the leaves along with cigarettes or sugar.

The social, ideological, historical, and political embedment of coca in Andean culture and society has not been explored, nor have the consequences of eradication been considered. It may not be too farfetched to state that coca is as Andean as apple pie is American. The link between coca and human life in the Andes must be taken into account when analyzing the coca-cocaine question.

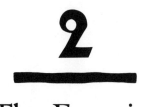

The Frontier

If one has never traveled in Peru before,
the first experience is exciting and unique;
and even those who know it
will never cease to find fascinating surprises
in its infinite diversity.

Fernando Belaúnde Terry (1965:131)

When the Spanish conquered the Incas in 1532, they found a divided empire. The empire was in downfall. The two sons of Huayna Capac, Huascar and Atahualpa, were disputing the throne. Atahualpa, imprisoned by Pizarro, suggested paying for his ransom with as much gold as the room in which he was imprisoned would hold. But this gold and silver did not satisfy the ambition of the conquerors. Atahualpa was executed in Cajamarca in August 1533.[1] The conquerors found Peru, then named Tahuantinsuyo, a country rich in silver and gold. Later, as a colony, Peru became primarily a mining possession.[2] Potosí (now in Bolivia) was the largest mining city.

Exploitation of the mines was done exclusively with forced labor imposed upon the native populations. There are historical indications that by 1548 Peru (Tahuantinsuyo) had about 8,285,000 inhabitants. The census of the Viceroyalty of Peru in 1561 established the number of Peruvians at 1,076,122.[3] The almost 90 percent decrease in the population was probably due to the forced labor and diseases brought to America from the Old World. Mining of silver and gold facilitated the rise of another source of wealth: agriculture and marketing of the coca leaf.

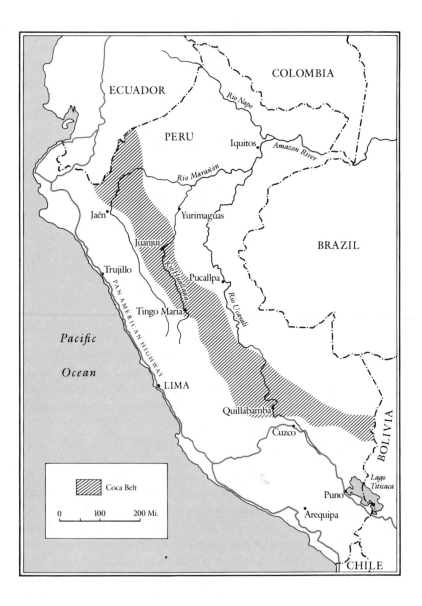

In the towering Andean highlands the Spanish colonizers were unable to exploit the environment as they did on the coast. They seized only the most productive land in the Andean valleys such as Vilcanota, Andahuaylas, Cajamarca, and Jauja and the "balconies to the *Jatún Yunka*" (the rain forests) such as Huánuco and Chachapoyas.[4] The latter were, and still are, pivotal in the exploitation of both the mountainous forests and the Amazon lowlands.

Before the demise of the Inca Empire, coca cultivation and usage had been limited to the nobility and a group of the privileged subjects dedicated to the service of the gods. However, it is uncertain whether the Incas controlled production and use of the shrub, took the economy and the habit from other conquered tribes, or used the leaf as a social control and status yardstick. The Huayna Capac Inca dominated some Arawakan (Antis) tribes near the rain forests of the eastern Andes as late as 1500; the Conchucos and the Huacrachucos were two ethnic groups who organized themselves into two large confederations to defend their territories from Inca invasion. After six months of fierce resistance, the Conchucos and the Huacrachucos surrendered and became part of the vast Empire.[5] Furthermore, the Conchucos and Huacrachucos most likely were part of the millenarian Chavín civilization that existed thousands of years before the emergence of the Incas as a powerful group in Peru. The jaguar and the snake from the jungles were worshipped in the Chavín civilization. It is also likely that the coca plant was also widely used by Chavín peoples.

To the Spanish, the practice of the neo-Aristotelian philosophy of European racial superiority, openly formulated by Juan Gines de Sepúlveda, may have been a political justification for their plunder of the millions of Indians. Thus, besides wealth collected from taxes imposed on the Indians and the mines exploited throughout the possession, the soil of the colonial territory was also perfect for the cultivation of the coca leaf, another source of wealth to the Spanish, the Creoles, and the rising mestizos.

Coca was so valuable in Peru in the years 1548, 1549, and 1551 that there has never been in the whole world a plant or root or any growing thing that bears and yields every year as coca does, aside from spices, which are a different thing, that are so highly valued.

In those years the *repartimientos*, that is to say, most of those of Cuzco, the city of La Plata [Bolivia], brought in an income of eighty thousand pesos, and sixty thousand, and forty thousand, and twenty thousand, some more, some less, all from coca. Anyone holding an *encomienda* of Indians considered his main crop the number of baskets of coca he gathered. This coca was taken to be sold at the mines of Potosí, and everyone began setting out bushes and gathering the leaves, so coca is not worth anything like what it used to be, but it is still valuable. There are those in Spain who became rich from this coca, buying it up and reselling it and trading in the *catus* or markets of the Indians.[6]

It was in the best interest of both the conquerors and the Spanish crown to allow the Indian population to consume what had been forbidden in the previous system. As production and marketing were restricted to the new landholding class, the indigenous peoples' coca-chewing practice became another source of wealth. This new economic system developed along with the biological rise of the mestizo, many of whom secured their middle-class status in the national society. Inca Garcilaso de la Vega, the son of a conqueror and an Indian woman, himself exemplifies the takeover of the coca economy by the mestizo rising class. In writing about the expansion of the Inca Empire during Inca Roca's period, he states that

From Pillcupata [the prince Yahuar Huacac] went to Huaisca and to Tunu, where the Incas had laid out their first coca plantations. The government of Huaisca was later entrusted to my father, Garcilaso de la Vega, and he, in turn, donated it to me for all my life, but I lost the benefit of this gift when I left Peru.[7]

Thus, progressively, the eastern side of the Andes lured individuals and entire families who envisaged the jungles to be the solutions to their social problems and economic quandaries. The national government also visualized the colonization of the rain forests as that historical missing link which would close the gap between the national peripheral groups and the industrial metropolis.

The exploitation of rubber during the nineteenth century, air trans-

Table 1
Coca-Belt Departments by Size and Population (1981)

State	Total Size (Km²)	Selva Alta (Km²)	Selva Alata Pop.
Amazonas	41,297	29,685	161,979
Ayacucho	44,181	5,210	74,455
Cajamarca	35,417	2,224	208,546
Cuzco	76,224	43,421	139,683
Huánuco	35,314	19,106	134,564
Junín	43,384	19,648	155,960
Pasco	21,854	15,437	52,642
Puno	72,382	27,797	80,450
San Martín	53,063	53,063	319,751
TOTAL	423,116	215,591	1,328,030

SOURCE: Instituto Nacional de Estadística. Censos Nacionales, 1981.

portation to major cities in the jungles, and road service helped the colonization of the Amazon basin.[8] The drive to win the high jungles began with the construction of the *carreteras de penetración* (inland roads). Two decades ago, most of the rain forests of the eastern slopes of the Peruvian Andes were inhabited only by native tribes and some new settlers. To encourage colonization in the late fifties the Peruvian government distributed land to families who were willing to relocate in the forests. To facilitate communications between the frontier lands and metropolitan areas, the government started the construction of a road that has not yet been completed. As of 1987, this road is paved to Tingo María. The Carretera Marginal, which runs along the Huallaga River, continues to the departments of Amazonas and Cajamarca. Although this dusty road leaves much to be desired, it connects the eastern rain forests and the Amazon lowlands with the central Andes, the capital city of Lima, and the northern coast.

The Carretera Marginal was probably the biggest step a Peruvian middle-class government took in its effort to develop the country. Fernando Belaúnde Terry's ambitious plan was

integrating vast regions into the social and economic fabric of the nation. . . . Road-Colonization will give the peasant a permanent, stable, happy place to live. Our program will banish the old practices of favoritism and abuse which harmed the colonist and only benefitted influential speculators who trafficked in jungle lands for selfish ends. The dispossessed will find a home where they can put down roots and look to the future with optimism and confidence. The age of parasitic land misers is closed and a new era is dawning. The future belongs to a new generation of "builders of land," men who will tame the rain forests and bring them to fruition for the benefit of all Peruvians.[9]

The population transfer to the jungles of Peru presents an interesting record. The Incas used the *mitimaes* (labor system)[10] to cultivate coca in their native section (Cuzco). Serfdom, forced labor, and slavery were the methods practiced during the colonial period. In the first independent years, a shortage of labor opened the way to Chinese and African immigrants. At this point, food supply and population were balanced. The total population of Peru in 1850 was 2,001,123.[11] Therefore, migration forced by economic need did not take place. Aside from the traditional ecological exchange between the jungles and the rest of the country, most of what is now the booming coca-producing area was almost untouched. The use of land in the highest points of the jungles was almost exclusively in the hands of the same families who had inherited landownership from old Spanish settlers. Many of these longtime landowners had their administrative seats in highland towns and cities from which they controlled the production of coca.

As the population increased, migration from all over the country to the capital city of Lima also increased tremendously. In the twenty years between 1961 and 1981, the population of the coast jumped from 3,859,000 to 8,513,000, a 220 percent increase. By 1984, 27 percent of the national population, 69 percent of the industrial production, and 73 percent of hospital and medical doctors were concentrated in Lima.[12] On the other hand, between 1961 and 1981, the population in the highlands increased from 5 million to 6 million. There was a need to steer the migration to other areas with better economic potential than Lima, where economic resources were very limited. The new demographic and economic policies were to encourage highland migrants and urban

Population migration from highland communities (top) to the jungle has increased. Sometimes entire families move to the new frontierland, which includes the town of Tingo María (bottom).

surplus populations to relocate voluntarily in the foothills of the eastern Andes ranges, for

> Demographic saturation is evident in the highlands of Cajamarca, Ancash, Junín, Cuzco and Puno. The restricted areas of the inter-Andean valleys, rigidly limited by surrounding mountains, caused the population excess to overflow towards the coast, where the limited oases of the seaboard were already saturated. This was evidenced by the alarming growth of marginal slums. Here, the highland inhabitants are defrauded of their hopes; they do not find the opportunities in the search for which they abandoned their natal soil.[13]

Of the five departments mentioned above, Ancash extends from the coast to the highlands. Cajamarca, Cuzco, Junín, and Puno have their eastern sections on the Amazon basin.[14]

The inter-Andean departments (Ancash, Cajamarca, Cuzco, Junín, and Puno) exhibit like patterns of emigration. In the period between 1967 and 1972 they all present higher emigration rates than in the period between 1976 and 1981. This phenomenon may be a good indication of the failure of the reforms dictated by the military government in power from 1968 to 1980. The land reform law of 1969 pushed the poor and the landless out of rural areas into the industrial metropolitan centers. By 1972, 45 percent of Lima's population was made up of migrants. It also seems that unemployment, among other factors resulting from the industrial reform, contributed to an almost 7 percent increase in emigration from Lima. In the jungle departments, migration has been rather stable. The only significant change seems to have been displayed by the department of San Martín, where by 1981 5 percent of the population came from outside. The Amazon lowland departments (Loreto, Ucayali, and Madre de Dios) have shown no major population fluctuations.

Data on migration collected by the Peruvian government does not realistically convey population migration in the country. This information becomes even less clear when one looks into the mass population movements to the "green mines." In order to establish an accurate measure of population movement within the country, a migration census detailing the provincial, district, and village levels may be necessary. This may be even more decisive given that the eastern coca-producing provinces (see Table 2, p. 57) are becoming the targets for seasonal workers as well as new settlers. This side of the Andes may be regarded as both the origin of riches and the source of the subsistence economy, for different groups and individuals who moved to the jungles had varying ambitions and expectations.

The New Agricultural Frontier

Many Andean people have knowledge of what exists beyond their regions only through oral accounts passed on from generation to generation. The eastern side of the Andes range was always a mysterious land that only a few brave men dared enter. The mysteries and myths of unknown places have inspired renowned authors such as Ciro Alegría (1935), who in his *La Serpiente de Oro* describes some of the social beliefs that Indians and mestizos knitted around the ecology of the mountains, also known as the Selva Alta. Thus Alegría relates the devastation of some populations such as Pajatén, Contumarca, and Collai by Hibito and Cholón, Indians who, after ravaging the settlements, took the women and children with them.[15]

Today in many communities in the northeastern highlands of the Andes there are still some folk rituals which indicate that, in fact, the contact between peoples in the highlands and the rain forests was hostile. Some of the many traditional folk enactments in many places that are a few days' walking distance from the Upper Huallaga are the *Antis*, *Aucas*, and *Chunchos*.[16] The *Aucas* is a dramatization of the struggle between the highland Indians and the jungle tribes. A group of men in costumes that indicate their jungle origin come to the population. Another party of women (*pallas*), guided by an old man (*ruku*) and singing prayers in Quechua to the patron saint, affront the Aucas, who respond to the pallas with obscenities. At the end of the skirmish, the Aucas surrender one by one and are presented to the church for their conversion to the Catholic religion. The jungles were also, and still are, pictured as that magic land where witchcraft and folk medicine flourish.

The methods used to conquer the Amazon basin were quite different from the violence employed by the Spanish to subdue the Incas. The "uncivilized" inhabitants of the Amazon and their lands were integrated gradually to the market economy and their landownership and agriculture were modified to fit the material demands of the Western culture. The "civilized" people's needs, such as rubber, oil, precious stones, gold, wood, and hides, were critical for the formulation of policies to integrate the natives with the international mainstream economy and the exploration and exploitation of new frontier lands.[17]

Because major metropolitan areas, especially Lima, did not offer adequate opportunities to migrants from the countryside, it was necessary to implement new policies that would change the population movement, spur economic development, and stop migration to metropolitan areas. The Amazon basin mountains and lowlands were envisioned as the new frontier lands.

The migrants or settlers are motivated by economic need to abandon their original or temporary habitat. Migration to the Peruvian Amazon basins occurs in two different patterns: steered and spontaneous. Steered or directed migration, known as colonization, is the relocation of individuals and families through official economic-development schemes carried out by the Ministerio de Agricultura, the office of Asentamiento Rural, the Consejo Nacional de Población (CNP) and the Instituto Nacional de Desarrollo (INADE).[18]

Spontaneous migration refers to cases in which persons or families from other parts of the country come to the rain forests on their own. Change in residence in the jungles may be due to many factors and causes. Some may be drawn by friends or relatives who seem to be "making it," others may stay after their seasonal labor or visits, and some may even be outlaws who have fled from the police. Spontaneous migrants usually join the groups who have established themselves in hamlets, villages, or towns.

Migration to the jungles, especially among the Andean peasants, as formulated by Aramburú, takes three clearly defined stages: penetration, settlement, and urbanization. In the penetration process the Andean migrants acquire land and exploit it without disjoining themselves from their area of original or native residence. During the settlement phase, colonists change their permanent residence and are tied to their place of origin only through kinship. If it is large enough, exploitation of land and division of labor are within the family, a social characteristic brought from the Andes. Once the migrant is secure in his occupation of land and the economy is secure by local standards, or if his land becomes unproductive, he finds a more productive plot of farmland or moves to the city.[19]

Another group of families has a permanent dual residence both in the highlands and the rain forests. Many families from the central Andes who live in areas located at about two days' walking distance from the rain forests spend about half of the year in each ecological region. For instance, peasants from many highland towns in the provinces of Marañón, Huamalíes, and Panao hold land deep in the jungles of the Upper Huallaga section. Because their barren lands in the Cordilleras yield only one crop per year, the family labor force is divided between the two agricultural domains. Generally, shortly after planting wheat and corn in late spring (October–December), depending upon the type of labor required in their jungle crops, some or all members of the family move temporarily, and their stay in the tropical landholdings depends on the type of labor to be had.

In theory, the new agricultural frontier lands in the Selva Alta and the Ceja de Selva (eyebrows of the jungle) are conquered, colonized, or "civilized," mainly employing official channels to direct the process.[20] The National Institute of Development (Instituto Nacional Desarrollo [INADE]) is the parent office whose role in rural development is commissioned to nine special projects (*proyectos especiales*) which are situated on the eastern side of the Amazon basin.

Some of the special projects are Proyecto Especial de Jaen-San Ignacio-Bagua, covering parts of the Department of Amazonas and Cajamarca bordering with Ecuador; Proyecto Especial Alto Mayo in the southeast Amazonas, north of San Martín and west of Loreto; Proyecto Especial Huallaga Central-Bajo Mayo on the northeastern side of San Martín; Proyecto Especial del Alto Huallaga including the province of Mariscal Cáceres in San Martín and the provinces of Leoncio Prado and Monzón in Huánuco; the Proyecto Especial de Oxapampa, Pichis-Palcazu-Pachitea, and Satipo-Chanchamayo enclosing parts of the rain forests of Junín, Huánuco, and Pasco; and the Proyecto Especial Madre de Dios and Chontayacu-Purus-Ucayali, consisting of sections of Puno and Cuzco and the entire department of Madre de Dios. The nine Proyectos Especiales comprise a total of 7,716,149 hectares of land, of which 1,605,125 hectares have priority for agricultural development. A total of about 125,000 families benefit from these nine Proyectos Especiales.[21]

The main goals of these frontiers are to open new farming land, to expand development based on agriculture, and to capitalize on the available resources in the regions, such as gold, oil, and fish. But because of conditions unique to the country and the area, immediate mass exploitation of land resources is difficult, and the ambitious goals of the new frontier land projects overshadow the small investments that depend on foreign aid.

Speaking of the investment-credit-peasant relationship, an illiterate but experienced farmer in the Upper Huallaga humorously concluded that "both the government and the farmer could be compared to a person who is handed a clew of thread whose end is tied to the funding source (aid); as the peasant walks away from the starting point, his clew grows smaller and smaller, so that when he reaches his destination (farm), the creditor starts rolling his clew back; both the peasant and the government end up empty-handed." The relevance of this analogy to the special projects of the mountainous forests of the Peruvian Andes may not be too far-fetched.

The Proyectos Especiales are victims of their own dreams, for their limited funds are spent in projects and programs that retard the agricultural frontier and create other nonagricultural sectors. Because of the workings of urbanization, service sector activities far exceed the needs of an economy that is based on an irrational use of land. Uninformed, capricious bureaucrats tell farmers what to plant and cultivate in the land alloted to them. Highland peasants and poor metropolitan migrants, who are frequently unfamiliar with soil conditions, many times end up planting crops inappropriate for the soil. Even experienced and knowledgeable farmers are restricted by the procedures of those funding the project. Rational and scientific use of land is overridden by petty politics.

The "agricultural frontier" projects are estimated for six years of operation. The total estimated investment between 1982 and 1987 was $515,000,000, of which 29 percent ($149,063,500) was spent in the construction and maintenance of roads and other works connected to transportation infrastructures; only 12 percent ($59,579,600) was appropriated directly for agricultural development.[22] Transportation infrastructures are necessary, obviously, to connect the farmer to the consumer markets. Although the intent of the government may have been the transportation of jungle products to the rest of the country, the real effect of the "road boom" has been the opposite. Sixty percent ($208,643,100) of the "frontier money" is invested in cosmetic development programs, a policy that makes the colonists dependent on food imported from other parts of the country and world rather than on food supply from within the region.

The nonagricultural priorities of the projects may indicate that the "jungle alternative," like most policies of development, was improvised and failed to take into account the real situation in the rest of the country. Thus, the "frontier land" was but another tactic for exploiting the Indian ideology which, obviously, was to the benefit of contractors and planners whose identification with the colonists—Indians and peasants from the Andes—did not go any further than political and group interests.[23]

As it stands today, the goals of the frontier land are unattainable, and it is uncertain whether the present conditions and priorities can help establish a strong regional economy based on agricultural output. Many factors may hinder the rational exploitation of land in the eastern ranges: 1) conquest of the "green inferno" is not likely with the limited investment whose main funding source is foreign aid at interest rates ranging from 2 percent (West Germany) to 11 percent (the World Bank); 2) low prices paid for the products in the national market and the high cost of living governed by the illegal cocaine industry are heavy burdens the colonists bear; and 3) high interest rates charged by the national bank inflict permanent hardships upon migrant families.

The colonists are faced with making a choice between legal and illegal credit and the marketing channels available to them. But neither the illicit entrepreneurs nor the state bureaucrats let the farmers negotiate a fair deal. The peasants simply take what is offered to them, and many remain in permanent debt. As the cost of tools and other essential manufactured items continues to spiral, while prices for agricultural products stay constant, investment in agriculture exceeds the return.[24] The farmers' hopes of ever getting out of debt, much less realizing their dreams by legitimate means, dwindle constantly.

Because tea, coffee, and tobacco plantations did not yield the expected returns, most colonists have turned their lands into coca plantations. With the growth of the demand for cocaine in the international market, the need for coca increased and attracted the interest of other peasants from the central and western sides of the Andes. Parallel to the increased demand for cocaine, the reformist social programs infused by the military dictatorship of the early seventies seemed to boost the national economy through agricultural and industrial growth. Unfortunately, land distribution and the industrial reform yielded negative results. As a direct consequence, migration to the capital city of Lima and other urban areas increased tremendously. There was hunger among the unemployed, poverty among the landless peasants, and the ambition to regain social and economic power among those who had been stricken by the imposition of the new order.

The Green Ore Alternative

The postwar consumer drive of the fifties exerted an enormous influence on the development of the countryside. Construction of roads and the diffusion of radio and television became commonplace. In dormant villages and communities, imported goods such as household items and appliances became status symbols among Indians and peasants. Myriad imported items, such as radios and sewing machines, changed the attitudes and mores of the highland populations.

Indians and mestizos were attracted by industrial cities and by corporate sugar and cotton plantations on the coast. The pattern of seasonal migration to the coast was accelerated. Migrant laborers would bring along with them new cultural elements unknown in small populations. The classic example is the Singer sewing machine. This brand name was so fashionable that it became part of the folk lexicon as a synonym for sewing machines. Adults who owned a radio or a Singer machine were more desirable for marriage. Parents were more willing to consent to traditional marriage (*sirvinacuy*) petitions from males who guaranteed the comforts of life offered by modern technology. Children visited the newly arrived people to learn new words, obtain information on the outside world, and acquire goods that were either rare or not yet to be found in the highlands.

The almost autonomous traditional economy became more and more attached to cash source regions. By the late fifties, migration from the countryside to the metropolis had increased dramatically. The capital city of Lima grew from 749,171 inhabitants in 1940 to 2,093,435 in 1961, and to 4,954,787 in 1972.[25] The housing problem forced migrants and the urban poor to establish dozens of shantytowns on private and state land. The population movement to urban areas forced the government to look for new alternatives to curb the ever-increasing population. In addition to land reform, the government's response to this growth was twofold: colonization of the rain forests and free education. Primary schools were opened in hamlets and villages, and towns with populations as small as one thousand people boasted their own high schools.

In 1964, Fernando Belaúnde Terry signed land reform law 15037, but this law excluded large plantations and their industrial infrastructures.[26] He also tried to tamper with the issue of land reform with his proposition to colonize the eastern slopes of the Andes (Ceja de Selva). However, he and his party were unable to find a solution to the unequal distribution of land without affecting the interest of the oligarchy represented in the Congress. He found an alternative in the virgin lands in the forests. Belaúnde's misguided attempt to solve the problems of overpopulation of the cities, unemployment, and unfair land distribution was the voluntary relocation of migrant families to the frontier land, the eastern foothills of the Andes.

In the midst of national and racial unity wrought by the common denominator of *mestizaje*—the fusion of two cultures—it may be asked if we Peruvians have managed to fully conquer our own territory. The answer is negative. Although man has secured a place in the mountains and along the coast, he has only done so on a very small scale in the jungle. The ceja de montaña, a region full of promise for youth, remains almost untouched. The incorporation of the high jungle into the national economy—not in just a few spots, but along the entire length from north to south—is the great battle to be waged in the conquest of Peru.[27]

However, the government encouraged farmers to colonize the jungle with no regard for their material needs.

Before the gigantic land reform of 1969, Peruvian middle-class governments reacted to the problem of the national peripheral areas by formulating two policies of development: education and modernization. In the fifties, elementary schools were opened in every small town as well as in some estate headquarters. The population growth and freedom from earlier labor ties convinced the peasants to urge the government to open high schools in small towns and elementary schools in almost every village and hamlet. By 1975, every district town boasted its own coeducational high school.

In Peru, education is designed to maintain the traditional hierarchical Latin American paternalism that makes the countryside more dependent on the cash sources and prevents peasants from fulfilling their own potential. The peasant populations are coerced into developing in accordance with the ideas of outside planners. Education does not match the needs of the diverse ethnic and cultural enclaves. In a country with so many geographic, cultural, and environmental variations, education must be decentralized and designed to fit the needs of the three major regions. Education, in and of itself, does not change the peasant substantially or help him adjust to the process of change. Simply providing a mediocre education and giving voting rights to the illiterate does not guarantee participation in national life. On the contrary, local politicians exploit the Indians by buying their votes with a few grams of coca.

Faculty at both elementary and high-school levels were mostly high-school graduates who were not adequately equipped to teach. The unskilled teachers got on-the-job training by attending summer school at various colleges and universities to earn their degrees or by enrolling in home study programs sponsored by the ministry of education and taking their examinations at the ministry's branch offices in the capital towns.

Thousands of young adults have left their communities to get high-school educations at other locations with better economic opportunities. Education, however, has not proved to be an effective developing agent. It is just another cosmetic layer applied to the peasantry by the middle-class governments' "Indian ideology," for education cannot be democratized without also democratizing the economy and the political superstructure.

For a good-quality education, three fundamental ingredients are needed: populations who want education for the welfare of the community; an educational infrastructure; and properly trained teachers able to guide students in the fulfillment of their educational needs. Education in the highlands of Peru does not meet any of these elements. The immediate needs of the peasant child are material. The Andean people need agricultural and economic development before a formal education.

Entire families and communities from unproductive highland areas are settling in the Peruvian coca belt. In the earthquake of May 31, 1970, a town of about 30,000 people was totally buried by an avalanche caused by a landslide from the highest mountain in Peru. It had been one of the most successful towns in the northeastern highlands. Many peasants from the surrounding areas, who supplied labor to the town, migrated to the Upper Huallaga and lured other relatives, friends, and acquaintances to follow them. They all founded a hamlet, which today is one of the safest locations for the manufacture and international trafficking of coca paste in Peru. These northeastern highlanders all moved because, after the destruction of the town, no other city or town in the area could absorb their labor. Those who could not afford road transportation hiked for as many as fifteen days. To these highlanders, coca and cocaine were the way out, the means of starting a new life in a new place.

Between early 1970 and early 1980, migrating for wages from the highlands to industrial areas dropped dramatically. In 1981, in a community of 375 families, I found that only 21 percent of male wage-earners migrated to the coast for higher salaries. During that year 61 percent of the family wage earners worked as seasonal laborers in the jungle netting from 1,000 to 1,500 soles a day, while comparable work in Lima was worth only 800 soles a day.[28] In 1985, the percentage of migrants to the jungles for wages increased to 75 percent. From the 21 percent who depended on wages on the coast, 12 percent had shifted their migration routes to the northeastern rain forests.

A typical example of one of these migratory workers is Carlos Santos, a thirty-year-old peasant from a village near Paras, who never went to the coast. When I revisited Paras in the summer of 1985, Carlos invited me for a traditional lunch of guinea pig stew. He made me read the instructions for his Sony receiver and his Sankyo turntable, which had not been used since he bought them in 1983. We listened to a soccer game broadcast from Argentina and after lunch talked about what goes on in "coca land." Carlos makes three regular trips to the jungles per year, but only on his trip following the harvest does he take food for trade. Between September 1983 and August 1985 Carlos acquired two Seiko watches, one table-top sewing machine, one Sony stereo receiver, one Pioneer equalizer, and two ladies' Citizen watches, one for his wife and another one for his lover, who was also his sister-in-law. No other peasant in the village enjoys Carlos's affluence. Because of this peasant's economic position vis-à-vis the rest of the community, many young school boys are tempted to make the long trek across the eastern range of the Andes.

Each time Carlos makes a trip to Sodoma, a drug-producing village almost untouched by the police, he stays for about thirty days. His initial trips to the jungle were related exclusively to the traditional coca economy, but since he has learned the techniques of preparation of coca paste he has become a consumer, able to buy the goods he wants because of the underground cash economy. Because his regular cash earnings from his migratory labor cannot satisfy his needs as a consumer, he is active in the petty trafficking of coca paste. When he told me of the difficulties he had in dodging the police, I asked him how much coca he had brought with him. His answer was "just a few pounds." The real reason for his ordeal on the return trip was that he had smuggled 500 grams of coca paste to "show to his friends in the community."

Carlos is but one example of the thousands of peasants who migrate to the new frontier lands in the rain forests. Some peasants go as seasonal workers, while others move with the intention of relocating in the "promised land."

The [Peruvian] National Council of Population argues that only one of every four migrants from the highlands settles in the jungle areas of the country.[29] Consequently, the highland population may be decreasing in an order of 25 percent or higher. Intensification of population movement and migration from both the hinterland and urban areas is due solely to the lack of economic opportunities in metropolitan areas and the existence of subhuman conditions in the national peripheries. A brief description of some aspects of Andean material life will help in understanding some of the reasons for migration to the international "coca belt."

The size of an average house in the highlands is about twenty square meters. Bearing in mind that, in the best of cases, the family size is at least six, available space is limited. Rooms are used to store food provisions and timber for fuel, and to protect household animals such as chickens, dogs, and guinea pigs. Every highland house has benches attached to the walls inside or outside the rooms. In the kitchen or in the main room of one-room houses, the benches are hollow for use as guinea pig pens. The hearth (*tullpa*) consists of three stones or adobes placed on the floor to support the clay pots on the fire. Few households have kitchens. In the majority of cases, the hearth or *tullpa* is placed inside the main room or in the porch. A blower made out of reed is used to fan the wood to fire. Pots are made of clay and bought in stores or from traveling traders. Metal pots are uncommon, and those who have them keep them for special ceremonial events. Inside the rooms are wooden hooks on which to hang clothes, maize, baskets, and other items. A rustic table and a couple of homemade chairs are found in some houses. The traditional stool (*konko*) made from maguey trunk is present in every household.

Metal or wooden bedsteads are still luxury furniture affordable only by a few well-to-do peasants. For sleeping, they place sheepskins on the floor of the room or outside on the porch and huddle together covering themselves with heavy quilts. Folded *ponchos* and shawls are used as pillows. They go to bed without taking their clothes off, removing only their sandals or shoes. No household has a bathroom; some village school buildings have their own *silos*, underground deposits for human waste. To defecate, one goes to open areas, to corn or wheat fields, or just behind the house. Toilet paper costs about 2,600 soles per roll, so instead, they use stones, leaves, corncobs, or nothing at all.

Clothes are washed with plain water by beating them on stones with a bat; soap and detergents are too expensive. Women wash their hair with *creda* (white clay), lemon, or sometimes with fermented human urine. In some communities shampoo is used only as an external medicine for headaches. Babies are bathed (*arma*) every two or three months until they are approximately three years old. After this age, they rarely bathe or take a shower. Some, however, wash their bodies at least once a year when they have to attend patronal celebrations.

Because of the lack of hygiene, parasite infestation is a major problem, and it would be difficult to eradicate it without introducing comprehensive health services. Parasite infestation is so deeply rooted in the culture that the peasants even conceive of the parasites as parts of their bodies. They say (in Quechua) that "lice and fleas are signs of life." No insecticide is used. They catch the lice with their fingertips and kill them by biting them. Virtually no household is free from lice, flea, or tick infestation.

All these precarious health conditions predispose people to contracting illnesses that can become epidemic. Because of both ignorance and scarcity of basic medicines, such epidemics can devastate entire communities. In 1980, in a community of five villages, 102 children between the ages of one and seven died when a measles epidemic erupted. Many couples lost all their children. Because of massive burials, some families even omitted the traditional *parvulo* party. In some cases, two corpses were placed together, using U.S. AID cardboard food boxes as coffins.

Urbanization and the building of roads in order to develop the backward and economically peripheral areas are ongoing efforts of both the national government and international aid. In Peru, the well-known partisan state organization in charge of development was the Cooperación Popular, founded by Fernando Belaúnde Terry. In his second term in office, the Cooperación Popular became known as the Sistema Nacional de Cooperación Popular (SNCP). SNCP was founded to make the rural masses active in their own development. In its initial stages, SNCP received technical support and material subsidies totaling $600,000 from the U.S. Agency for International Development (AID) through its mission office in Lima.[30] Cooperación Popular provided materials and technical advice to the communities that needed schools, medical posts, and roads.

Besides the official agency committed to the modernization of the countryside, other independent agencies support food projects and provide other material aid. Each agency has its own method of operation. Caritas Peru, subsidiary of the Catholic Relief Service, distributes food as payment for labor performed in public works in small urban and rural areas. The Lutheran World Service of Switzerland also provides food-for-labor and technical advice in urbanization programs, education, and agriculture. It seems that the goal of these organizations is the improvement of living conditions in small populations in the countryside. But these projects and programs benefit a few local middle-class people rather than the peasantry at large.

At the village level peasants do not speak for themselves; aid to remote communities comes only if mestizos articulate their needs for it to the agencies, or if the agencies themselves come voluntarily to offer their support. Because the towns boast lawyers, doctors, engineers, and high-ranking police officers among their members, they usually realize all or part of their requests. Urbanization causes poor peasants to flock to towns and cities where they can work for payment in kind (food). Agriculture is becoming less important to the extent that the peasants no longer rely on its proceeds to support their families.

Furthermore, modernization through urbanization and transportation has destroyed traditional specialized craftsmanship that produced use-value commodities with which some groups supplemented their food shortages in times of drought, flood, or when the land was unproductive. For instance, two small towns whose inhabitants were clay potters and shoemakers have been affected by the modernization policies. Metal wares and synthetic rubber shoes have displaced the traditional local cottage industries. Even water mills, which were used to grind wheat, have disappeared. Currently, bakers in highland towns depend totally on wheat flour coming from Lima.

Modernization of highland populations through urbanization and education has had negative effects on the peasantry. Such efforts neither supported local traditional economies nor generated new economic activities. Education made peasants aware of their backwardness. Western culture became the yardstick for comparison with their own social, economic, and cultural realities. Construction of roads opened new markets for goods manufactured in the national and international metropolis. The traditional barter and the incipient cash economies were unable to meet the exigencies of the industrial markets.

Relief and philanthropic efforts satisfy peasants' needs only partially and temporarily. These humanistic actions not only make the indigenous people dependent upon outside sources but also discourage agriculture. In order to meet their new needs, villagers and urban people alike are compelled to seek other alternatives for raising cash. Ironically, in the process of trying to help the Indian and the peasant to meet their day-to-day needs, policies of development have created another social hunger. Thus, the ideological tenets of the dominant classes who remain aloof to the real Indian issue are responsible for the countryman's support of the underground economy.

The underground coca and cocaine economy stimulates crime such as thefts and homicides in highland communities whose economies are more dependent on the coca-producing foothills of the Andes than they are on urban areas. The need for pack animals to transport coca and cocaine, as well as the scarcity of food in the jungles, motivates thefts of mules, horses, and cows. One specific incident illustrates the many that happen every day. In a village on the eastern side of the central Andes, the horse belonging to a local teacher was stolen. Because police were unable to find either the animal or the suspect, the teacher started threatening publicly to kill the unknown thief. The unknown thief learned of the threat and tried to kill the teacher to prevent her from going to "the bad witch." Neighbors rescued their teacher and took the suspect to the police. He confessed his offense but the horse was never recovered.

Even in towns that do not produce much coca, religious feasts paying homage to local patron saints are financed by coca planters or cocaine traffickers or laborers. For three consecutive years in one particular town, celebrations were sponsored by active members of the coca and cocaine industry. Because of the country's depressed economy, religious festivities, which are symbols of status, are beyond any average peasant's reach because they require such immense outlays of cash.

By 1970, 16,906 hectares of land in Peru were dedicated to legal production of coca. To satisfy and protect the needs of coca-chewing Indians, the Peruvian government incorporated the production of coca into the national economy by creating an exclusive administrative office (Estanco de la Coca, now Empresa Nacional de la Coca) to collect tax revenues from the coca trade. Peru has also produced limited amounts of cocaine for scientific and medical purposes, which by 1984 had escalated to 54,770 hectares, a 324 percent increase since 1970. These legal cultivations produced 15,058 metric tons in 1970 and 59,859 metric tons in 1984.[31] In 1985, the Peruvian government recognized that the total production of coca was about 135,000 hectares[32] with a yearly average production of about 18,900,000 arrobas (214,704 metric tons) of coca, an enormous increase in illegal cultivation. On the other hand, 6 percent of the population in 1984 consumed 5,410 metric tons.[33]

Today, there are indications that the coca plant is cultivated in the upper Amazon basin of Brazil and to some extent in many sections of the Ecuadorian rain forests.[34] With good cultivation, the coca plant can yield as many as five crops per year. Taking a conservative position, the total legal and illegal production of coca in South America, excluding Brazil and Ecuador, may be safely estimated at 34,160,000 arrobas (388,057 metric tons) of coca.

Hideouts where coca paste is made are widespread, and many towns, isolated villages, and hamlets both in the highlands and the rain forests have become strategic locations for the mass production and distribution of coca paste.[35] The cocaine underground economy is an ongoing and constantly increasing activity that both satisfies the material needs of local economies and supplies an illicit product to international consumer centers.

The estimated production of 240,000 hectares of coca (excluding

Brazil and Ecuador), is enough to manufacture approximately 3,360 metric tons of coca paste, or about 900 metric tons of powerful cocaine hydrochloride.[36]

Excluding smuggling time, it takes about one hundred days before the crystalline "white gold" reaches the hands of high-level dealers in the United States.[37] The time needed depends on the age of leaves at harvest, the quality of materials used, and the expertise of mixers and chemists. The refining operation itself is another subculture which usually involves people from social strata very different from that of the coca growers and small coca-paste entrepreneurs. Once the shipments reach the United States, according to the President's Commission on Organized Crime, cocaine is responsible for about fifty percent of the $80 billion-a-year drug industry.[38]

The "green mines," which stretch across the eastern side of the gold and silver mines in the highlands, are as attractive to the peasant from the barren highlands as they are to national middle classes and international groups. The slopes, mountains, and long valleys represent a unique economic rush, which in essence may not be very different from other economic booms that Peru has had since its discovery by Europeans in the sixteenth century. Each and every economic rush satisfied varying tastes and groups. The mines of Potosí, for example, quenched the parasitic Spanish royalty's thirst for silver and supported the colonial hierarchy in America in the sixteenth century. The oil rush contributed to the advancement of multinational corporations and national middle classes who were at the service of powerful organizations. The coca industry fosters the same social and economic phenomena generated by other national and international economic establishments.

Suddenly in the 1970s, coca use, which had previously been a quiet pastime mainly of Indians, developed into an industry affecting farms, plantations, and entire provinces actively cultivating the "white gold." Craving for "white gold" and its economic rewards has seduced native populations, tempted new adventurers, and, more importantly, brought into the green mines another type of international investor, whose cash, to the illiterate Andean, represents the productive power of international monopolies. The green mines, which are between the humid, hot Amazon lowlands and the dry, cold Andean peaks, are backdrops for all kinds of human behavior generated by the "white gold

Almost every marketplace in the highlands of Peru has a coca section. Most coca retailers are women (top). Balls of *llipta* (quinua stalk ash) chewed with coca leaves are also sold in the marketplace (bottom).

rush." Before cocaine comes to parties in Hollywood, to the briefcases of Wall Street executives, or to "crack houses" of the Harlem low-level distributor, it generates a number of jobs that help support the ailing Peruvian economy. These mines satisfy the hunger of the indigenous people, the ambition and political interests of the national middle class, and the greed of international organized crime.

Coca Culture and Economy

Erythroxylon coca is a variety of shrub native to the tropical slopes of South America, but it is now found in other parts of the world with climates similar to the Amazon tropics.[1] A leading ethnobotanist maintains that the coca shrub is one of 250 species of Erythroxylon found in the tropics of the New World.[2] About ninety species of Erythroxylon coca shrub grow between Argentina and Colombia, of which Erythroxylon coca and Erythroxylon novogranatense are the most widely cultivated.[3] Edgardo Machado, in an article published in a Peruvian journal, maintains that E. coca lambran, E. coca mollecoca, E. coca fusiforme, and E. coca ovoide are all species from Erythroxylon coca Lam, and that the first species is grown in Cuzco and the other three species are distributed in Huánuco.

Plowman (1986) reports that Huánuco coca leaves vary in their cocaine content from 23 percent to 93 percent, with an average of 63 percent. Plowman's analyses show that the leaves from Chinchao (the highest point in the Upper Huallaga Valley), Huánuco, yield the highest cocaine from the coca leaves grown in Peru and Bolivia. Erythroxylon Truxillense, Trujillo coca, and Erythroxylon Novogranatense—Colombian coca—yield 72 percent and 77 percent respectively. Erythroxylon Ipadu—Amazonian coca leaves—average 25 percent in cocaine content.[4]

There seems to be a misunderstanding in the cultivation of the Erythroxylon Truxillense in Peru. Van Dyke and Byck argue that the Truxillense or "Trujillo" variety of the Erythroxylon species is now grown on the northern coast of Peru and in the valley of the Marañón River, a tributary of the Amazon River.[5] The Peruvian northern coast has an altitude ranging from 3 meters to 230 meters above sea level. The area in the province of Trujillo (Simbal) where some coca is grown is an inter-Andean valley that is more than 600 meters above sea level. It is inconceivable that coca shrubs could grow in low altitudes and desert climates. The misconception probably resides in the fact that the Marañón River touches the department of La Libertad whose capital city is Trujillo on the Pacific coast, where leaves are shipped to the United States for legal use by Coca-Cola.

From land acquisition to harvesting, coca-leaf farming has five distinct stages: slash and burn (*roso*), seedling preparation, hole digging (*poseada*), transplanting, and cultivation. The most arduous and fatiguing part of agriculture in the rain forests is keeping land cultivable. Lofty, thick, and towering trees are cut down using axes or chain saws. Smaller trees, bushes, and shrubs (*purma*) are usually cut in the traditional method, with a machete. Depending on the number of wood cutters (*rosadores*), clearing one hectare of land can take about thirty days of manual work. Contracted labor is the most practical method for clearing land in the dense forests.

To cut down trees and undergrowth, contractors charge about $300.00 per hectare. To meet a deadline, the contractor may hire help; however, he generally works by himself or with his partners if he has any. Greater labor supply does not make land-clearing prices cheaper. Daily wage labor used to clear land may, at times, be much more expensive than contracted labor. Daily laborers work exact hours. They also demand food and drink, which may result in higher costs. The average daily wage in the coca agricultural area is $2.50, but if three meals are added, actual daily wages may rise to as much as $6.00. Chopping and burning are not included in the contracts.

Farmers plan ahead so that their planting coincides with the clearing process. Land is prepared immediately after burning. Otherwise, weeds, shrubs, and bushes grow back in a few weeks. Also, within about three months, a thick wood would totally cover the soil, in which case another slash-and-burn operation would be required. Once land is cleared and the soil is ready for planting, the farmers dig holes (*posos*) of about 35 centimeters (14 inches) deep and about 22 centimeters (9 inches) in diameter. The *posero's* (digger's) tools are a large, narrow,

Clearing (slash-and-burn) of one hectare of land costs as much as $300.

spoonlike shovel and a stick about 1 meter long used to measure the distances between holes. About ten thousand holes are dug in one hectare of land to contain the same number of seedlings at a cost of about $90.00.

Seedlings either are bought from other specialized farmers or are prepared by the planters themselves. The coca seeds are dried indoors for about twenty days. Dirt is mixed with sand and fertilizers in a small plot, about 10 centimeters deep, called a *cama*. Once the seeds are planted in this bed, the farmers protect the plot from direct sunlight by making an awning (*tinlado*) with the plastic sheets that may have been used to make coca-paste pits. Before their transplanting, the seedlings are kept in the bed for about five months. If sold ready for transplanting, the young plants' prices are set at the going rate for coca leaves; that is, one arroba of seedlings costs the equivalent of the black-market value of one arroba of coca.

The transplanting method is used only during the rainy season. Some expert coca growers always transplant the seedlings during the full moon. Between the months of May and September, they plant the seeds directly; no seedling preparation is needed. This procedure cannot be followed during the summer rains, because seeds placed in the holes would putrefy. The age of the coca plant is counted from the day of transplanting or, if planted directly, from the time the new plant shows signs of growth, about five months after planting directly in the poso. About twenty days of manual labor are required for planting the seeds or transplanting ten thousand seedlings. If the seedlings do not sprout, they are replaced with new seeds. Extra seedlings are always kept ready to replace plants that do not take root. The total cost of planting ten thousand coca plants is approximately 1,100,000 soles including extra days of inspection and replanting work. The delicate young plants are ready for the first harvest six months after transplanting or about one year after direct planting.

Until the plants reach maturity, at about eighteen months, coca growers have to weed the coca plants. They also carefully hoe the field every six months. About 25 days of weeding and 75 days of manual hoeing are required, in five months of cultivation, before the plant reaches its full growth. The estimated cost for the total of 225 days of manual labor is about 1,100,000 soles at the daily wage of 250,000 soles plus 250,000 soles in meals. Periodic fumigations help the plant yield better crops. The cost of the fumigation of one hectare demands an extra investment of about 500,000 soles.

The first collection of leaves takes place six months after transplanting or about one year after direct planting. The selective picking (*tipleo*) is carried out without destroying the tip of the plant. In some areas with large Andean populations, the Quechua word *kiplla*, which means "to pick gently using the thumb and the forefinger," has been adopted. The initial five tipleos are usually done by the growers themselves or by workers paid on a daily basis. The average crop yield of tipleos is one arroba, three arrobas, and six arrobas of dried leaves at the first, second, and third pickings, respectively. The proportion of increase is constant until the plants are about two years old. The aggregate amount of leaves during the first eighteen months could safely be estimated at 45 arrobas (511 kilos) to 50 arrobas (568 kilos). Thus, at 1985 prices of 900,000 soles per arroba, total cash yield of one hectare of coca runs between 40,500,000 soles and 45,000,000 soles.

Hills and slopes are ideal for the coca plant. Depending on altitude and soil conditions, the same plant yields as many as five harvests per year for about thirty-five years.

Subsequent collections are done by the olive-picking method, that is, by placing the branches between the fingers and pulling the leaves along with the seeds. This random picking helps in pruning the branches, which makes the plants more leafy. Both piecework and day labor are employed. Experienced pickers are paid at the rate of 35,000 soles per arroba; daily workers get the current earnings of 250,000 soles per day. Meals are provided for all workers regardless of the nature of their work. Some planters pay their workers in coca leaves. Workers who receive coca for their labor may sell or save the leaves to make their own coca paste. There are well-cultivated fields which produce as much as 60 arrobas per season, but the average output of one hectare of coca at its full production is 35 arrobas, or 140 arrobas per year, a total cash yield of 126,000,000 soles.

The pickers collect the leaves in large baskets, which they take to the grower's headquarters. The green leaves are deposited indoors on dry floors to avoid decomposition. The next step is to dry the leaves for shipment, storing, or cocaine production. The leaves may be dried industrially or on a small scale. The industrial and legal method of drying is rarely found now. The use of specially built drying houses owned by legal coca growers was the technique established in traditional coca agriculture. Legal coca planters charge about 10,000 soles for drying every arroba of coca. With the growth of illegal farming, the number of drying houses (*secadoras*) also increased. The drug eradication drive which began in 1978 has destroyed most of these drying buildings. It is curious to note that the national police force in charge of controlling illegal coca farming and cocaine production and traffic reported the blasting of the drying houses as demolitions of "cocaine laboratories."

Drying and packing processes have changed. Every farmer controls his own drying and packing, for legal planters take advantage of the other farmers' illegal status. They withhold for themselves a percentage of the coca, arguing loss of weight in the drying operation. For instance, for every 100 pounds brought into the drier, many legal farmers deliver only one 25-pound bale. Thus, the illegal coca planter who contracts driers loses about 17 pounds for every 100 pounds of green leaves. Today, coca planters dry their leaves by spreading the green leaves on a threshing floor or in the concrete pools built to make coca paste. Baling is done only when coca is sold legally to the government. Otherwise, the coca is deposited in blankets, sacks, baskets, and so forth, until sold in the black market or reduced to coca paste.

In Peru, the more than 100,000 hectares of coca yield approximately 160,000 metric tons of coca,[6] or about three times as much as legal production for 1984 (see Table 2). The official legal distributor of coca is the Empresa Nacional de Coca (ENACO) but, obviously, only a fraction of the crops reach ENACO's warehouses throughout the country. It is argued that coca leaves are also shipped to Colombia for further processing into cocaine.[7] This may not be true, for the transportation of the bulky bales requires the use of large vehicles. Theoretically, the 60,000 hectares of coca are for the routine traditional chewing in the highlands of the country. However, the historical use, the cultural influence, and the ecological exchange of coca have changed tremendously from local barter economies to international, sophisticated underground production and use.

Table 2
Coca Leaf Production 1980–1984 (Metric Tons)

Department	1980	1981	1982	1983	1984
Amazonas	235	482	436	521	437
Ayacucho	160	150	160	134	138
Cajamarca	71	101	110	118	119
Cuzco	3,161	8,169	3,170	3,800	4,180
Huánuco	18,000	21,600	24,000	24,000	24,000
Junín	2	4	5	5	5
La Libertad	607	621	622	620	617
Loreto	108	135	152	167	180
Puno	158	143	120	123	130
San Martín	18,000	24,000	30,000	30,000	30,000
TOTAL	40,502	55,405	58,775	59,488	59,806

SOURCE: Ministerio de Agricultura, Unidad de Estadística Agrícola, Lima, Peru.

In addition to satisfying the demand for coca leaves in the black market, there are other reasons and justifications for the cultivation of coca rather than other cash crops.

Ecologically, coca will thrive in areas where there are marginal soil conditions, little water, high elevations and steep hillsides, conditions to which the other principal crops are not suited. Many [peasants] have land with poor soil, where crops other than coca do not produce well. Coffee and cocoa require very fertile soil and a hot climate which are found in lower elevations. Another reason for not producing coffee is because of quotas on the international trade.[8]

Unlike other short-term cash crops such as rice and maize, coca makes better use of the soil, is not susceptible to diseases—except occasional fungus, which affects only old plants—and has a higher market value. Officials and authorities who control distribution of land often discriminate against poor migrant peasants and settlers who cannot afford to bribe them. Furthermore, even if the farmers succeed in acquiring land with good soil conditions, they cannot gamble on crops that take years to produce, such as tea, coffee, and palm oil trees.

Coca: The Andean Crossroads

Andean culture has three elements that are almost universal: the guinea pig, chicha, and coca. Of the three, guinea pigs and chicha either remain basically unchanged or are undergoing slow transformation. Unlike chicha, coca has not been controlled by the Indian populations at any given time in Peruvian history. Rather, coca has always conditioned the culture and economy. Many local economies that generated revenues for the national government functioned around coca trade. Before the advent of modern communications, it was the Andean montañero's role to bring coca up to the highlands. Although this ecological movement of coca still continues, new types and methods of trade have evolved with the rush of cocaine production to satisfy international demand. By 1951, the tax was about 11.50 soles per arroba of coca.

Prior to the cocaine boom, there were two kinds of montañeros in the highlands: the commercial voyagers who went to the forests to bring coca, coffee grains, and sun-dried fruits to sell to local bodegueros in small towns and cities; and peasants who went occasionally to the closest coca fields to buy one or two arrobas of coca, mostly for their own use. The former took food from the highlands to the jungles in order to trade for coca. The latter worked in coca plantations for payment in kind, for coca. Because of government control, the number of commercial travelers has diminished tremendously. However, peasants from remote rural areas have increased the frequency of their trading trips to the eastern foothills of the Andes so much that they are becoming dependent on the new coca economy. Today, crossing the high mountain ranges has come to be part of the subsistence economy.

Until the sixties, coca was mostly produced for traditional chewing. The Peruvian government established an official bureau to control coca agriculture and to collect tax revenues from coca trade. The agency, Estanco de la Coca, was a subdivision of the Department of the Treasury. Tax collectors (*recaudadores*) were posted in towns and strategic locations where the movement of montañeros could be controlled more effectively. Before 1938, the coca tradesman in the jungles bought one arroba of coca for about 4 soles, and the tax rate was 48.75 percent, or 1.95 soles per arroba of coca. One arroba of coca in cities and towns sold for 10 soles.

Between 1962 and 1972, each arroba of coca was taxed at the rate of 35 soles and 54 soles, respectively. Several old-time travelers asserted that, in addition to paying their taxes, the peasants were forced to work for the tax collectors. Many government employees themselves were coca planters and legal cocaine manufacturers. Up in the highlands, the recaudadores made the travelers labor in the fields or do private construction work. Outsiders appointed as tax collectors would demand pork legs, lamb, or wheat from coca traders.

Once the traveler sold his coca to the stores, retailers paid another excise tax. By 1972, the Estanco de la Coca disappeared and the National Bank (Banco de la Nación) took over coca-tax collection. Later, the Empresa Nacional de la Coca (ENACO) was organized, and it was announced that distribution and sale of coca was free of taxes. As local farmers turned their land to coca cultivation, production of the coca leaf increased rapidly. Traveling to the forests was no longer reserved only for experienced Andean peasants and merchants. The forests attracted new tradesmen and laborers who intensified the old system of making local economies dependent on cash supply in the jungles. Today, the number of montañeros has increased significantly. Hundreds of peasants still follow the same trade routes established hundreds of years ago.

The season during which montañeros make long trips depends on conditions in the jungle. The peasants who take their goods to trade for coca make the trip only during the dry season (winter), immediately after the collection of their crops. Dried coca leaves are very sensitive to humidity so that it is safer to transport them in winter. Besides, in the highlands the peasants are free from their agricultural activities. Other peasants who migrate for wages need take nothing with them that could be spoiled by the rain; they go whenever they have time or need cash.

After storing a food supply to last his family at least seven months, the montañero begins preparation for the long trip. The first thing he chooses is his companion, generally a *compadre* (a close relative) or a close friend from the community. His second immediate task is to secure good transportation—mules and donkeys. Horses are not used because they are not as strong. The owner of the pack animal to be used on the trip receives a *llanqui* (advanced partial payment) in money or in kind.⁹ Only after both companion and animals for transportation are procured does the montañero peasant fix an approximate date of departure. The best trading goods are wheat, broad beans, common vetch (*arvejas*), meal, dried pork, and lamb. Often the montañero peasants buy dried pork and lamb from their communities in order to satisfy their customers in the jungles.

The peasants take their grains to the water mills to have them milled. Once back from the mills, meal is sifted and put in either sacks weighing four arrobas each to pack on donkeys or sacks of six arrobas to pack on mules. The housewives prepare traditional *fiambre* (snacks), which consist of parched corn, toasted broad beans, heavily spiced fried guinea pigs, and smoked pork to last as long as two weeks. The peasants provide themselves with one box of matches, one tin pot, coca, and other herbs good for colic, diarrhea, and so forth. One of the peculiar characteristics of long-range travelers in many parts of the Andes is that they always bring home the skull of the guinea pig. They believe that, otherwise, there would be no guinea pig for the next fiambre.

On the day of departure, the montañeros pack their cargo and, commending themselves to their favorite saints, take whatever route is familiar to at least one of them. Distances traveled vary from one day to one week, depending on the location of the community in relation to the coca fields. Generally, a day's travel lasts from dawn to dark, about fourteen to sixteen hours. The hours of actual walking are determined by the distance to pasture for their animals from one day's trip to the next. They usually spend the night in caves, under leafy trees, or in abandoned houses, or they are sheltered by friends and acquaintances along the way.

In coca-producing communities, the peasants either exchange their foods directly with the planters or with the stores established in the towns. They get the same amounts of coca from either source. Exchange is established at the rate of two units of the peasants' products for one unit of coca. The exceptions to the latter are broad-bean flour and dried meat (lamb or pork), which are traded at equal weight. One of the problems montañeros have to deal with is that, in many communities in the jungle, food prices drop with the decline in the production of cocaine; that is, if their production of coca is greater than the demand for cocaine, peasants are paid in coca leaves. However, if coca-paste pits absorb the coca crops, the peasants are forced to accept payments in cash. To the illiterate highlanders, extra days of hiking to find better market conditions are the alternative.

These traders always return immediately following the transactions, for they cannot afford the high cost of living in the jungle. They pack their coca-leaf bales and leave for their communities in the highlands. The logical supposition would be that the peasants could take their loads of coca back to the villages where they would sell them at the legal market prices. But such is not the case. In cities near the jungle, such as Huánuco, peasants sell two qualities of coca. The retail price for select coca leaves is about 5,000 soles, and the lower (*segunda*) quality leaves sell for about 3,000 soles. The peasants carry just enough coca to pay for pack animals and for their own use. Owners of the animals rent their mules and donkeys on condition that they be paid in coca leaves. Mules earn half an arroba (5.75 kilos) and donkeys six pounds (3.0 kilos). The peasants sell the rest of their loads of coca leaves at macerating pools set up along the treks in the rain forests, highland villages, and towns. Very often they sell the leaves to the same planters who initially had refused to pay them in coca for their goods.

In high altitude, the coca leaf is a costly and esteemed item. Friends, relatives, and neighbors visit the montañero peasant. They come with eggs, guinea pigs, and chicha to welcome the traveler back home. The visit implies a token exchange of coca leaves for their highly valued goods. But, unfortunately, visitors are very often disappointed, for new regulations forbid any traveler to transport more than two arrobas of coca leaves. Often the montañeros are unable to transport coca to pay for the rent of animals used on the trip. Police confiscate their bales and parcels containing coca leaves. In order to meet payment agreements, the peasants take secret and unpatrolled routes to smuggle coca. Thus, wage laborers who travel light have better chances of supplying coca to their communities. Wage earners and pack-animal owners are the best sources for obtaining coca leaves.

While among small groups the prevailing practice is exchange, coca is also sold for cash. Like any other commodity, coca is subject to the laws of supply and demand, which are governed by availability, rather than by production and scarcity. Traditional practices, cultural habits, and, to some extent, individual biological needs are other determining factors in the cost and value of coca.

In high-altitude villages and communities where cash flow is minimal, coca is obtained in exchange for Andean grains and roots.[10] The trader usually visits communities at least one month before harvest activities begin, knowing that the crops are promising. If, because of drought or flood, the quality of grains or roots does not meet market standards, the trader does not come to the villages at all.

The *cuca-tumasik* (coca trader) brings with him a few pounds of coca, clothing, tools, and plastic wares. The peasants have the choice of either taking a partial payment in coca for their products or the full amount in advance. Others take only llanqui consisting of a fistful of coca. Between 1981 and 1985, in many villages the rate of exchange was half a pound of coca leaves for two arrobas of select Andean grains. The cuca-tamasik does not go from house to house. Translated, the Quechua term *tumasik* means he "just walks around" the villages with his load of coca and other goods on his burro. Weeks later, the trader comes back to the communities to pick up his commodities with as many pack animals as are needed to transport their grain.

The coca trader takes the grain to towns that have road service to Lima and other cities. Here, he sells the grain (mostly wheat and barley) to truckers for about 13,000 soles per arroba. The peasant is paid 16,000 soles in coca leaves for two arrobas of grain worth 26,000 soles. This type of transaction is carried on despite the fact that the villagers are aware of the current cash prices of both coca and their crops. When the peasants bring their products to town, they sell them at regular prices, and sometimes they even want higher prices. But when coca leaves are used as the medium of exchange, regardless of the setting of the transaction, the peasants accept the rate established by the other party. Thus the coca trader makes almost a tenfold profit.

In many parts of the Andes, coca leaf is so precious a commodity that it may well be compared with credit cards or traveler's checks in the modern world. In locations where cash flow is minimal, chewers and non-chewers alike prefer coca to any other goods brought for exchange or sale; in this respect, Indians and peasants operate similarly to merchants in modern consumer societies who prefer bank cards to charge cards.

) When I paid a short visit to my community of fieldwork in the summer of 1985, I took with me two pounds of coca leaves, three kilos of brown sugar, and five kilos of salt. In this community, restaurants and boardinghouses do not yet exist, and cash cannot buy food. The first thing my research assistant (a local teacher) asked me was, "Did you bring coca with you?" Many peasant friends who saw me arriving came to visit and to welcome me back in the village. I told them that I needed guinea pigs, chickens, eggs, and so forth. Their direct response was, "If you had coca we could provide you what you want." In other instances, I would just invite the peasants to pay me a visit. After our routine conversations, I would give them a fistful of coca. The peasants always react to gifts by asking what one's immediate needs are. The six dollars I spent on the coca leaves, sugar, and salt satisfied my food needs for one week.

The Coca Black Market

Both legal and illegal growers are more attracted to the cocaine black market than to legitimate means of distribution. The shift in the use of coca seriously affects the traditional chewer. The impoverished, coca-chewing Indians are paying higher prices for their traditional pastime. Many of the thousands of bales of dried leaves distributed by the Empresa Nacional de la Coca end up in illegitimate enterprise.

Legal coca growers sell their crops to ENACO at the fixed price of 200,000 soles per arroba. The highland retailer buys coca from ENACO for about 250,000 soles per arroba. The coca retailers are regular store owners who are certified to sell coca leaves. The legal retail price in small highland towns and cities is 1,000 soles per ounce. Thus, the coca retailer gets 400,000 soles per arroba. ENACO offices are always located in urban areas. The legal coca retailer has to pay for the transportation of the bales. Transporting coca from ENACO warehouses involves the use of motorized transportation and pack animals for a total cost of about 50,000 soles per arroba. The coca seller makes a total profit of about 100,000 soles per arroba. Depending on the size of the population, he may sell from one to as many as three arrobas per day.

In cities and towns near coca-producing provinces, coca leaves are much more expensive than in highland communities. For example, in the streets of Tingo María a bag of coca of about three grams sells for 1,000 soles. High demand for coca leaves in the black market also has a direct effect on the quality of coca leaves. Legal coca growers sell their crops to the government every three months, or four times a year. In order to provide coca for both the government and the underground market, the legal coca growers pick the leaves every two months. The obvious consequence is lower quality coca. The black market pays 900,000 soles per arroba of dried coca leaves. Actual legal producers survive only because the cocaine economy subsidizes them. Because of the high cost of living, they have to keep wages and working conditions competitive.

When the legal Andean retailer buys coca from ENACO, he makes sure that he is given the best quality available in the ENACO premises. He brings a turkey (an expensive, luxurious food), a sheep, guinea pigs, and so forth, to give ENACO employees on special occasions, or he bribes them with cash. Occasionally, he obtains the traditional *huanta* (coca leaves picked when mature and dried indoors) to satisfy his customers. However, large quantities of huanta as well as standard leaves are consolidated for their shipment to the black market in the jungles or else used in coca-paste production in the highlands.

The highland retailer may also be a coca-paste manufacturer or a black-market distributor. He always has one or two bales of low-quality coca in the store. The peasant or the Indian chewer sees the condition of the leaves and buys his provision from some other storekeeper. Some experienced coca chewers, who are also familiar with the details of coca-paste manufacture, argue that there have been cases of adulteration of legal coca leaves. They contend that legal coca handlers (ENACO, legal coca growers, or licensed retailers) are mixing regular coca leaves with the leaves collected from the coca-paste pits, that is, the leaves that were soaked in the fluid containing sulfuric acid. These claims are based on much infection and inflammation found in the mouths and throats of coca chewers, which may have been caused by contaminated leaves.

As seen above, in the traditional marketing, coca from the jungles was transported on pack animals. Currently, the legal supply of coca travels almost exclusively via the roads. The legal coca leaves collected in the highland black market are shipped back to the rain forests on pack animals, and in trucks and cars. Legal coca merchants send the bales holding coca to small populations in the highlands.

The technique of trafficking coca leaves in the woods is usually legal distribution. There are populations that lie in one or two days' walking distance of the coca-producing forests. The legal distribution of coca is in the exclusive realm of ENACO. Therefore, nearby communities, who earlier had secured their provisions directly from the growers, now purchase supplies from the ENACO offices. The latter are set up generally in large towns and cities or in the capitals of the departments (states). To small populations, coca travels via the roads and on mules and donkeys. The storekeeper or the small bodeguero sells the bales of coca to full-time independent coca-paste entrepreneurs. These illegal cocaine manufacturers may be friends, relatives, or associates of the highland coca suppliers. In highland black markets, one arroba of coca leaves sells for about 400,000 soles. Cost of transportation is about 5,000 soles per arroba, and it is carried either on pack animals or by the peasants.

It would be misleading to argue that all coca leaves brought from the jungles take only the route described above. The highland black market also transports coca from cities and towns by truck. One arroba of legal coca going into the jungle is sold for about 500,000 soles, which is 44 percent cheaper than the current local black-market prices. One interesting characteristic of this type of black market is the legal use of the coca black market as an effective interrelationship between different coca-producing regions. Thus, coca leaves produced in the southeastern foothills of the Andes may, via the legal market, travel as far as the northeastern mountainous forests to link up with processing chemicals.

Both coca leaves from the black market and those collected in the region are combined for their use in the macerating pools and pits. In the northeastern rain forests, coca leaves are sold publicly. Initially, they are gathered in trucks and cars, then the bales, bundles, and baskets of coca leaves are carried to the coca-paste hideouts located deep in the woods. The economics of the process of making coca paste, and its refinement into cocaine hydrochloride, are the topics of chapter 4.

Given the average yield per harvest per hectare (35 arrobas), the 100,000 hectares of coca farming may yield an annual total crop of about 14,000,000 arrobas of dried leaves or about 160,000 metric tons.[11] It is estimated that 1.5 million people chew coca.[12] Assuming that 5,410 metric tons of coca leaves are consumed by the traditional coca-chewing Indians and peasants,[13] 164,990 metric tons per year are absorbed by the illicit economy. Thus, after allocation for national consumption, the black-market value of this yearly surplus production (164,990 metric tons) is estimated to be at least $1 billion.

The Cocaine Economy

Before the cocaine boom in the seventies, coca was produced primarily for traditional consumption and legally for medical purposes. This trend has changed. In the eighties, the primary focus of coca producers is the use of the leaves in the preparation of coca paste. The traditional coca-leaf market in the highlands is no longer the main interest of coca planters.

After harvesting the coca leaves comes the extraction of the alkaloids from the plant. This process, resulting in cocaine, is an enterprise unto itself. Although the basic raw material is locally produced and readily available, other ingredients required come from outside. The cocaine economy supports both legal and illegal markets. The need for chemical agents generates a gamut of mechanisms for smuggling, which creates new sets of social interrelationships, each of which adds to the value of the final product. In the underground economy, the move from coca farming to manufacture of coca paste and cocaine does not require the use of complex technological and organizational structures. Thus, the bulk of the cost of cocaine as an illegal commodity is not determined totally by costs of production but by the rewards paid to those individuals involved in the distribution—from coca-paste pits to cocaine-refining laboratories to the consumer.

Beginnings of the Underground Economy

The most expensive materials in the jungle are those that are illegally transported or smuggled. Of the four chemical agents used in the preparation of coca paste, only one is locally produced: calcium oxide (unslaked lime). The calcining kilns built alongside the roads operate legally and regularly. Lime from the furnaces is relatively cheap because the kilns are set right at the foot of lime rock hills, and fuel (timber) is abundant. Production of calcium oxide in the smallest kiln is about 800 kilos per day, and it employs many local and migrant workers. The unslaked lime is packed in bags of 8 kilos each. Truckers buy the bags of lime for about 7,000 soles per bag. They then sell them to retailers for about 11,000 soles each. Retailers sell them for 15,000 soles per bag, and usually get hundreds of bags of calcium oxide on a three-to-four-day consignment. Retailers always have another supply store deep in the woods where prices are from 20 percent to 25 percent higher.

Peru is not a country with a marked industrial division of labor like the United States or other European countries. The capital city of Lima absorbs almost every activity in the industrial sector. Therefore, Lima is the main national supplier of materials to the underground economy, especially sulfuric acid and sodium carbonate. Some chemicals, except lime, cement, and kerosene, may come from Colombia, Brazil, and Bolivia by air, river, or land. Kerosene does not necessarily have its shipping points in Lima. It can be brought from any point in the country. Kerosene is transported to the jungle to be sold as domestic fuel. However, people would rather cook with timber and save kerosene for maceration purposes. Domestic kerosene is used because it is cheaper than industrial kerosene and sold in the legal market without any restrictions.

Three brands of cement—Andino, Pacasmayo, and Lima—are available. Cemento Andino comes from Huancayo, a city which is about ten hours from the largest town in the rain forests. Cemento Pacasmayo travels more than thirty hours from the small northern seaport of Pacasmayo. Despite the differences in transportation to the market, retail prices for the three trade names are about the same. A fifty-kilo bag of cement sells for 75,000 soles or 56 percent more than the price outside the drug area.

The best place to buy sodium carbonate and sulfuric acid is in Lima, the largest industrial city in Peru. The manufacturer's prices are 2,600 soles per kilo of sulfuric acid and 10,000 soles per kilo of sodium carbonate. In the jungle, one kilo of sulfuric acid sells for 15,000 soles and one kilo of sodium carbonate for 40,000 soles. The sale of chemicals used in the preparation of coca paste, as well as cocaine itself, is controlled by the government. The restrictions, however, benefit both manufacturers and black-market jobbers connected to factories and distributors.

Chemical smugglers themselves rarely buy directly from the factory or from the distributor. They always know a jobber connected to the industry. The illegal jobber may be a factory employee or a licensed distributor, charging twice as much as the legally established prices. Thus, sulfuric acid and sodium carbonate in Lima are available in the black market for about 5,000 soles and 20,000 soles, respectively. Demand for materials used in the underground industry is so high that people tend to suffer from almost permanent shortages when their livelihoods depend on any of the chemicals. For instance, small manufacturers of car batteries complain that factories always claim to be out of sulfuric acid, and these manufacturers cannot afford black-market prices. Shipments are sent by itinerant buses and trucks that travel between shipping points and the jungle. Sodium carbonate is shipped as foodstuff manufactured on the coast.

Smuggled chemicals are discovered every now and then, but never to the point that supply to the jungle is completely cut off. Luckily, control of traffic on the roads is organized in such a way that it eases the smuggling of these two elements. It is difficult for the police to control every single bag or sack in very large loads of merchandise and foodstuffs displaying original factory packaging. Besides failing to detect the contraband, the police let trucks and buses pass by controls with little or no inspection. Every commercial vehicle stops at stations established alongside roads and highways. Either the driver or his helpers take the cargo or passenger inventory into the office or the sentry-box. They place some money in the control book. Then the officer takes his routine bribe, stamps the control book, and the vehicle continues on its way.[1]

Shipping is not limited to the use of motorized vehicles. It is also done on mules, donkeys, and on human backs. This type of transportation is used, not because of tight police control, but because of the lack of road service to many sections of the rain forests. Despite the fact that it takes longer to get the chemicals to coca-paste pits and that transportation costs are lower, the prices are comparable to those for substances carried by trucks and cars. The routes taken to smuggle sodium carbonate and sulfuric acid into the forests are the same treks and trails followed by highland peasant travelers. The hiker or the muleteer "chemical smuggler" is, at times, just a wage earner; the cargo is usually someone else's.

Caution, experience, and a good sense of direction are the preconditions for a safe and effective delivery of materials. The nature of the substance, variations in altitude and weather, and other exigencies are taken into account only by expert and knowledgeable travelers. Often the risk of being caught by the police is taken care of before the outset of travel. However, if provision does not include waterproof packing and sealed containers, the chances of losing the cargo, as well as of physical damage, are high.

When I visited Paras, my village of research in 1981, I asked to see a man named Tomás, one of the masters of the Andean treks. When I saw Tomás on the outskirts of Orangetown, he told me of his latest experience. The cap of two plastic containers of sulfuric acid had not been tightly closed, and the leaking acid had actually cut a rented mule in half. Tomás buried the two plastic containers of sulfuric acid and then hiked four hours to reach the nearest town. He rented another mule and managed to bring the sulfuric acid to the town, where he found help. The peasant smuggler sold his acid without making any profit and continued his trip to his usual place in the jungle. Tomás was compelled to stay longer because he had to save money to pay $100 to the mule's owner.

Accidents may also be caused by confusing sulfuric acid with the name under which it is sold. Cases of confusing sodium carbonate and sulfuric acid with other goods are also very common. I myself had to be very careful with these two elements during my first weeks in the field, for my host in Free Village owned a small hardware store, which I occasionally tended for a few hours. One morning, a peasant came into the store and ordered foodstuff sold by the kilo. I weighed, packed, and gave him what I thought he wanted. Later, he came back to exchange this for what he really needed, which was sodium carbonate.

This supplier alone sells an average of 50 kilos of sulfuric acid daily at 15,000 soles per kilo and from 20 to 30 kilos of sodium carbonate at 40,000 soles per kilo. The empty sugar and cement bags are sold to lime truckers for 500 soles.

While calcium oxide and kerosene are sold legally and may be substituted for cement and gasoline respectively, sodium carbonate and sulfuric acid are basic and indispensable; they are brought to the area exclusively for use in the coca-paste industry. There is no legal demand for them. During the dry winter, the chemical elements are regularly available, but in the summer there is a marked shortage due to the heavy rains which make the roads impassable. Buying materials and putting them away is a good practice.

Capital and Materials

The next step is the preparation of the coca paste. Depending on the location of the pit, the whole process of coca-paste manufacture takes from four to five days. That process is so common and natural that everyone in a community knows who is preparing how much.

As the final step in the manufacture of coca paste, the separation of the alkaloid cocaine from the leaves by maceration—that is, the reduction of the coca leaves to a coarse substance—is achieved in three chemical-processing steps. These chemical processes are commonly known as "preparation." Calculations of the amounts of leaves that the harvest will yield are usually done prior to coca picking. Based on the amount of the basic raw material expected, the macerator secures supplies from the four agents needed to make the coca paste: sulfuric acid, calcium oxide (lime), kerosene, and sodium carbonate. For a variety of reasons, such as excessive demand, heavy summer rains, or mechanical failures in the kilns, there are occasional shortages of calcium oxide for which cement may be substituted.

The first day of work is limited to collecting coca leaves and transporting them to the macerating sites, cleaning the concrete pools, and setting up the portable plastic pits. Although hundreds of concrete pits have been destroyed by the United States drug eradication program, this type of infrastructure is still predominant in the industry. The sizes of concrete pits visited during my research ranged from 7.2 meters long, 3.6 meters wide, and .9 meters deep (288 × 144 × 36 inches) to 8.0 meters long, 5.0 meters wide, and 1.6 meters high (315 × 197 × 39 inches). The pliable pit consists of a large heavy plastic sheet tied to a timber frame. In either case, the pit resembles a large halved decanter placed on the ground. In the selected spot, they plant sticks (approximately 1.6 meters high) 50 centimeters apart, forming a large irregular rectangle. The sticks shape the synthetic flat material and can withstand the pressure of the mixture of coca and acid fluid.

The ground on which the plastic pit rests must be smooth and free of any pointed or sharp objects such as nails or stones. Cleaning the floor and setting up the pit takes about three hours. Concrete pools require only the removal of branches and leaves that were used to hide the pit. Only those who have pits for their own exclusive use are compelled to cover them. That is, some planters make coca paste only once every three months or after every harvest period and do not let others use their private pools. Other manufacturers make regular use of their pits and sometimes let friends, relatives, and neighbors use them.

Depending upon the size of the pits and the amount of coca, the actual preparation of the raw drug itself requires the labor of two to five workers. During the process, the leader is the experienced mixer or "chemist"; the rest are general helpers. The mixer acquires his trade from serving as an apprentice or learns the role from parents or other models. Of the thirty mixers interviewed and observed, 75 percent were younger than thirty years and half of this group were natives of the rain forests. To all of the natives, the coca-paste industry was the first and the only economic activity they had known in their lives.

There are two kinds of mixers. One is the professional mixer whose main livelihood is his expertise in making coca paste. The second type is the planter-entrepreneur. He has total control of his business. The mixer always has his own band of loyal helpers. Unless the helpers or pit laborers are immediate relatives or very close friends, the mixer does not let them actively participate in the critical step of the preparation. The mixer is jealous of his formula. When he is about to make crucial combinations, he almost always asks his helpers to bring more water, or simply to remain seated away from his place of work. Some pit work-

A coca-paste pit. Most coca-paste entrepreneurs make their portable pits using plastic sheets sold in hardware stores.

ers have been working for many months and do not know how to make a good mix.

Generally, the mixer gets high wages for his work; his salary averages about ten dollars per day plus meals. As an added incentive some planters or entrepreneurs offer the mixer partnership in the business. Helpers are paid about nine dollars plus meals for three days' work. Pit helpers are always picked from teams of laborers who have maintained good conduct and have been loyal in keeping the operation secret. Not many wage laborers become maceration workers.

The mixer directs helpers to fill the coca-paste pit with the indicated volume of water. Since the pits are set up near streams or rivers, filling the pit takes only about an hour. The proportions of materials needed to make good quality coca paste are shown in Table 3. Many variables determine the quantity of leaves required to make three kilos of coca paste. The age of the leaves is important, but not critical.

In some places where slope and climate conditions are different from the coca core area, twenty-one arrobas (238.5 kilos) to twenty-four ar-

Table 3

Materials Required to Prepare Three Kilos of Coca Paste

Material	Quantities	Prices ($US) in the upper Huallaga	Prices ($US) in the Highland
Coca leaves	340.8 kilos (30 arrobas)	2,700.00	$900.0
Sulfuric acid	15 kilos	21.00	11.0
Kerosene	20 gallons	21.00	10.0
Lime	24 kilos	5.60	2.5
Sodium carbonate	3 kilos	12.00	8.0
Water	3900 litres	00.000	0.0
TOTAL		2,760.60	$931.5

robas (272.6 kilos) of leaves are enough to make three kilos of paste. In the southeastern section of the Peruvian coca belt, as many as thirty-six arrobas (409 kilos) of leaves are needed to prepare three kilos of coca paste. The best coca I found during my research was in a small village located at 2,100 meters above sea level, coinciding with Chinchao's (Huánuco) altitude, far away from the Peruvian coca core area where about ninety-five kilos of dried leaves yield one kilo of good coca paste.

The total amount of investment in materials presented in Table 3 applies only to those who do not produce their own coca leaves. (Those who do produce their own also have their own provisions of chemicals, which they get at prices lower than those in local black markets.) They get their supplies of coca in two ways: exchange and purchase. They exchange sulfuric acid and sodium carbonate for coca leaves with the planters and also buy dried leaves at the current black-market rates. In the summer of 1985, the price of one arroba of coca was 900,000 soles.

The profit for full-time coca-paste entrepreneurs is determined by the volume of production. If the entrepreneur's supply of coca depends on the planters, his cash investment in the leaves is about $950 per kilo of coca paste, including labor and meals provided to workers. But because of his exclusive year-round operation, by national standards, his income is very high. Besides constant production, this type of operation is often connected to the next chemical step, refining centers. Thus, low profits or losses are offset by higher market values of cocaine hydrochloride.

Isaias is a twenty-one-year-old peasant who has never been outside the jungle. He says he is the third generation of a family whose exclusive economic activity has been the manufacture of cocaine. His eighty-year-old grandfather talks about some Germans (he probably means Anglos) who came to the area to set up their cocaine laboratories. Isaias bought four hectares of a coca plantation, of which two hectares had mature, fully productive coca plants.

When Isaias went to supervise his pickers, he invited me to join him. We rode on his Honda motorcycle for about half an hour. Then, we hiked for another hour to reach his plantation. I asked him whether he could go to town the following day. His answer was, "It depends on the weather, for if it is cloudy and humid I have got to prepare." Indeed, the following day was cloudy and humid. He decided to "soak" his *mato* (fresh coca leaf). For macerating the equivalent of thirty arrobas of dried leaves (sixty arrobas before drying) five more kilos of sulfuric acid were required. However, the coca paste yield was higher. Isaias got 3.2 kilos of good quality coca paste.

If mato yields were higher, then why dry the leaves before macerating them? Drying the leaves is a traditional practice and agricultural ritual. But the coca-paste industry does not abide rituals, traditions, and habits. Leaves are dried because of both transportation difficulties and changes in coca-paste prices. When coca leaves are properly dried and packed in bales, they can be stored for long periods without losing much of their alkaloid content. Furthermore, coca leaves are raw material useful only in conjunction with chemicals such as sulfuric acid.

From Leaves to Rocks

The first step in the long process of breaking down the chemical content of coca to obtain cocaine is to add five kilos of sulfuric acid to every 1300 liters of water in the cement or plastic pit. No instrument is used to test the ideal relative acidity (pH) of the combination. At this point the expert mixer plays a very important role. He dips his hand into the acid fluid, brings up a few drops of the liquid on his palm and tastes it in a mouth-washing manner. Coca leaves are soaked in the acid fluid for twelve to eighteen hours. Journalists have erroneously reported (e.g., *Time*, Feb. 25, 1985) that "coca leaves are soaked in a solution of water and kerosene, which releases the cocaine contained in the leaves." Because of differences in the molecular weights, water and kerosene (carbon oil) cannot be chemically combined. Kerosene is not used in the extraction of cocaine from the leaves but instead at a later stage.

When the work is carried out in a concrete pit, some human labor is needed to help soak the leaves. Pit laborers stomp on the floating bundles of leaves for about one hour. The acid fluid containing alkaloids (cocaine), resins, tar, and so forth, takes on a light brown color. This fluid is commonly called *caldo* (broth). To me, the taste is like a heavy coca tea (*mate de coca*) with its characteristic smell. After required soaking time, caldo without the leaves is decanted to another pit.

In the second pit, the acid fluid containing alkaloid is neutralized by adding a base, that is, a compound capable of mixing with an acid. The chemical base could be sodium carbonate, calcium oxide, or cement. In the Peruvian cocaine industry, calcium oxide (lime) is used. The base element is stirred into the "soup" with a wooden instrument resembling a capital T whose flat crossbar has perforations to ease the blending process. After fifteen minutes of agitation, until the acid has been neutralized, the "soup" becomes alkaloid in basic fluid.

At this point, the basic fluid containing alkaloid is mixed with an organic solvent (kerosene). The same blending procedure is performed again for about fifteen minutes. The fluid is decanted and, because of its lighter weight, the kerosene remains on the surface. It is separated and used again and again until the process is finished.

In a separate plastic container with a capacity of about twenty gallons, water is mixed with sulfuric acid in the proportion of one-and-a-half tablespoons of sulfuric acid to one liter of water. This is the second critical formula, for an error in the water/sulfuric acid ratio will result in bad coca paste. (If either of the two formulas has too much sulfuric acid, then the mistake will be evident in the color of the acid. If not right, the liquid takes on a pale tone the color of tea, and when it is stirred, a sticky substance builds up on the stirring stick. This poor-quality coca paste is known as "chicle," and it is sold as "bazooka" in the streets of New York and Miami. The correct formula yields a crystal-clear liquid.) The fluid obtained in the second step is poured into this acid solution and stirred with a stick.

Sodium carbonate is then added to the solution. A dirty white substance (coca paste) forms at the bottom of the plastic container. The substance is placed on a piece of fine cloth and squeezed to expel the water; then it is dried in the sun. The acid fluid is disposed of. New acid fluid is made to soak the leaves in the pit for the second and third times. A batch is considered successful when at least 80 percent of the expected amount of substance is obtained in the first round. The remaining 20 percent comes from the second round. In this case, the entrepreneurs often let their workers do the third round for themselves. At the end of the preparation, thousands of gallons of polluted water are drained into streams and rivers.

Often, pit laborers may end up with as much as thirty grams of paste. Thus, a successful "preparation" benefits both coca-paste entrepreneurs and pit laborers. Social bonds are developed during coca-paste production. The bonds are the result of participation in this illegal economy, and from them spring friendships, marriages, and compadrazgo.

In addition to the miscalculation in the mixture of one of the two acid-liquid preparations, many other things contribute to low-quality coca paste. First, it is more difficult to extract coca from some varieties of coca leaves such as erythroxylon Novogranatense, known as Colombian coca, and erythroxylon Truxillense. Next, coca leaves sold to coca-paste entrepreneurs may have been picked prematurely or been grown in different areas. Finally, the most frequent cause for bad quality is use of a lighter sulfuric acid sold by some suppliers. Usually, mixers or "chemists" are experts who control successful production. Normally, the mixers buy the materials; if hired only for the manufacturing process, they always try to learn the origin of the leaves and approximate dates when they were picked. What this means is that the mixers are experienced persons who know their environment so well that cultivation and mixing are almost second nature. Thus, their mastery of their specialty in one area is not necessarily easily duplicated in other areas of coca planting and cocaine manufacturing where circumstances differ. In addition to the pits that are operated in the rain forests, the preparation of coca paste takes place in some villages or on the outskirts of some towns along the central Andes. This backyard cottage-type industry is attracting more and more people, both urban and rural. In most cases, for the sake of security the highland processor sets up his pit in isolated areas where he has a peasant compadre or debtor, because the characteristic smell from the mixture of dried coca leaves and other agents is difficult to hide. If the pit is discovered by police, the peasant in charge is usually the only suspect, and often he goes to county jail for a few days until the mestizo townsman "clears" his status with the local police.

In the highlands, coca for the preparation of coca paste comes from the leaves transported for legal chewing or sometimes is smuggled into the area in large amounts from bribing authorities and the police. The two primary differences between full-time coca-paste entrepreneurs from the jungles and highland producers are variations in prices for coca leaves and amounts of coca paste produced. First, the highland cocaine entrepreneur's cost of production is lower than his jungle counterpart's investment. Material, including coca leaves, is cheaper in the highlands. Most highland cocaine manufacturers are licensed coca traders; thus their provisions of coca are much cheaper and more secure. Their cash investment in coca leaves for three kilos of coca paste is about 9,000,000 soles. This sum can change to about 12,300,000 if the coca-paste manufacturer buys coca leaves from the black market, which sells ENACO coca leaves.

Second, unlike the manufacturer in the rain forest, the highland coca producer is a small, cottage-industry merchant. Because the clandestine activity demands an exclusive "workplace," mass production in the barren *cordilleras* (mountain ranges) is rarely seen. Thus, making three kilos of coca paste that takes three days in the jungle can take as long as ten days in the highlands. Although labor is cheaper in the highlands, helpers are seldom hired. Secrecy is an important factor. Frequently, families and relatives are ignorant of the entrepreneur's operation. Leftover coca leaves are generally disposed of in two ways. After the insipid and powerless leaves are dried, they are burned and the ashes are used as fertilizer. Other times the dry remnants are used as fuel to calcine limestone in order to make calcium oxide. The highland coca-paste entrepreneurs are not directly tied to the international underworld.

The fine and coarse rocks smell something like slaked lime. The balls of *merca* (merchandise) are kept in empty cement or lime paper bags, usually in their original shapes. They look like balls made out of white sand that disintegrate when they are squeezed. The next immediate chemical process is removal of impurities from coca paste to make cocaine hydrochloride.

Distribution and Market

Both the international drug syndicate and cocaine-producing countries have their own social division of labor, rituals, and practices. There is an intermarriage between the national economic needs and the international underworld economy. The result of this unique union is manifested in social and economic behavior of the groups that participate in production, distribution, and marketing of coca paste and other goods related to the industry.

Before leaving the "green mines" for the national or international markets, the white, sandlike balls of coca paste circulate in communities, hamlets, and towns. Then they take diverse routes. Coca-paste producers sell their "stuff" a few hours after manufacture, for if it is kept for many days, the substance's weight is reduced.

Large-scale buyers are known as *corredores* (see pages 86–93). In each territory dominated by one boss there are two kinds of buyers: independent and contracted. Independent buyers operate their own business; contracted collectors work for commissions, averaging about $100 per week. Few independent operators survive long in the business because they cannot afford to buy wet coca paste. Coca-paste manufacturers resist doing business with independent buyers, because they demand more money.

Furthermore, if independent buyers pay better prices than "official buyers," contracted collectors complain to their bosses. Their bosses get rid of the "unfair competition." Independent buyers can continue their operations only by paying the same prices stipulated by the local organized group. Small entrepreneurs survive only in cases in which the independent buyer's operation is believed insignificant, that is, if the volume handled by independent operators does not affect local supply.

Because the *patrón* (boss) is aware that the merchandise is bought wet and knows that coca paste loses weight in a few days, the suppliers deliver lesser amounts than the boss purchased. As much as two kilos are retained. Bosses accept the arrangement without objection. They do not consider the moisture that chemical components of the raw drug absorb from the environment to be part of the product's actual weight. Another method of cheating the international mafia consists in lumping "chicle," bought for lower prices, with regular coca paste.

Again, chicle is the fruit of a miscalculation in the amounts of sulfuric acid added. The error may take place during one of the two preparations of acid fluid. When dry, chicle is harder and more solid than regular coca paste. If the error takes place in the first stage, the formula extracts more of other components (resins, tar, and other impurities) from the coca leaves than a correct formula would. If amounts of sulfuric acid are exceeded in the third step, the alkaloid cocaine contents are destroyed (reduced).

Although the alkaloid cocaine contents may be present, chicle is considered to be of lower quality. Therefore, it is sold for about 30 percent less than the regular price. Those who can afford to put away the merchandise until the next picking season and preparation are able to include part of the chicle in the sale. Others, especially small-scale producers who take cash advances or loans, are compelled to take the loss. If a *cocalero* (coca planter) controls the whole process, chicle still accounts for some profit, for the most expensive ingredient (coca) comes from his own production.

Fluctuations in prices are functions of international demand, presence of organized crime, police control, and distances to shipping points (airports). Primarily, Peru supplies coca paste to the international refining center, Colombia.[2] Nevertheless, between 1980 and 1985, large-scale refining centers were set up in the country (see pages 000–000).

When the bosses in "Colombia" send more cash requesting greater amounts of coca paste, the local boss authorizes raising prices 20 percent more. For instance, during the first two weeks of July 1985, one kilo of coca paste was sold for $1,000, but later in the same month, it dropped to $900 per kilo.

Arguments for stipulating new prices can be attributed to the saturation of the international market or heavy competition. The most naive argument, however effective, to maintain or lower prices of coca paste is competition from coca produced in the United States. Coca planters and coca-paste manufacturers are made to believe that the United States produces coca leaves. One day I was sitting on the porch of a hardware store when two regular customers came in and sat next to me. One of them commented on the latest news of American coca-leaf prices, quality, and crop yields. International traffickers have spread the idea that United States coca plantations yield only one crop per year and that forty arrobas of American coca are required to make one kilo of coca paste. At first, I thought that this finding was an isolated case, but as I moved around various communities and provinces I found people explaining to others the characteristics of American coca. In some places where they knew I came from New York, they even asked me to lecture to them about coca-farming technology in America.

Some towns and cities are territorial dominions of some secret societies. Organized crime stipulates prices based on seniority in the territory. One "big fish," whose brother represents the business in Colombia, states clearly that he had a difficult time establishing the business in his locality. In no case, he said, was he going to let newcomers try to take over the market. This "white gentleman," as some local people call him, buys coca paste at prices he believes are just. In the summer of 1985, while prices fluctuated in other areas, his price for one kilo of paste was fixed at $800, or 20 percent less than prices paid in the core drug district.

Like other legal consumer commodities, coca-paste market values add expenses such as human labor required for transportation, the use of secret routes to mislead police, and other unexpected expenditures. Besides being heavily concentrated in drug-terminal towns and using regular transit roads, coca paste also moves through villages and communities in the highlands as it proceeds on its way to national and international markets. Some of the latter are isolated strategic locations whose economies are fit to cover and ease circulation of coca paste in Peru.

Before getting mixed with commercial shipments and thus disguised, drug parcels emerge from the jungle as valuable "rocks" and come first to small towns and villages at three to four days' walking distance from their point of manufacture. From these locations, motorized shipping terminals are just a few hours' hiking distance away. In Andean shipping points, some wholesale dealers buy the "stuff" coming directly from the villages and towns where it was made.

Two kinds of people are involved in the local trafficking of cocaine. The petty trader either buys coca paste at the first stage or he goes to the jungle to bring paste to towns for resale to wholesale dealers. The resale of coca paste brought from the jungle reports a profit of about 30 percent, less if brought from first-stage markets. The second type of drug dealer is the local middle-class bodeguero or the public employee. Town wholesalers always have the petty traders in their power in that they lend money at high interest or pay lower prices by arguing an overstock. Petty traders are always out of cash because they splurge in the towns. They are the best consumers of the services available in the coca-paste terminal settings. Commercial movement of coca paste in the second stage is almost completely open. Everyone knows who is who in the business, and it is not rare to observe local and nonlocal petty dealers walking around with their merca in their *alforjas* (traditional saddlebags) hung over their shoulders.

Coca paste from the second stage goes to the national market via surface transportation. Buses, trucks, and private cars carry the drug, declaring it as food being transported to Lima and other cities on the coast. Some police stations control traffic coming to Lima. Usually, the dirt roads are closed for twelve hours, from 6:00 P.M. to 6:00 A.M. of the next day. In theory, these stations are responsible for searching for cocaine in the vehicles traveling the route. However, it is an impossible task for the two or three policemen to do more than simply check personal identifications, detain suspects, or accidentally discover smuggled coca paste.

Smugglers and dealers have their own ways of finding out their status with the police. When they suspect or know that police are expecting them, they use specialized *pasadores* (hikers) or muleteers. The latter take the load on pack animals, or on their backs, along unpatrolled passages to specific points of pickup. Once coca paste is in Lima or other cities in the central Andes, depending on who the carrier is, it is transported to various other places. In the cities, some sell their merca to customers or people to whom they were recommended, and some are caught by police.

Important reasons for bringing coca paste to the market in the cities are to satisfy individual consumption and to supply it to refining laboratories. Slums and shantytowns are ideal settings for cutting, packaging, distributing, and establishing smoking galleries. It would be misleading to affirm that all coca paste entering the cities is either smoked or further processed into pure cocaine. It takes unsuspected roads and routes to international markets. The most outstanding feature of distribution and marketing of coca paste is its return to the jungle.

The distance from Sodoma to Peachtown is only thirty-six kilometers, and there is regular road service between these towns. Probably more than 75 percent of land in the outskirts of Sodoma consists of coca plantations. The obvious assumption to make would be that the coca paste made in Sodoma is sent to Peachtown, since these two towns are only fifteen hours' walking distance apart. Peachtown is under tight police control, and is managed with little or no difficulty. But the problem is that coca paste coming from Sodoma is hard to market in Peachtown because the drug traffic in this town is controlled by a European family that migrated to the area during the Second World War.

Although small amounts of coca paste are smuggled into Peachtown, the bulk of the product goes by way of the northern route. The trip to make the deliveries takes from two to three days on pack animals, boats, in canoes, and rafts. When these means of transportation are not available or trails are inaccessible to animals, human beings become the "two-footed jackasses" of the cocaine industry, transporting on their backs as much as fifty kilos of coca paste for wages of about 30,000 soles. Shipments from Sodoma heading for the western route take as long as eight to ten days to arrive at mass transportation terminals.

As cargo going to the jungles in trucks, buses, and airplanes is superficially checked, the outlawed freight is dispatched by unsuspected methods. It is interesting to see how most of the coca paste manufactured in Sodoma travels through highland communities, touches cities on the Pacific, and continues to the jungles via Peachtown on its way to "Colombia." Because the method and the route present minimum risks, either the dealers travel in the same vehicles, or they send their parcels and packages ahead and pick them up later themselves. If the "stuff" was bought in the province of Sodoma at the current local price of 6,000,000 soles per kilo, and sold at the average national market price of 10,000,000 soles, except for Peachtown, the long journey would report high profits.

Kitchens and Cooks

Shipments of "white gold ore" that leave for "Colombia," as well as the fractions that remain in Peru, go through the second and last chemical treatment that results in the substance craved by millions of cocaine addicts.

Refining coca paste to make cocaine is a subculture in its own right, and as such it practices a jargon and rituals unique to its function. In describing the process of cocaine making in the following pages, only names and phrases that do not jeopardize the more or less normal functioning of the industry are used.

The nature of chemical materials used requires that "kitchens" (laboratories) be set up in houses or other places with safe electrical outlets and good security. Suburban middle-class houses and lower-class areas are ideal locations for establishing such kitchens. Sophistication in the process, quality of the end product, and type of markets are matters that uneducated lower-class individuals cannot consider. Production of coca and coca paste is, in most cases, a subsistence economy for farmers, peasants, and migrants. However, manufacture, distribution, and marketing of cocaine hydrochloride is controlled by professionals and middle-class families or individuals.

Coca paste that stays in the country goes to refining laboratories in two different ways. Some coca-paste entrepreneurs either have their own refining laboratories or are associated with such laboratories. Others get their supplies of coca paste from the national black market. Only in rare cases do coca-paste traffickers and cocaine refiners transport their merchandise themselves. *Burros* or *correos*, described in the next section, diffuse the goods throughout the country.

Finishing the coca paste to extract the alkaloid cocaine from its basic form may be done either hot or cold. In the hot procedure, laboratory (kitchen) distillers are used. The use of the traditional chemistry infrastructure calls for fixed or permanent workplaces. The distillers are ideal when the transformation involves large amounts of coca paste.

More and more kitchens are adopting the practical method of cold cooking (refining). What is ordinarily called the "cold method" is practiced by a great majority of independent individual entrepreneurs and small clans of traffickers related to international marketing. Provided that chemicals are available, cold kitchens can even be set up in the places where coca paste is produced. Although there are some problems and difficulties in getting materials and good "cooks," the enterprise is worth undertaking. Setting up a cold kitchen suggests taking or sending materials and chemists to perform on-site assignments. The cook may be a professional chemist running his own operation, may be a partner in the business, or may be hired for a good salary. In all cases I observed, the cook was either a partner or owner of the small business. Large-scale refiners hire professionals, paying salaries of from $10,000 to $15,000 per year; that is, 1,190 percent to 1,786 percent higher than a full-time high school teacher's annual income of 8,400,000 soles.

Chemicals used to wash and to refine coca paste are extremely corrosive. Glass, porcelain, or pyrex bowls have to be used. These containers may be purchased from regular hardware stores or even from street peddlers. A good working set of wares consists of six or seven porcelain or glass vessels. As to chemicals, 300 milliliters of hydrochloric acid, eight gallons of acetone, and one gallon of ether combine to form one kilo of cocaine hydrochloride. The total black-market price for these three elements is about $700, 500 percent higher than legally established prices. Quantities and prices of materials may vary, depending on the coca paste to be refined, that is, on the quality of the leaves, determined by the area where the leaves are produced.

From my observation of four "cold kitchens," I calculate the average amount of coca paste needed to get 1.0 kilo of cocaine hydrochloride to be 3.75 kilos of coca paste. Three and a half (3.5) kilos of coca paste from the plantations in the far northeastern slopes contain 1.0 kilo of cocaine, whereas in the southeastern area, for the same amount of cocaine hydrochloride, it takes 4.0 kilos of coca paste.

Once coca paste reaches the refining site, the cook evaluates the quality of the material and estimates the amount of chemicals needed in processing. The whitish substance is crumbled and diluted in acetone. The fluid containing alkaloid, resins, and water is decanted. Some impurities remain at the bottom of the vessel. In the second container, hot air is added to separate the acetone, which then evaporates, while alkaloid and other substances condense on the base of the receptacle. Then the wet substance is forced through a heavy-duty press until water and remaining resins drip through. The result is washed coca paste.

Next, two solutions are prepared in two separate vessels. In one of the containers, washed coca is diluted in acetone. In another, acetone, ether, and hydrochloric acid are mixed. Now the two fluids are poured through a special filter into a third vessel and stirred briefly. A solution containing ether and acetone is decanted and a humid crystalline substance remains in the bowl. Both hot and cold refining methods use electricity to dry the cocaine, with high-voltage bulbs hung above the pyrex or porcelain bowl containing the final product—export-quality cocaine hydrochloride powder.

Prices for cocaine in Peru vary according to the costs of production and operation. Those who control production—from coca farming, to maceration of coca paste, to the refining stage—can afford to sell one kilo of pure cocaine for as low as $7,000. However, those refiners who buy coca paste from the black market sell their cocaine in the national market for approximately $10,000.[3]

Structure and Division of Labor

The people who participate in the national and international underground economy are organized and labeled according to production, distribution, and marketing of both the "white gold ore," coca paste, and the "white gold," cocaine hydrochloride. One of the peculiarities of the people of the Peruvian Amazon basin is that they use diminutive nicknames for some cultural elements that come from outside. Thus, among others, they call those people who come from Colombia colochos. The term "colocho" in the drug world implies more than being a Colombian national; it refers to a person who has either come from or by way of Colombia and is connected to the international underworld through that country. The colochos play an important role in unifying the Latin American cocaine network with the international drug markets where many major distribution networks are controlled by Colombians. In 1986, 42 percent (1,224) of the persons arrested for narcotics trafficking in the United States were Colombian nationals.[4] However, this does not mean that the traffic in cocaine is totally controlled by Colombians. Many nationals from other Latin American countries are connected directly to the United States. For instance, in the summer of 1986, two Peruvian traffickers transported 450 kilos of washed coca paste each to two midwestern cities in the United States.[5]

Another social label that is widely, and somewhat loosely, used in Peru is the word "narco," applied to those persons who participate in the traffic of coca paste or cocaine. Actually, "narco" is a new social category that carries recognition, respect, and prestige based on economic power on the local and, to some extent, national level. A narco always has an investment in one of the sectors of the economy. His legal activity is to incorporate "white money" into the legal economy and thereby to participate in every aspect of national life. This phenomenon is known as "bleaching cocaine money." Finally, a narco may be a jungle crime boss who is stipulating prices and controlling local populations.

In all instances, the underworld organization in coca-paste production has five different players with strictly defined roles: the big outside boss; the international link man; the local boss and his personal bodyguards; the runners or collectors of coca paste; and transportation and security support-staff members.

The big outside boss is always a colocho. He comes to the area once or twice a month, or whenever his presence is necessary. Besides his routine visits, he comes to brief the local boss. He stays no longer than two days, and he always leaves for Colombia "before the police smell money." To most people in villages and hamlets, he is a mysterious person known only by his code name. When a team is not yet well organized, the big boss appears in every pick-up flight. In this instance, if the head leaves, the organization vanishes. To illustrate: a colocho, after previous trips to negotiate a deal, had come to name a coca planter as his local boss. This colocho was killed in an accident on his way back to Colombia. He had left $100,000 with a farmer to buy coca paste from other planters and coca-paste entrepreneurs. No one representing the colocho came to claim the money. The farmer, who had migrated to the community two years before, thus found himself a rich person, a dream few migrants realize.

The pick-up man, also known as the "money man" or "bag man," comes in an airplane to transport the merchandise to Colombia. The plane is loaded with contraband such as watches, appliances, liquor, arms, canned food, and so forth—high-quality products that can be purchased at prices comparable to New York discount rates. The pick-up man and the pilot are the only occupants of the small plane. Because of their skill and critical role in the business, the pilots are paid well. However, they are the ones who are at a permanent risk. (When the plane cannot land because of bad weather, they always joke, saying that "it is too bad that Mother Nature does not take bribes.") Successful transport of coca paste from Peru to Colombia depends on the pilots' knowledge of the jungle and their experience in air navigation.

Fuel supplies and the size of airfields and planes are decisive factors in landing. Because some small planes do not have the fuel capacity to cross the borders they often refuel or leave their loads at points where several smaller loads are collected for transport in larger planes. Because of their longer haul capability, large planes may fly as far as the Caribbean or south Florida, but they need longer runways. Commercial, private, and air force airstrips are sometimes used with the cooperation of corrupt officials. In some private airstrips, planes carrying cocaine just "drop in." Although the communication with Colombia is critical, because of tight control, new methods and routes of transportation and communications are developed constantly.[6]

The airfield closest to a boss's site that I observed was a three-hour walk, and the most distant five hours. (There are airfields at greater distances than those I observed.) After landing, the plane stations itself at an established spot. Neither the pilot nor the pick-up man leave the plane. The operation is so synchronized that from landing to departure takes less than ten minutes. The delivery men carry a full load of coca paste to within a few steps of the airfield. Two specialists climb the tallest trees located at both ends of the ramp in order to signal the pilot either to land or fly over and come back later. If, in some cases, landing attempts are not successful, the planes return to Colombia without the expected cargo. Then the "stuff" is buried in a secure spot until the next flight at a later date. If the landing is successful, the bodyguards and two or three gunmen position themselves on the ground with their fingers on the trigger, and there they stay until the plane leaves with the merchandise.[7]

The third important member in the organization is the patrón, who may be a colocho or a narco. If he is a colocho, almost as a rule he lives in a totally isolated place known as a *caleta* (creek or cove). However, the actual location of the patrón's headquarters is never in a creek or cove but at a good walking distance from the river or the nearest village. By local and national standards, the patrón has an enviable lifestyle. His residence is full of luxuries. Color television sets, stereo components, home video equipment, and imported liquor are commonplace there. In towns and villages, the patrón can eat, drink, and entertain his friends without any cash in his pockets; his name and reputation are the best guarantees of payment. Although his involvement in the drug business makes him seem like a dangerous villain to many local town people, he acts like a gentleman and a humanitarian. He helps the poor; he makes sure that his bodyguards "fix" or push out some crooks that are either disturbing the community or suspected of being against his clique.

On the average, a patrón has four bodyguards. The number depends upon the size of the territory under control, presence of law-enforcement agents, relationship with the police heads, and size of the population. The fearless bodyguards are mercenaries who may be either colochos or Peruvian nationals. Among the former, more than two claimed to have served as personal security guards for two Central American presidents (both deceased).[8]

The personal security force is divided into two types of specialists: the hit men (sharp shooters) and karate experts. The "karate boys" settle some routine quarrels that the boss has, and also frighten reporters and suspected police informants. The hit men's missions range from executing traitors to silencing the media people and killing "fool" (honest) law enforcers. Because the bodyguards are appendages of the boss, it is part of their fringe benefits to share the boss's lifestyle. The salaries offered for these types of jobs are so tempting that some soldiers join the underworld right after discharge from the army. Besides having the asset of military training, the ex-servicemen are best informed on the tastes, needs, and personality features of high-ranking officers. They also tend to be loyal and follow orders.

Continuing down the structure, the organization presents a group of people known in the jargon as "runners" or collectors of coca paste. They are known by these names because at the beginning of the coca-paste boom, they literally did the footwork. But now coca production is permanent and supplies are so large that collectors wait for the producers to bring "merchandise," and they select from several suppliers.

Depending on the number of runners and pick-up flights, the local boss gives the runners cash to buy coca paste. The range of maximum amounts collected by the runners is between 50 and 100 kilos. Translated into cash, the range is from $50,000 to $100,000. Cash at this stage is almost exclusively in U.S. dollars, and it is all in ten- or twenty-dollar bills. Nobody would accept a bill larger than $20 for fear it would be counterfeit.

The coca-paste collector gets a commission of about $50 to $100 per assignment, which takes from three to five days. If he is raided, he usually claims to be an independent entrepreneur. Although he may lose his load and his cash to the police, he is typically set free a few hours later. Because the money he gets is not enough for the risk he takes, the trade allows him some opportunity to make "big bucks." He buys chicle and passes it mixed with regular coca paste, cheating both his boss and the producers.

The lowest subjects who handle the "white gold ore" are the delivery men. These "burros" of the underground economy are mostly unemployed migrants and highland peasants who transport the drugs for extra income. In their regular activities they may be coca-leaf pickers, high-school students, teachers, or any persons who want to make from five to ten dollars in a few hours, depending on distances walked and their physical strength.

The structured participation of individuals in the coca-paste economy and its concomitant social division of labor discussed above applies only to coca-paste manufacturing settings. But, as has been stated before, the "white gold ore" is spread throughout the country. *Correos* (mailmen) and *burros* (donkeys) deliver the illegal goods to consumer markets and refining laboratories. Correos and burros are intermediaries between sellers and buyers of coca paste or cocaine hydrochloride. The seller may be a producer or a drug dealer; the buyer may be a coca-paste or cocaine retailer or both, or a national and international wholesaler.

According to their modus operandi, drug carriers may be classified as motorized large-scale transporters or as small wage earners. Hundreds of kilos can be easily camouflaged in commercial vehicles and passenger buses, and it is too much work for the police to unload tons of lumber, rice, bananas, and so forth, for a routine check. Truck and bus drivers are ideal mass drug transporters, and economic circumstances often drive them to become smugglers. Despite the type of work they perform, truck and bus drivers are paid very low wages. The average salary for a long-distance driver is about sixty dollars per month plus expenses. A driver can make ten times that for one delivery of coca paste or cocaine.

In addition, long-distance drivers have an advantage in that they can handle police searches fairly easily. A kind of informal social contract exists between highway police and route drivers in which there is an implicit exchange of favors and services. Police very often ask drivers to transport packages, letters, or even members of their families without paying the corresponding fees for the services rendered. In return for their favors, the drivers are treated with special deference. This type of relationship can make policemen ignore major traffic infractions or even cover up crimes such as drug trafficking.

Small carriers take with them as many as five kilos of either unrefined paste or pure cocaine. Given the kind of goods transported and the risks faced, a burro's wages are very low. The average pay for a delivery job that takes from three to five days is $40 to $60, or the equivalent of two month's worth of minimum salary. Burros usually do not know whether they are carrying unrefined, washed, or pure cocaine. For this reason they are called burros, since they carry whatever is loaded on them. They cannot reveal the owner's name or the final destination of shipments.

"Burras" (female carriers) generally conceal their cargo on their bodies, using false breasts or disguising the load as an unborn child. María, one such burra, is a twenty-three-year-old, good-looking blond who supports both her mother and a younger brother by smuggling coca paste from the jungles to Lima. She makes five trips per month for a total of $300. In addition she earns income from her smuggling skills and, as she says, "other womanly jobs" she performs while in the "green mines." She said she was once contracted to make a trip to Miami, but, because the American Embassy denied her issuance of a visitor's visa, she missed the opportunity to become an international carrier, for which she might have been paid two to three thousand dollars per one or two kilos of cocaine. When I met her she was buying a house in a middle-class section of Lima. The house mortgage was the equivalent of $25,000, the balance of which she anticipated paying in a few months.

The underground economy helps maintain legal industries that produce materials for the preparation of coca paste and the manufacture of cocaine. High demands for lime, sulfuric acid, kerosene, and sodium carbonate in the jungle cause supply shortages in industries that depend on the same materials. As we have seen, the illegal trade generates a variety of occupations and activities that support both legal and illegal economies.

Some 1500 metric tons of coca paste are produced annually, earning at least $1.5 billion; this amount yields 400 metric tons of high-quality (uncut) cocaine hydrochloride. The estimated cost of 3.75 kilos of paste required for one kilo of pure cocaine is $3,525. There are added costs for transportation of the product from manufacturing sites to refining laboratories, and for ether, acetone, and hydrochloric acid. The total cost of production for one kilo of cocaine is $4,275. This estimate does not take into account other expenses such as rent, electricity, telephone calls, and parcel postage. Even if all other conceivable petty-cash expenses are added up, the total cost of the "white gold," with a purity ranging from 90 to 95 percent of alkaloid cocaine, is $5,000. Reliable sources indicate that in New York wholesale prices of cocaine with 50 percent purity are $35,000 per kilo; when retailed, cash yields from one kilo of adulterated cocaine (50 percent) can be as high as $200,000. Thus the production costs of cocaine in Peru constitute only a fraction of the wholesale and retail value.

The effects of the cocaine economy are directly reflected in the culture, economy, and behavior of groups actively participating in the creation and marketing of a restricted consumer commodity. Participants become economically dependent. Cultural dispersion through education, sports, entertainment, and the mass media bring into the countryside new standards, wielding pressure on indigenous behavior. Changes in the behavior of both indigenous and industrialized people brought about by the presence of coca dollars can well be termed merely cosmetic development.

5

Cosmetic Development and Coca-Dollar Dependency

For those of us living in relative prosperity
even in the very poor countries,
it is difficult to conceptualize
the true dimensions of everyday poverty—
the battles people fight
to acquire a thousand calories or just to survive.
It is such endemic poverty that
the better off fail to comprehend or understand.
Yet for those in poverty
every day is a struggle to survive.

(Khan 1986:55)

In our modern, competitive world, maintenance of one's appearance calls for the use of contemporary fashionable items as well as superfluous commodities that modify or perfect our personal appearance. Aesthetic products such as cosmetics make the ugly pretty and the pretty prettier. They present us to the world as we would like to be and not as we really are. Thanks to makeup, a corpse is presented at funeral services as more beautiful or more handsome than the person was in life. With cosmetics, a sick woman can look healthy and a poor man can hide his pale, malnourished face. The fantasy world of fashion and cosmetics has spread faster than other cultural products. To use such products is to be "modern."

Imagine a peasant or an Indian woman living at an altitude of three thousand meters above sea level or higher, sharing a one-room house with the rest of her family, her guinea pigs, and so forth, lacking essential items for personal hygiene or household cleanliness, which obviously translates into high parasite infestation and infections. Now, let us take this peasant woman and make her look like the rest of the women in the modern world. Cover her tattered traditional outfit with new-fashioned clothes and apply a layer of cosmetics to her face. Doubtless anyone who has not seen what we have done to her may say "she looks beautiful." The peasant woman has changed in appearance but not in essence.

The booming underground coca-leaf and cocaine economy may be characterized as the cosmetic modernization of the Peruvian countryside, as an economy that is totally subject to international organized crime. An illustration of cosmetic development is the well-known case of Tingo María, often cited as the "white city." When in 1966 I visited Tingo María for the first time, it was a small town whose main street was the dirt road connecting Lima with the town of Pucallpa (a city in the lowlands of the Amazon basin). The town counted three roach-ridden hotels and one tourist hotel, a few mediocre restaurants, and a whorehouse about five hundred meters from the main street. At that time, the recently colonized forest lands around Tingo María were not yet in full production.

Twelve years later, the main street was the commercial center. Major national banks had opened their branch offices there. The city boasted a university campus, the Universidad Nacional Agraria de la Selva, and scores of average restaurants and hotels had been opened. The town was so busy and lively that even the same roach-ridden hotel built in the sixties was always overbooked. Tingo María had become a center of cocaine traffic.

Currently, Tingo María is a city which already shows segregated residential areas. It has a local middle-class section, working-class neighborhoods, and large shantytowns such as "Chicago," originally called "Bamboo." It has its own regional medical center, elementary and secondary schools, and a very busy marketplace. As one of the major cities in the jungles, Tingo María is an administrative and commercial seat

The cocaine industry has boosted the need for public accommodations in the Upper Huallaga. A three-star hotel in an ex-cocaine magnet town is named after one of the biggest cocaine-consuming cities.

for the Upper Huallaga region. Many national governmental organizations, including the five forces of social control and political repression, have their regional headquarters in Tingo María. Three major Japanese car and truck dealers have their showrooms and warehouses located on the main street.[1] Scores of physicians and lawyers have their private offices concentrated in one section of the city.

Bars and nightclubs are new cultural elements that provide expensive drinks, food, and entertainment to local residents and visitors. The two whorehouses satisfy two different types of patrons. In addition, young streetwalkers, homosexuals, and drug addicts are always hustling on crowded corners and at bus stops. Beggars, pickpockets, and shoeshine and newspaper boys hanging around at the doors of banks, restaurants, and bars complete the image of the "white city."

Local residents complain about the condition of their streets and services such as electricity and water supply. They argue that given the tremendous amounts of money handled, "the city should be paved with marble." It is true that Tingalenses (people from Tingo María) come in contact with large amounts of cash, yet, unfortunately, money that comes to Tingo María is neither invested to create a solid and independent local economy nor used to generate tax revenues for the welfare of the community. Tingo María is a consumer marketplace for goods brought from outside. Money coming from coca agriculture, other cash crops, and cattleraising in nearby areas is either spent on luxury items or it leaves the area. More importantly, the local economy does not have sources of cash income other than agriculture and service jobs.

Beneath the attractive cosmetic facade built by cocaine dollars lies a city in decay. Not only are modernization and development supported by organized crime, they are also promoting the spread of physical and social disease of epidemic proportions.

Chasing Coca Dollars

In its attempt to avoid choosing either of two extremes—communism or capitalism—the military dictatorship that governed Peru from 1968 to 1980 imposed a centralized state capitalism in the primary and industrial sectors. In the highlands, traditional groups were labeled "peasant communities." The government organized these communities around the common use of land. That is, it intended to revive the *sui generis* social organization of the Inca empire, the ayllu system.[2] However, this policy did not develop the countryside. It was just another political cosmetic layer applied to the problems of the Peruvian Indian.

For the last thirty years, Peruvian governments have attempted to put into practice different models of development. However, all developmental programs have been designed to connect the rest of the country to the industrial city of Lima. Capital investment in education, transportation, and health services made the countryside more dependent on the metropolis. In 1969, the radical military junta flamboyantly decreed land-reform laws. The peasantry considered this action as the second national grant of independence, but neither it nor the paternalistic junta were ready for such a giant step. The failure of land reform due to many social and political factors led to increased unemployment, inflation, and the depopulation of the countryside.[3]

Thousands of peasants, migrants, and ambitious professionals now place their hopes in the virgin lands of the jungle. Their quest for better living conditions makes them depend upon the underground coca and cocaine economy. Production, marketing, and control of coca and cocaine totally condition populations and communities near drug-producing sites. People for whom coca and cocaine make the difference between poverty and plenty openly admit that "thanks to coca and cocaine, we can dress and eat well." At the collective level, the general public recognizes the importance of cocaine in their lives. Their position could be summarized by the Peruvian proverb: "When there is bread in Gomorrah there is bread for everybody" (*cuando hay pan en Gomorra, hay pan para todos*).

In the early sixties, the Peruvian government's first step to try to develop the city of Tingo María was the installation of a wood-processing factory, Madera Prensada Sociedad Anónima (MAPRESA), which was built in the outskirts of the town. The military dictatorship's industrial policy made this industrial complex a cooperative that, theoretically, was controlled by the workers themselves.[4] As a consequence of the failure of the cooperative system, this manufacturing complex was closed down and hundreds of workers were without jobs. The government now hopes that the industrial exploitation of cacao plantations in Naranjillo will generate jobs and revenues in the near future. The cacao-producing cooperative of Naranjillo is implementing a processing factory a few blocks from downtown Tingo María. However, there are indications that the cooperative of Naranjillo may follow the same fate as MAPRESA. Cooperative workers (*obreros*) and employees (*empleados*) of Naranjillo argue that their wages are not enough to pay inflationary prices and meet the high cost of living inherited from the cocaine boom era. Workers see every day how the product of their labor is spent to support teams of foreign technicians and managers. European and Latin American professionals specializing in cacao agriculture and processing come to Naranjillo to train workers and to organize the factory based on experiences in other societies. Workers say that these expensive technicians "cost thousands of dollars while our wages are shrinking more and more."

I met and interviewed five ex-clerical workers of Naranjillo who had resigned to go into agriculture. They all agreed that "the last thing we want to do is the pain of clearing land and having to face the rugged and dense forests." But agriculture was their only alternative. Their 750,000 soles weekly salaries for six days' work was not enough income to support their families.[5] "We had enough," they said. So they decided to plant coca and have a "more decent life than toiling for a wage of 12,000 soles per day." For these five ex-cooperative workers things have changed. Thanks to coca, they say, their children can attend expensive private schools and enjoy the otherwise unattainable comforts of modern life.

In Tingo María, a family of four living in "Chicago," the slum section of the city, has a weekly budget of about 100,000 soles. They cannot afford meat and milk. For local residents, as well as outsiders, it is hard to accept misery when, as they say, others are "making it." Poverty and misery are ongoing social problems as old as the country. However, because of the tremendous influx of cash coming from drug production and traffic, people are becoming aware of their own realistic possibilities for material gain.

Fernanda (not her real name) is a senior at Universidad Nacional Agraria de la Selva (UNAS). We became acquainted in the university library. After reading my letter of introduction, signed by the head of the fellowship program, she tried to stop me from going to Sodom and Gomorrah. We had long discussions and friendly arguments on many political and social issues. The most interesting point she made was that drug traffic and production were analogous to "economic prostitution."

Like hundreds of other college students, Fernanda makes ends meet either by working in different jobs generated by coca agriculture and cocaine production or by becoming a coca planter herself. People are so caught up in the economy that they are not concerned with the legal definitions of their behavior. Reliance on future coca-leaf collection is so high that peasants and farmers are backed by their crops. They get cash loans to buy uniforms for their children, for medicine, clothing, fertilizer, and so forth, and later they pay their debt with cash from coca or cocaine sales.

It is no exaggeration to contend that, while in the rest of the country people have incomes below the subsistence level, native coca planters and coca-paste manufacturers in core drug communities spend their cash in a lavish and wasteful manner. Imported consumer goods are available and affordable. All of them, except cars, trucks, and motor-cycles, are contraband, coming to the Amazon basin cities and towns directly from Panama and other countries with duty-free facilities and smuggled in on drug pick-up planes or boats coming upstream via the Amazon and other major rivers. Many unscrupulous individuals also sell counterfeit goods, using labels and brand names of internationally known products. For instance, on more than one occasion, I met a hiking peddler who was selling a major Japanese camera for about 25 percent less than the New York discount price. This is not to say that all goods sold under foreign labels are counterfeit.

In Peru, generally, the purchase of appliances such as television sets, stereo components, and radios is made on credit. Creditors require a cash down payment of at least 50 percent of the total amount. The debtor signs a bill of credit for the balance. Only in rare cases do monthly installments exceed thirty-six months. Thus, to buy a color television set, the purchaser must have at least the equivalent of $450 in cash for the down payment. Due to high prices and interest, and due to low national per-capita income, home appliances are luxuries that are practically out of reach for a good portion of the population. In slums and working-class sections of Lima, for example, those who have television sets charge a fee for letting their neighbors' children watch movies or educational programs.

Despite the fact that acquisition and use of modern technological goods is limited to small groups, the government is expanding the na-tional telecommunication system to small towns and villages in the hin-terland. The money to pay for installation, maintenance, and bureau-cracy of that system always comes from foreign aid. Cultural diffusion through mass media has a negative effect on the countryside. It not only disturbs the traditional culture and society, it also prompts the

Indian and the peasant to seek commodities that, as their economic and cultural conditions now stand, are not essential for their subsistence. The desire to obtain Western manufactured commodities dislocates traditional values and priorities. Possessing them adds new distinctive variables to the centuries-old traditional social structure. Andean natives want modern Western goods so badly that they often over-esteem them. When they see pocket radios or recorders, some would say *"ma kuyaykuska"* (let me touch it and love it); others even decide to trade their best crops or animals to obtain them.[6]

One of the advantages of making transactions in U.S. dollars is that the equivalent of tens of millions of soles* can be carried in small bundles. But the use of dollars also presents some disadvantages. Because of its illegal source, people keep U.S. dollars in their houses hidden in boxes, bags, and baskets. Large amounts, however, are put in briefcases and crates and buried in secret spots. U.S. dollars cannot be deposited in banks or safe vaults. Besides, in populations where coca dollars are widespread, there are no bank representatives or agents at all. Investments are always made in goods and items that directly benefit automobile and truck dealers, appliance stores, beer companies, and so forth. The lack of investment opportunities induces villagers and townspeople to spend their cash on unnecessary and extravagant items.

Criminal or illegal income from participation in the underground economy is flaunted, openly spent on entertainment, personal services, and status goods such as cars which, in the long run, may not be good investment decisions. This is true especially among peasants and uneducated people. To many, money is no problem at all; the problem is what to do with it.

In a highland city about eight hours from Gomorrah, one of my research assistants suggested that I meet an Indian who, six months earlier, had quit his job to become a coca planter, coca-paste manufacturer, and dealer. We agreed to meet at the park bench opposite a designated hotel. My assistant (a law-school student) and the subject ar-

---

*The new Peruvian currency is inti. One inti is worth 1,000 soles. The current exchange rate for U.S. dollars is 150 intis or 150,000 soles. In 1985, one dollar was worth 10,000 soles or 10 intis.

rived in a 1985 Toyota streamlined automobile, equipped with the best Pioneer car stereo. Yony (for Johnny) spoke Spanish with a heavy highland accent. I suggested that we have coffee in a modest restaurant. My new friend answered, "No, brother. You guys are my guests. Get your asses in the car and let's go to a nice place."

He drove us in his "Linda" to an expensive traditional restaurant. We ordered barbecued lamb and beer. He asked the waiter to keep the music on for as long as we were in the restaurant. Since he knew that I came from the United States and that I was trying to go to Sodom and Gomorrah, he asked me a very straightforward question: "Do you work for DEA or for the CIA?" Neither, I said. He kept staring at my camera bag and wanted to know what I had in it. I opened it and showed him my cameras. He grabbed one and said, "This is mine now," and counted the price of the camera in twenty-dollar bills. When I came up with some expressions in Quechua, he was immediately interested in knowing where and how the hell I had learned that language. This was my best opportunity to gain his confidence and make him understand my position. I told him my life story and my experiences exactly as they had been. In his rudimentary Spanish he said to me, "Brother, you are a real man." I had won his respect.

Besides supporting his family in the city and his parents back home in the highlands, Yony supports a very attractive medical student, his lover. He talked about "the old days" when he used to work loading and unloading trucks. "Thank God I quit that shit for good, and I do not intend to take another 2,500-soles-a-day job ever again." Yony's immediate goal was to fulfill his promise to buy another Toyota—for his lover—for Christmas. (The girl wrote me a letter before Christmas, saying she had already received her Toyota.) He also plans to buy a condominium in a posh section of Lima.

Yony has spent more than $22,000 in cash in one year on the two cars alone. Every month, Yony sends about the equivalent of $100 to his mother and other close relatives which, compared to what he wastes in the city where he lives, is insignificant. In June 1985, by Yony's own calculations, his "Linda" represented more than forty years' salary had he stayed in his "old crappy job"—an impossible dream for any Indian or highland peasant and, for that matter, for many middle-class people.

Some peasants think that cars, trucks, and appliances, besides being status indicators, are savings investments that can be translated into cash when needed. Others store them until the national government builds roads or power generators. In either case, they want to see their wealth in material things, not in cash. Moreover, because of the high inflation rate, prices change almost every month. The peasants are afraid to deposit their cash in the banks because they think that evidence of their income from cocaine would be obvious. They cover their four-wheel drive Japanese trucks and cars with leaves or worn-out plastic sheets previously used as pliable coca-paste pits. Then they park the trucks until someone in the family learns how to drive. From time to time, they ask friends and passers-by to start their vehicles or to read instructions for their electronic equipment.

As the area is flooded with money from coca and cocaine production, some local governments also get their share. Two municipalities impose tolls on cars and trucks that travel through their boroughs. Tingo María and Aucayacu collect 1,000 soles from every car or truck that comes in their jurisdiction. Farther north, there is a group of persons who have organized a cooperative to operate the "Balsa Exclava" ferry, consisting of a large raft propelled by two outboard motors. Heavily loaded trucks and passenger cars cross the Huallaga River using this ferry. The fee is 20,000 soles per crossing.

The Social Impact of the White Gold Rush

The consumer attitude has also changed because of the white gold rush, as is especially evident among adolescents, homosexuals, and prostitutes. Drugs bring in money, and money opens up new opportunities. Spectator sports are promoted and sponsored. Routine games and parties become expressions of opulence for those who engage in local drug subeconomies.

In 1978, in one of the hamlets along the road, a group of people organized a soccer team, which later moved to a nearby town and is today recognized as the major team in the region. Most of its players, including the coach, have been recruited from professional teams in Lima. On many occasions, the team has defeated major national-league clubs. Thousands of spectators from all over the Upper Huallaga crowd the small stadium and spend hundreds of millions of soles.

In farmlands and neighborhoods, workers, housewives, and school-children play volleyball and soccer every day after their regular activities. The very afternoon I arrived at one of the drug hamlets, a group of housewives invited me to join their volleyball team. Since I had not practiced this sport for years, I volunteered to be the official score-keeper, to hold pool money and to be, as they called me, the "official photographer" for both teams. At about 4:00 P.M., the local teacher and his wife started setting up the volleyball net and marking the dirt playground with gypsum. Once both teams selected their players, my duty was to collect the cash pool which would go to the winning team. Daily pools varied from 5,000 to 20,000 soles per competing player. The winnings were always spent for refreshments like Coca-Cola or beer. In other settings where populations are predominantly male, because of the nature of the work, field and coca-paste pit workers gather on river shores or coca-leaf drying floors to play soccer. Prizes range from one or two cases of beer to packs of American cigarettes.

Sometimes the cocaine manufacturers and local bosses treat their workers and friends by donating money and beverages or by offering surprise awards. One Sunday was a local boss's birthday, and his four bodyguards barbecued wild pig, beef, and fish. They also bought many cases of beer, Coca-Cola, and Pepsi Cola. Before the feast, some of the hosts played mini-soccer. The boss stopped the game and said "the winning party will get a damn good prize later tonight." Everyone except me knew what the boss meant. Late that afternoon we all walked through the woods toward the road that leads to a very busy town. One of the fellows told me in Quechua where we were headed. All ten of us went in different mini-buses and met at the point indicated by the boss. "Wonder Woman" was the final destination.

"Wonder Woman" may be one of the most expensive disco houses in Peru, but it is not located in an exclusive section of Lima. The regular full-time staff included a manager, one cashier, two doormen, one cook, and three "first-class girls." Some regular customers had arrived before us, so suddenly we found ourselves with no girls at all. This inconvenience was solved promptly and efficiently. The manager called four additional girls to "wait on us." The only problem was that all four girls wanted to stay with the boss. It was even worse for me when they heard me chatting in Quechua with my loyal highland *paisano*, who was from

A local whorehouse open twenty-four hours a day. Coca dollars attract many metropolitan and foreign women to work as prostitutes.

the same Andes ranges where I was born. Everyone in the group, including my countryman, knew that I had come from Lima to visit friends in a nearby hamlet, and they assumed I was penniless. Because the boss could not deal with all the girls at the same time, one of them approached us saying "Hi, *cholitos*" (a pejorative term for highlanders). As drinks and food were on the boss, we invited her for many drinks and a tuna salad platter. Guessing she was Brazilian, I asked whether she had ever been to "Papagallo," a disco in Río de Janeiro. For the rest of the night, I controlled the conversation.

"Wonder Woman's" prices are so high that few people can afford to spend even a few hours there. A fifth of Chivas Regal costs $100 or its equivalent in soles. Johnny Walker black label and Cutty Sark are priced at $80, while the matches that in America are given away with cigarettes are sold for the equivalent of about fifteen cents a box.

Of the seven girls who had been assigned to us, three were foreigners who had come through Colombia; the rest were Peruvian nationals. The girls do not get any salary at all. Their entire earnings come from prostitution; compared to that of metropolitan prostitutes, their income is high. "Wonder Woman" is not a whorehouse, because it has no rooms where intercourse can take place. Sex is performed outside the disco. The setting may be the house of one of the partners or even the open woods. This is decided mutually between the girl and the client. Once both parties reach an agreement as to the price for the service, the number of hours the client wants to spend with the girl, and the place of exchange, the patrón pays the manager the "nominal" fee of $30 for taking the girl out. If the customer accepts her conditions, the girl charges about $80 per service, more if conditions are set by the patrón. Earnings of from $300 to $500 per night are not unusual in "Wonder Woman." By common standards, in order to have a nice night, one must have no less than $300 in cash, something only those in the drug industry can afford.

Whorehouses are licensed and registered establishments. They are, by rule, located on the outskirts of town, and these locations create occupations for local people. Taxi cabs, gypsies, and motorcycles transport men of every age and social condition from town to the *chongo* (legal whorehouse). Transportation tickets and sex-service rates are fixed by municipal authorities. Prostitutes are duly cleared and identified by police, and they must hold periodic health-inspection cards.

As one travels north from the largest city in the area, the quality of service, prices, and sophistication increases in proportion to the volume of coca and coca-paste production. The two brothels in Tingo María average about 30,000 soles per service. Eighty kilometers to the north, the fee determined by the local city hall is 70,000 soles, but actual rates paid for the services exceed 120,000 soles. As rates increase, so do the youth and attractiveness of the prostitutes displayed in shacks and small tin houses. A poetic migrant observer says that "here things increase and get better, just as they worsen with the flow of the [Huallaga] river" (*aquí las cosas aumentan, mejoran, como también empeoran con el curso del río*). What this means is that as one follows the river, coca and its social and economic consequences multiply.

Only in cities like Tingo María, Pucallpa, and Iquitos are street hookers visible. In small towns and villages, and deep in the forests, single mothers, schoolteachers, and students subsist or supplement their cash needs practicing "snowball" prostitution. Men tell others of women who "render good services" and how to approach them. In

Peru, there are even cases where housewives have to perform prostitution to feed their children. However, this is not as common in the jungle, where the economy is not so impoverished, as it is in Lima. Pathetic instances of housewives walking around with empty market bags are most typical of Lima. On more than one occasion, I have seen mothers on the street in marketplaces trying to give their children away because they are unable to feed them.

To satisfy special personal needs, there is also an escort type of prostitution in the jungle. The escort is a contracted female companion obligated to live with and render sexual services to a man for a time agreed upon by both parties. She receives food, drinks, and other personal expenses during her stay. On holidays and weekends, young girls come from cities and towns on the coast and in the highlands to spend a few days with "friends."

Besides seeking pleasure in sex, individuals and families show off their wealth in social manifestations such as birthday parties and other ritualistic events. Baptisms, weddings, and birthdays are expensive and pompous ceremonies. Saturday evenings are reserved for parties, drinking, playing cards, and traveling. Local and migrant workers spend their wages on beer and liquor in bars and restaurants. One bottle of national beer costs 15,000 soles (in Lima it costs 6,000 soles). On weekends, an average wage laborer spends about 250,000 soles on jukebox tunes, beer, and cigarettes.

Professional musical groups which have come from Lima and other large cities to the Upper Huallaga are hired to play in both private and neighborhood parties (*fiestas sociales*). The three top groups, for example, do not sign any contract for less than six hours. Their rates are a little more than 1,000,000 soles per hour, plus food and drinks. To keep a band for six hours, the host institution or individual must spend at least 7,000,000 soles. If the party is a private one, the host also provides food, beer, cigarettes, and liquor.

Saint John, whose feast day is June 24, is the patrón of most of the cities and towns in the Peruvian Amazon basin. Contracts with bands and caterers for the feast of San Juan are secured many months ahead, as are airline and bus tickets to the area. During the week of June 24, it is almost impossible to travel to the Upper Huallaga or any other place in the jungle. Hotels and boardinghouses are crammed with merchants.

Many family and community events such as birthdays are planned to coincide with this traditional holiday.

An ex-police officer who is now a coca planter invited me to his fifteen-year-old daughter's birthday party. The party was organized in such a way that the girl's friends, as well as the parents', were in two separate spots on the large, flat floor used to dry coca leaves. The house was about one hour's walking distance from the road that runs along the Huallaga River. Not counting food, specially ordered ball dresses, and other cosmetic expenses, the host parents spent approximately 25 million soles. The host bought thirty-five dozen cases of beer, more than fifteen bottles of imported whiskey, and ten packs of instant film. The band played *cumbia* and Peruvian creole music for eight hours. Those who stayed after 4:00 A.M. the next day were served a heavy breakfast consisting of *ceviche* (a traditional Peruvian meal of raw fish, lemon, and onions) and chicken soup. When two other guests and I left, we all thanked the parents for the attention paid to us. The father's reaction to our politeness was the common expression, "Thank God coca makes dreams happen."

Dollars in Action

Cocaine money not only makes some dreams come true in the areas of production, but also brings into the scene traveling money brokers who spread coca dollars throughout the country. Money exchangers travel back and forth through the cocaine cities and towns, collecting coca dollars and concentrating them in Lima and, to some extent, disseminating them throughout the country. In addition to making U.S. dollars available to the general public, coca-dollar brokers funnel the American currency back to the United States. Because of its underground roots, it is extremely difficult to know or estimate the amount and proportion of coca dollars that remain in Peru or leave the country.

There are two kinds of foreign currency dealers: independent and salaried. Due to the high inflation rate, cost of living, and lack of other viable cash resources, many affluent Peruvians speculate in foreign-currency exchange markets. Independent U.S. dollar dealers borrow their initial investments from friends, banks, and cooperatives or use their own savings. Salaried or contracted dollar collectors are either money-exchange company employees or people hired temporarily for that purpose. The amount of cash they carry either in soles or dollars and the number of trips they make to the jungle depend on the supply of U.S. dollars in the coca belt. Hired travelers take advantage of their position to change their salaries into dollars and thus supplement their income. Some money exchangers also get involved in petty drug trafficking. Since foreign currency is controlled by the government, these money brokers are double violators of the law. Sacks and bundles of dollars come from the international market to the hands of organized crime bosses. In the jungle it is rare to see one-dollar bills or notes larger than twenty dollars. In fact, in cocaine communities, it is almost impossible to change fifty-or one hundred-dollar bills. The rationale for not accepting large bills is that, allegedly, "Colombians" counterfeit them, and coca-paste manufacturers claim that they have thus been cheated on various occasions. Hundreds of thousands of dollars are handed to the local bosses who distribute the American currency to their collectors of coca paste. Once large amounts are dispersed, it is difficult to trace the order in which dollars circulate. When there is a shortage of national currency, many agricultural and service jobs pay in dollars. Cocaine producers, traffickers, and wage laborers alike spend their coca dollars in consumer and service centers.

Buyers of American currency have their own methods of collecting U.S. dollars. In cities and towns, they go to stores, pharmacies, restaurants, hotels, bars, and whorehouses. Others, especially independent exchangers, go deeper into villages and coca plantations in the forests to buy directly from coca planters and coca-paste manufacturers. In Lima in the summer of 1985, the official exchange rate was 10,000 soles for each American dollar. However, in cocaine-producing areas, the price of the dollar was from 9,000 to 9,500 soles. In the same period, the black-market value for the U.S. dollar in Lima was 12,500 soles or higher, so that $1,000 in capital could yield earnings of about $300 per trip.

From 1980 to 1985, circulation of coca dollars was wide open and legal. Dozens of new money-exchange offices were opened in downtown and middle-class suburban sections of Lima. In particular, Lima's financial district was flooded with U.S. dollars. Hundreds of dealers holding their calculators and bundles of dollars, bonds, and soles hustled passers-by. Tourists, businessmen, and others who needed to buy or sell dollars would go to the "Wall Street of Lima."

There are two commonsense reasons for nourishing the open black market. First, because of the underdeveloped bureaucracy, transactions in financial institutions, especially banks, require long and tedious paperwork. Customers wait for hours and sometimes days to exchange foreign currency or cash their money orders. Second, the black market purchases dollars at higher rates than banks and, more importantly, transactions take only as long as it does to count notes.

Competition from the black market has been so high that legally established money-exchange offices assign their employees—probably the same employees who traveled back and forth through the jungle—to deal out in "Wall Street." The new government's first attempt to stop the black market was on July 30, 1985. Approximately two hundred street-money exchangers were arrested and hundreds of millions of soles and thousands of dollars were seized. One arrested dealer confessed that he was, in fact, an employee of a money exchange office whose owners were high-ranking police officers.[7] New foreign currency policies established that any transaction in foreign currency was to be made in the national bank.

The national bank charges five different fees for exchanging foreign money. This control policy creates an artificial scarcity of dollars as well as high prices. At the same time, the flow of dollars to Peru is constant, because it moves in conjunction with the production of cocaine. The fact that the government controls the circulation of U.S. dollars does not mean that the approximately $1.5 billion coming to Peru from the cocaine trade goes to the national bank. The fact of the matter is that the ruling sectors of Peruvian society benefit from the economic power of coca dollars: indeed, the biggest national drug-trafficking cases have involved members of the national elite and middle-class officials and authorities.

In a small town with about three thousand inhabitants, one person, allegedly a "big fish," built a two-story concrete house. Builders were

Table 4
Independent Money Exchangers

Initial Cap.	Current Cap.	Freq.	# Trips	Prev. Occ.	Oper Time
Less than 1,000	3,000–5,000	5	4	Peddling	12 Mo.
1,000–2,000	5,001–10,000	8	3	Factory	9
2,001–3,000	10,001–15,000	3	4	Teacher	15
3,001–4,000	15,001–20,000	2	1	Civ. Service	6
$\bar{X}$ = 1,611.00	2,278.00		3		10.5

contracted from Lima and glass was imported from Europe. The owner opened the "best pharmacy in the Upper Huallaga" in the building. But, because it could not compete with the established and well-supplied drugstores in a nearby city, the pharmacy was closed down. Commonsense market research, or even the fear of losing capital, does not concern some stores and small corporations like this short-lived drugstore. In fact, the underground economy can afford to support many activities operating with little or no profit at all.

Bleaching or laundering money usually takes place in cocaine centers, whether in the countryside or in urban areas. This laundering yields excellent returns that, along with the wealth produced by other illicit businesses, have created a class of nouveaux-riches families throughout Peru. Rather than integrate their new wealth into the often unstable legitimate economy, they usually divert it into foreign investments.[8]

In a central Andean city, I met a cocaine entrepreneur who owns twenty van-type Toyota minibuses. The twenty vehicles were bought for cash in three purchase orders for a total price of $300,000. After deducting costs of operation (gasoline, drivers, tolls, and helpers), the owner nets the equivalent of about $500 per day from the minibuses, transporting passengers between two busy cities in the northeastern and central ranges of the Andes. Because car parts are extremely expensive and difficult to find, the owner sells his vehicles after approximately two years' use at prices which allow him to recover more than 50 percent of his initial investment. Because of his healthy and solvent economic status, he has an outstanding credit record and is planning to make a big financial move. Those who have international perspectives, especially professionals and middle-class traffickers, deposit their money in Europe or the United States.

Contrary to the popular belief that narcotics money is crucial to the economic health of these [producer] countries, in fact the great majority of [the] illicit gains flow out of these countries and into off-shore bank accounts in the Caribbean and the United States.[9]

To cite an instance, one independent entrepreneur who handles his own operations from planting coca to maceration to refining and international marketing, ships an average of two kilos of high-quality cocaine hydrochloride to the United States every three months. He plans to send his children to private American colleges and is laundering his coca dollars through foreign bank accounts and business investments; he has opened a joint savings account with an immediate relative who resides in the United States, and part of his profits from the lucrative underground entrepreneurship have gone into the assets of a legally constituted corporation on a Caribbean island.

People try to emulate others who are "making it." The desire to satisfy material needs by participating in the production, trafficking, and other kinds of activity supporting the industry is contagious and almost beyond control. Never before have so many people in Peru been so dependent on an illegitimate income as they are today. Besides the changes in attitudes, language, and traditions, the cocaine economic movement brings along other human degenerative epidemics and deviant behaviors such as drug addiction.

Coca-Paste Addiction

Traditionally, the indigenous populations of the two Andean countries, Bolivia and Peru, were always associated with their habitual coca chewing. This traditional social and cultural practice has changed to more sophisticated and addictive behaviors. Cigarette smoking and alcohol abuse are probably still the most serious health hazards and social problems affecting traditional and modern societies alike. But another, coca-paste smoking, has appeared in Peru and some Latin American countries, as well as the United States. The language of the drug subculture may assign different terms to coca-paste or cocaine smoking. However, in essence, they all are the same drug with variations in the alkaloid cocaine content.

In the 1970s, coca paste among rural and highland urban addicts was known under two different terms: *tangana* and "bazooka." Probably, tangana comes from the Quechua word *tanga*, a variation of *tangay*, which can be translated "to push" or "to shove." In northeastern Quechua dialect, tangana is a noun which means "something to push or propel with"; in many jungle areas, tangana is still used to mean "oar." In the highlands, when peasants feel fatigue, or are hungry or thirsty, they chew their coca leaves saying *mama cuca ma tangarkamay*, meaning "magic coca, please give me strength."

New terms were coined as migration to the jungle increased. "Bazooka," *cuete* or *cuetón* (firecracker), *cohete* (rocket), and *sharuta* (cigar made out of whole tobacco leaves) were used interchangeably. As consumption of the raw drug spread to the rest of the country and across the continent, packaging of the substance was adopted. The initial retail distribution code name may have been *"un paquete de cuete, cuetón, cohete."* This long and cacophonous phrase was contracted to a single word, *quete* or *kete*, which described both the package (*paquete*) and its contents (*cohete*). The word *cuetón*, meaning good-quality coca paste, is still used among addicts in the jungle.

In Peru in the early 1980s, coca paste was retailed under the name of *quete* or *kete*, while cocaine was commonly sold as coca. Ketes containing about two milligrams of coca paste were packaged in used newspapers picked up from garbage cans and bags. Individual ketes were consolidated in plastic bags, empty match boxes, or cigarette boxes. Prices for ketes ranged from 5,000 to 15,000 soles per package. Despite availability in nearby production centers, in Chicago (a slum section of Tingo María) one kete costs 5,000 soles. Outside Chicago, prices varied according to the setting and the buyer. Just a few blocks from these slum areas, a *kete* could be sold for as much as 10,000 soles. In Lima, adulterated coca-paste kete sold for about 15,000 soles. In many urban populations of the country, coca paste and cocaine retail distribution became an informal income that supplemented the low wages paid to teenagers, women, and unskilled laborers. Many low-paying service jobs were held more for their drug-market advantages than for their legal wages. Drug-sale incomes were much higher than those from other service employment. For example, four employees of a roach-ridden hotel made about 100,000 soles a day cash income from the sale of coca paste. The customer paid in advance 10,000 soles per kete. With the customer's money, the workers went to Chicago or a nearby dealer to buy the requested supply. All four employees were from Lima. They sold an average of twenty ketes per day, which yields daily earnings of about 25,000 soles for each employee, that is, 330 percent more than their legal daily wages. These four employees, similar to many other low-income and unemployed people, were totally dependent on the sale and resale of coca paste.

While production of coca paste and the retailing of ketes have created an economic dependence and caused inflationary prices, they have also brought about physical and psychological dependence. Other than some isolated research supported by foreign money, nothing had been done as of 1986 to solve the problem of coca-paste addiction. Ramirez and Ruiz report that in 1978 in Peru the police arrested 630 coca-paste addicts of whom 98 percent were Peruvian nationals.[10] Now, *keteros* (coca-paste smokers) have spread all over the country.

Besides economically supporting the underworld, the highland peasants undergo the social consequences of using coca paste. Their trend of coca chewing, especially among young male peasants, is now changing to the use of coca paste, that is, to a more addictive and dangerous habit. Those who work for wages in the underground laboratories have relatively easy access to coca paste and cocaine hydrochloride. During their stay, peasant laborers consume the drug without having to pay for it. As one informant asserted, "To them it is just like they were working in a bake shop and taking home some bread."

When they return to their communities, some migrant laborers or travelers come back home with both coca leaves and coca paste. In 1981, of the sixty-one peasants who went to the jungle (60 percent of the sample), forty-eight had used coca paste regularly. Thirty-six of these coca-paste users were in favor of cocaine in its rock form because it was "more convenient to carry along." Veteran coca chewers, who tended to be the older group of the sample, preferred to continue their traditional habit. They argued that coca paste was too strong and made them "feel strange." An overwhelming majority of the young bring coca leaves from the jungle only to give them to their relatives or to sell them; for themselves, they take coca paste.

Random measurements of coca-paste possession in a small community in the highlands ranged between 200 and 400 grams. These calculations showed only the amounts the respondents had with them for their own use; they did not reveal their actual personal "stock" at home. The existence of more substance in stock was obvious, for some peasants who came back from the jungle exchanged part of their coca paste for other consumer goods from the metropolitan areas. For instance, a local community teacher secured his supply of coca paste by trading two vaginal contraceptive inserts or three condoms for about one gram of coca paste. These items are difficult to buy in the highlands of Peru.

Here, what is at stake is not the possession of coca paste as a source of income, but the spread of the use of the drug among indigenous people. To the peasant, coca chewing is a part of culture. However, even before his traditional vice has been scientifically analyzed, he is now exposing himself to an even more severe health hazard by smoking a drug that contains the elements utilized to make coca paste. At best, coca paste has only about 27 percent of alkaloid cocaine content. Thus, coca-paste addicts are smoking more impurities than they are cocaine. Also alarming is the fact that coca paste manufacturers are getting rid of bad quality material—chicle—in the market.

The peasants informed me that, in coca-paste manufacturing settings, they smoked coca paste mixed with tobacco or marijuana. But in the highlands, because cigarettes and marijuana are expensive, the peasants licked the little brownish rocks. I did not see other forms of coca-paste use during my fieldwork in the highlands.

Besides the obvious availability of coca paste, there are two main reasons for the consumption of the substance in the jungle: economic and social. In the jungle, food is expensive. Since the cocaine entrepreneur has to provide the peasant with food during his employment, it is to the entrepreneur's advantage to keep production expenses low by letting his laborers consume coca paste. Socially, the Andean peasant is used to working under the stimulation of coca. However, the low status assigned to the coca chewer makes some of the young peasants and Indians aware of the social stigma that has been attached to coca chewing. Furthermore, since cocaine use is a vice of Western culture, they believe that being modern implies imitation of the drug's fashionable use in modern societies. Cigarette smoking is probably the most dangerous and negative cultural element that modern societies have imposed upon indigenous groups. But because of tax revenues generated by the tobacco industry, cigarette smoking, as well as the consumption of alcohol, have become political sacred cows.

In the highlands in the 1950s and 1960s, cigarette smoking among peasants and Indians was restricted to traditional medical use, and it was appended to the supernatural and curing properties of coca leaf. Now both American brand-name cigarettes manufactured in Peru as well as national brands are sold in the most remote communities. The subtle advertisement methods used by Peruvian cigarette manufacturers appeal to the indigenous people. That appeal carries over to cocaine smoking.

In order to be *fumones* (coca-paste smokers), potential addicts must first have knowledge of cigarette-smoking rituals such as inhaling the smoke. Otherwise, they are subject to ridicule and mockery from other addicts. Smoking coca paste mixed with cigarettes or tobacco is a universal practice in the drug subculture. About one fourth of the tobacco from a cigarette is taken out, coca paste is poured into the cigarette, and then the tobacco that was removed is replaced to secure the coca paste. Deep in the jungle, coca paste is smoked in *sharuta*, a cigar made out of local tobacco leaves.

The small town of Aucayacu and the city of Tingo María are well known for their coca-paste addict populations. The fumones in Tingo María and Aucayacu are localized near the Huallaga River. The addicts build their cardboard huts on mounds of garbage which they share with flies, rats, and other rodents. The smoking quarters have an indescribable characteristic smell that comes from the mixture of sewage, organic wastes, lack of hygiene, and the nauseating smoke of coca paste. A walk along Puno Street and Raimondi Avenue, especially the blocks where the fumones hang out, is for the most part avoided by local residents and tourists. Before 11:00 A.M., the Datsun dealership and the Tropicana movie theater are quiet, almost deserted. Fumones of every age and both sexes sleep on newspapers, pieces of cardboard, or on cement pavements in the streets and parks. Since banks, offices, and some stores close at noon, downtown Tingo María is even more silent and empty. The fumones sleep or hang around in their usual haunts.

Many local residents know that Chicago exists, but they learn about what goes on there through other people. Even taxi drivers decline trips to these places. Anyone who goes to Chicago is suspected of drug addiction. One woman who had been observing my daily visit to Chicago whispered to her neighbor, "He does not seem to be, but I bet he is one of the new fumones." She only changed her opinion about my activity when she saw me taking photographs of children smoking coca paste near the local theater.

In 1983, the Iglesia Alianza Cristiana y Misionera de Tingo María numbered 215 coca-paste addicts whose ages ranged from ten to fifteen years. In this group seventy-five children were from ten to fourteen years old and the rest were fifteen-year-olds; almost a third were females. [11] The statistics presented by this church depict smoking problems among local resident children, not just the derelict and hopeless addicts of Chicago. In the beginning, I thought this picture was an exaggeration. However, my visits to Chicago and Aucayacu to gather some figures on groups smoking coca paste proved me wrong.

The figures presented here are the result of observation, interviews, and conversations with some addicts and local informants. The seventy-three fumones come from Tingo María, Aucayacu, and other small villages along the Huallaga River. Three addicts who have been in the area more than two years indirectly helped collect data on ages for most of the sample. Addicts who are still conscious of their status seem more difficult to approach, while those who are totally alienated and have lost their identities with normal society seem more accessible. The former perhaps provide more accurate information on themselves and others. The latter, because of their psychological and physical deterioration, are less than ideal subjects. Many, especially the children, hardly remember their names or nicknames, ages, and places of birth.

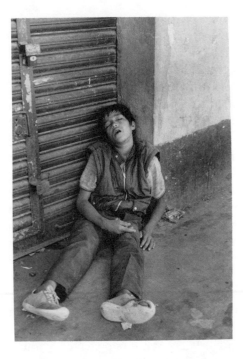

Coca-paste addicts of the
"Chicago" section of Tingo
María take over sidewalks
in front of banks and stores
after business hours.

The most damaging effect of addiction to the impurity-laden drug
is the self-destruction of hundreds and thousands of children who enter
the drug subculture very early in their lives. Twenty-seven percent of
the population surveyed began smoking coca paste when they were
nine or ten years old, and across the board, they have been smoking
coca paste for one to five years. One third of them came from nearby
cities or claimed to be natives of the area.

Theft, robbery, prostitution, and homosexual activity are the most
common methods of getting money for ketes. The younger addicts
usually get their daily dosages by way of homosexual services or exchange of sexual gratification. Nonaddicted homosexuals and hetero-
sexuals also trade coca paste for sexual gratification.

David is a fourteen-year-old Caucasian boy. He has been smoking
coca paste for the last four years. Black lice run about on his long hair

like ants on an anthill and white (body) lice cover his neck. "How did you become an addict, David?" I ask him.

"Like everyone else," he responds.

"What do you mean, like everyone else?"

"Who the fuck cares anyway, and stop asking questions you mother ——— and get lost, will you?"

Next morning (Saturday) I find David sleeping on the porch of a state office building along with two other addicts. I sit on the sidewalk to hear their morning conversation as they awaken. The three of them scratch their bodies constantly while they talk.

"Wake up, fucking José. Do you have a kete on you?"

José folds the newspaper (headlining the results of the national beauty pageant) with which he covers his body, and replies, "Shit, I do not have any even for myself. Maybe our new friend has some ketes left. Yesterday he traded his asshole for ten ketes. The owner of the bodega, that old man who likes kids, came and gave him coca paste."

"Let me check him out," says David. He gets up and leaves for downtown. He stands by the market street for a few minutes. He goes to the back of a bank only to find empty paper "beds." Then he walks along the main street and turns left toward Chicago.

David's portrait is just one of the many hopeless children who now wander along the Huallaga River. Their desperate efforts to satisfy their craving for drugs even cause violent deaths. Cupizo, a seventeen-year-old boy who had started smoking coca paste when he was ten years old, was stabbed by a local fruit peddler. The peddler was a kete retailer, and the addict had been his regular customer. One day Cupizo walked to the peddler's spot and decided to rob the peddler of his ketes. The fruit seller knifed Cupizo, who died pleading for coca paste.[12]

The economic influence of coca dollars on a large number of populations has been very significant in the changes that have taken place in traditional as well as modern Peruvian groups. Coca-dollar traffickers, prostitutes, and merchants are effective agents of social change and modernization. Production of cocaine as a commodity for an international market has many of the features of legally produced commodities. Resulting inflation, high cost of living, sophisticated tastes, and new lifestyles are not unlike the influence of oil on the economies of oil-producing countries. However, the millions of coca dollars coming to Peru from the drug industry do not help support a sound, healthy, independent national economy. The advent of coca dollars might well be compared to the American tourist who travels around Peru, makes indigenous groups aware of the existence of another world, pays inflationary prices, and leaves for home.

The Politics of Control and Eradication

*We believe that politics is the science or art of government
or the administration and management of public or state affairs.
But, if we revise our elementary biology
we could look at politics as a social subsistence chain
where individuals and groups in power
strive for the survival of their own well-being
at the cost of the majority.*

Drug production and distribution in the world's major coca and cocaine-producing countries—Bolivia, Colombia, and Peru—have emerged as national and international political issues. Due to heavy international pressure and economic aid, mainly from the United States, the Peruvian government has implemented different programs for control of coca cultivation and cocaine production. The U.S. Agency for International Development (AID) and the U.S. Bureau of International Narcotics Matters (INM) also sponsor programs and projects that aim to reduce the production of coca and to control trafficking of cocaine. However, these eradication and control policies are opposed by organized crime, which has filtered into the indigenous economy, traditional culture, and national politics.

The survival of thousands of individuals and the livelihood of the population on the eastern slopes of the Andes depend upon how these conflicting groups function in relation to one another. Political conditions are shaped by the balance of two opposing forces, each of which satisfies different interest groups. That is, the actual functions and interrelationships of these forces are critical in the maintenance and demise of eradication programs and control policies. In the interrelationships among labor, production processes, and capital, the class that creates wealth in the form of coca dollars is ultimately the group that carries the burden of repression, punishment, and the social and political adversities resulting from control and eradication.

Survival vs. Subsistence

The legal, national, social, and political structures of Peru are made up of individuals from all social spheres, whose role is to maintain the dictates of a normal society. Nevertheless, their survival as individuals has higher priority than the preservation of norms, rules, and laws. On the other hand, those whose behavior is considered deviant according to the legal structure resist complying with the standards imposed by groups who are alien to their reality. It is a struggle resembling the battle between a wasp and a spider.

The Peruvian government has installed five forces to control cocaine. These forces are the Guardia Civil (regular police), the Guardia Republicana, the Policía de Investigaciones del Peru, the Unidad Movil de Patrullaje Rural (UMOPAR), and the Sinchis (a special anti-subversive unit). Of the five bodies, UMOPAR exclusively has the job of controlling the increasing production of coca and manufacture of cocaine in the mountainous jungles. These anti-cocaine police have established their headquarters in a town which, in the late seventies, emerged as the center of the cocaine industry. The UMOPAR policemen are popularly known as *upachos*, which in Quechua is a diminutive for "foolish people." Because of the increase in social problems accompanying the cocaine boom, other agencies of social control and repression have been established.

The unique features of the setting, the populations involved, and their relationships to one another present a host of problems and continuing conflicts. Duties and responsibilities of the five agencies of social control and political repression are not coordinated for effective action. Each task force has specific duties limited to particular aspects or a broader problem. Thus, for instance, a drug trafficker caught with large amounts of money, cocaine, and arms is generally suspected of being a trafficker or a guerrilla member or both. Should this suspect be detained by the anti-subversive unit, he would automatically be accused of being a terrorist, since the anti-subversive unit's main interest is not drug trafficking but the guerrillas. Sinchi unit members tend to ignore cocaine production and traffic. The military does not view narcotics control as part of its mandate.[1]

North of Tingo María, there are three police checkpoints that cover roads for about seventy-five kilometers. There the police make routine checks of passengers entering or leaving the jungle. One or two agents get on the buses and minibuses (*colectivos*), ask all passengers for their national personal identification cards, and have them open their bags to search for cocaine, foreign currency (dollars), contraband appliances bought inland, and so forth. Often, they check the hands of peasants. If they find signs of their having worked in coca-paste pits, the police thoroughly search the belongings of the peasants or the young urban migrant workers. Police know that these peasants have saved money and that they are taking with them no less than $100 or its equivalent in national currency. Occasionally, they seize large amounts of money from exchangers and detain cocaine dealers.

If a peasant shows signs of having worked in coca-paste manufacturing sites, he is charged with drug dealing. The peasant suspect has the choice of either going to jail for his crime or giving up his savings and being set free. These abuses are not limited to laborers and petty dealers. Any person carrying money or valuables is suspected of direct participation in cocaine traffic, the U.S. dollar black market, or smuggling out contraband goods.

Police literally go after any person who "smells" of money. For instance, an honest butcher came to the outskirts of Oaktown to buy cattle. Two customs employees "caught" him carrying 29 million soles in cash. He was then coerced into signing a report and told to come back the next day to pick up his cash. When the butcher went back the officers refuted his claim to the money, and the case was not included in the record book.[2]

On rare occasions, these abuses appear in news headlines. But even if they do get publicized, they often are distorted or disguised to protect the officers. In the worst of cases, the officers are only suspended or fired. For example, one night the UMOPAR organized a raid on one of the drug hamlets. They broke into one trafficker's house when he and his band were sleeping. The UMOPAR reported to the joint chief of staff in Tingo María that "there had been a clean-up operation in which action one suspect had been killed and sixty kilos of coca paste had been seized."

The mother of the twenty-four-year-old victim took the case to court. She said that, in fact, UMOPAR had killed her son and three more individuals and that the police had seized 48 million soles and U.S. $100,000 cash. The judge inspected the site and found human viscera that did not belong to the victim the police claimed to have killed. Residents of the hamlet also assured the court that three more members of the band had been killed, their stomachs opened, filled up with sand, and dumped in the river. A fellow colocho paid $1,000 to a diver to find the bodies of the victims of the vicious killings of the UMOPAR. The bodies of the young traffickers had been transported by plane to "Colombia."

Policemen usually come to the area without their families. They live in the police quarters and have their meals in restaurants and boarding-houses (*pensiones*) where they pay on a monthly basis. It is not unusual to find cases of a policeman going to pay for his meals, only to find out that someone has already taken care of his debt.

When the police want very large sums of money, they follow narcos or small dealers until they seize them. During my research, one local boss was about to "make a pass" (sell some cocaine to other dealers) in a local bar and earn U.S. $30,000 in the transaction. At the very minute of "making the pass," the boss and the buyer were caught red-handed. The following evening, when a "humble public employee" treated me to a couple of drinks, I saw the boss having his drink in the same spot. My host asked the boss about what had happened to him. The answer was simply, "You know what they want[ed]."

Another means of making a good living while in "coca-land" is to become an accomplice of the underworld. The work can vary from collaborating in the trafficking of materials, such as sulfuric acid, to knowingly ignoring the existence of secret airfields. The most sophis-ticated accomplices, however, arrange for organized and planned collaboration in the shipping of coca paste using legal airports. Negotiations are done with heads of police. At a time and date set by those who pay for use of the runway, a plane lands and two or three men rush the cargo to the plane. The craft takes off and only when it is out of range will the guards fire on it.

The cocaine economy and coca dollars corrupt the society at every level. When officials detain a cocaine smuggler, they "negotiate a commonsense solution" before other officials and authorities can take advantage of the situation. One migrant peasant had a large coca plantation where he himself manufactured coca paste. On their way to detain a cocaine trafficker, the anti-drug police groups stopped at the peasant's house and found eighty arrobas of dried coca leaves, 6 million soles in cash (of which 1 million were counterfeit), two shotguns, eight Seiko watches, videocassette players, and stereos, but no coca paste. Based on the amount of coca, arms, money, and other commodities found, the police assumed the peasant was a "big fish." He was detained and charged with drug trafficking and arms possession. The police and the local judge "gave the peasant a break" with the provision that he forfeit all his cash and the properties the police had seized. The police kept 5 million soles and the goods. The judge took the 1 million counterfeit soles (only the peasant and the police knew which bundle of bills was worthless). Later, the officer in charge of the station went to the judge's office and played victim, arguing that all the money was counterfeit. The peasant moved his living quarters to a less accessible place, for the "green dogs had already tasted easy money."

The "white gold rush" is so contagious that bribes and payoffs have almost become the rule rather than the exception. Since people are on the defensive, they operate on the principle that the best strategy is to attack the suspect. Definitions of innocence or guilt are situational.

Anyone who goes to the eastern slopes, regardless of profession or occupation, does it because, in one way or another, he or she is attracted by economic opportunities growing out of the "cocaine rush." One policeman, who later was a subject, described the difficulties he faced in becoming a member of the UMOPAR police. At national drug-control offices, a policeman was collecting information for the American Embassy on behalf of the Bureau of International Narcotics Matters. However, he was trying hard to save money to "pay for his transfer

somewhere in the forests." The difficulty in getting transferred or relocated to the jungles resides not in the lack of special professionalism
or skills determined by the institutions. On the contrary, there are long,
secret waiting lists, and the decision-making officers are greedy about
demanding payoffs for assignments in the jungles.

Civil servants and professionals, especially lawyers, know that they
can make far more money in small villages or communities where drug
production and marketing are the main economic activities. In fact,
before the seventies, the same towns and cities which are now viewed
advantageously were once looked on as a kind of Siberia, where policemen, teachers, judges, and new graduates were sent for disciplinary
measures. Village and town leaders had constantly to appeal directly to
the central government to appoint teachers, policemen, and other authorities to represent the national political structure. As a response to
social pressure, the military government established a minimum intern-
ship in communities in isolated areas as a requirement for a B.A. degree
in education, nursing, and other health professions. Now the shortage
of professionals is present only in drug-free highland populations,
while the opposite is true in drug-terminal highland communities and
in the "green mines" where, in addition to their high salaries, police
profit from enforcement of drug laws by taking small properties from
wage laborers, farmers, or petty traffickers.[3]

Cocaine and Class Division

The movement of cocaine within the country is almost exclusively in
the hands of small-town middle-class people, traveling merchants,
truckers, and so forth. The international marketing of the drug falls in
the realm of the metropolitan middle class operating at the national
level and connected to large-scale consumer centers in industrial countries. Engineers, lawyers, and airline executives either establish their
middle-class status or emerge as new economic power groups. These
white-collar "cocaine gentlemen" have, in some cases, lost their economic power due to the social and political conditions imposed by the
military dictatorship which ruled Peru in the seventies.[4]

In February 1980, 5.3 kilos of cocaine hydrochloride were found in the suitcase of a retired air force general and ex-president of a Peruvian airline who was traveling to Miami. The package containing the drug had been addressed to a fictitious person in the United States. The general ordered the luggage handler to put his baggage in the cabin. A customs inspector, who previously had been told "not to check the general," got his hands on the suitcase. At first, the general's reaction was to claim that he had been framed, that "it was a fix." He even blamed it on the "idiot luggage handler's work." Only later did he admit that the case containing the drug was his.[5]

Decree 22095, section 56, establishes draconically that the minimum sentence for drug trafficking is fifteen years; section 64 makes clear that drug traffickers cannot enjoy any conditional release whatsoever. The general in question was "sentenced" to "work" on an air force base in northern Peru. He was released in March 1986 and by now is probably enjoying a luxurious retirement somewhere. In contrast, thousands of petty dealers and innocent wage laborers who are caught with small amounts of coca paste are serving maximum sentences.

A twenty-two-year-old single mother of four children was caught with 500 grams of coca paste in a town in the central highlands. The peasant woman claimed she had traded three rams for the drug. She expected to earn about 2 million soles from the sale (she swore that it was her first deal), with which she was planning to purchase clothing for her school-aged children. She was sent to jail, leaving her children with their ailing elderly grandmother. Assuming that the coca paste the peasant woman was transporting was good-quality raw material, the 500 grams was the approximate equivalent of only 130 grams of cocaine hydrochloride, or 2.64 percent of what the retired general was smuggling. It is clear that preferential treatment and social bias influence the interpretation of the law in the cocaine business and perpetuate the already deep social divisions in Peru.

This highly lucrative business of drug trafficking is almost ubiquitous. Nonetheless, the wage earner and the petty dealer are the scapegoats in a society trapped in an illegal enterprise as its only effective source of cash. The loopholes in the national legal system protect the dominant classes' control of the international traffic in cocaine. Low-ranking customs and police officers, who come mostly from working or lower classes, are prohibited from enforcing the laws against cocaine traffickers. Government officials and the middle class use their social prestige and economic power to shun control. Thus, if a customs officer or a policeman tries to inspect a politician, a prestigious businessman, or a member of the national social and economic establishment, others will always try to stop the officer from making even routine checks. Those who act stubbornly to insist on equal application of the law are in danger of losing their positions or being reassigned to remote areas.

Because it is difficult to swim against the current, and because everyone in the system is corrupt—so popular belief insists—policemen, employees, and workers follow their leaders. They turn into support groups for cocaine trafficking. In many instances, their indirect participation results in better or higher-paying jobs in the bureaucratic system. For the collaborators, direct cooperation can mean economic rewards, but also it can lead to bearing others' blame. As the folk saying goes, "The ass always throws the blame on the pack saddle."

A major contraband scandal involving many government and police heads was discovered in December 1968. Allegedly, the secretary of the treasury, the head of one of the police forces, and the director of customs were all directly involved in the smuggling of goods into Peru. The head of the organization was a member of a European merchant family established in the country. Among other contraband goods, oriental rugs and English fabrics were illegally imported. A major international carrier with stopover flights in New York and two Caribbean islands was the transporter. Many airline staff members cooperated in the enterprise. The cargo showed a Chilean city as the final destination. By rule, in-transit cargo is forwarded on another airline without going through customs. In this instance, the freight was picked up a few minutes after the airplane's arrival and the paperwork properly signed by the second carrier. On many occasions, the open platform truck carrying the contraband was escorted and protected by a police patrol car.

On Christmas Eve of 1968, the organization was unmasked. Two cargo clerks claimed responsibility and were sentenced accordingly. A few months later, one of the employees who volunteered to be the scapegoat was leaving jail every two weeks to pick up his salary, collected by former fellow workers. One of the staff members argued that the convict had also been getting payoffs from the other party.[6]

Seventeen years later, just three days before officially ending its term in office, the same political group was embarrassingly accused by the mass media of participation in cocaine traffic. Supposedly, a plumber's error caused the explosion of a well-established "kitchen" in a middle-class residential area of Lima. The accident led to the discovery of a national organization with international connections. As is generally the rule, only the "little guys" such as the "cook" were detained. Judging by the closely knit nature of the organization, only an accident could have uncovered the powerful alliance between the middle-class leaders and the representatives of the international cocaine network.

The heads of the operation were three brothers who, thanks to cocaine, had shed their working-class garb and were becoming very active in the national society and economy. The "front" for the syndicate was a travel agency. The pseudo-agency was used to smuggle illegal aliens into the United States through Mexico and probably to launder cocaine dollars in this country, using the illegal aliens as "burros." The day the "kitchen" exploded, an official car, which was for the personal use of the top advisor of the premier, was found parked at the front door.

The president of the travel agency, who also was the "money man," and his sister had enjoyed open access to the ramp of the international airport, were close friends of the ex-premier, and were spiritually related (*compadres*) to one of the heads of the police charged with controlling cocaine traffic in Peru. Evidences of close social relationships were documented by home movies filmed in the trafficker's house. The general of the police force (the trafficker's *compadre*) denied any involvement beyond friendship with his *compadre*. Yet here are some facts published by local newspapers: The general's annual salary was about $5,000; one of his houses was estimated to cost about $200,000; he owned a yacht, which he said "was a gift from an unknown friend in the jungles." On repeated occasions, the cocaine trafficker's travel agency had issued tickets to many officials at gracious discount rates. Furthermore, one congressman stated publicly that the premier's office had been warned of the travel agent's link to international traffic in cocaine. The congressman said that his finding was ignored and nothing was done to stop the organization.

The second week of August 1985, the government seized the largest cocaine laboratory set up on the border between Peru and Colombia.

A local newspaper, *La República*, accused the premier of knowingly having ignored the existence of this cocaine "industrial complex." Whether the government knew or not, the large-scale laboratory found in the lowlands of the Amazon was most likely part of the international mafia with operations based throughout Colombia.

In light of the active participation of some police members, there is ample reason to believe that costs of production were much lower than in any regular refining enterprise. Supply of coca paste was constant and abundant. As people argue in Peru: "It is very likely that most, if not all, coca paste seized from petty dealers and traffickers was refined in the laboratories protected by police and some government officials." Besides export of drugs, the national middle class's control of the international traffic in cocaine brings to the United States and some European countries another social problem: the smuggling of illegal aliens into the United States through Mexico.

One Mexican consul was the trafficker's tenant living in a house directly opposite the "cocaine industrial complex." The consul admitted friendship with the "Padrino" of the Peruvian connection. It has been proven that the Padrino's travel agency had obtained visas to Mexico and the United States with little or no difficulty at all. Allegedly, his passengers were used also as "burros" to transport cocaine or American dollars to Mexico or the United States. Many illegal aliens living in the New York metropolitan area stated that visitors' B-2 visas to the United States were somewhat difficult to obtain, but not impossible. Savings and checking accounts were forged, or bank affidavits "bought" from some bank clerks, and letters of employment issued by fictitious employers. All of these papers were the travel agency's responsibility. Some illegal aliens argued that the agent would assure them issuance of a visa to the United States for a $500 fee, for the agency "had its contacts in the American Embassy." This claim may or may not have been true, but the fact of the matter is that hundreds of Peruvians entered the U.S. legally under a B-2 visa, or illegally through Mexico and Canada.

Hundreds of aliens were "exported" by the Padrino's agency. I have had the opportunity of interviewing fifteen of them who lived and worked in northern New Jersey and New York City. Once the visa to visit either Mexico or the United States was secured, groups of at least

A refining laboratory in a middle-class section of Lima (top). An explosion here (results visible at center) led to the discovery of a major Peruvian international trafficker who allegedly had enjoyed protection from some government officials. Today the former cocaine complex, covering nearly a square block, is used as a shelter for orphans and homeless children (bottom).

ten tourists were scheduled to fly to Mexico City, Miami, or New York via Panama. The agent helped those passengers who did not have cash for payment of the round-trip tickets, hotels, and surface transportation expenses to finance their trip through a national bank. Many of them are still sending money to Peru to meet their obligations to the lending institutions.

Furthermore, passengers were provided with considerable amounts of cash in U.S. dollars as travel-expense money. These amounts were handed back to the group leader in Panama, Mexico, or Miami. Some aliens were even asked to take small packages which supposedly contained traditional food and pastries. The packages, along with the cash, were collected after clearing customs in the cities of destination. The aliens, who apparently acted as unwitting "burros," did not know the real contents of the boxes they transported.[7] In Bolivia, the world's second largest coca and cocaine producer,

> senior military officers have been involved in extraordinarily lucrative drug trafficking and other corruption. . . . Some officers have received millions of dollars for protecting traffickers or for trafficking themselves in the processed and semi-processed cocaine leaving Bolivia. Many military officers are not bashful in displaying their new wealth. They drive flashy cars and live in expensive homes. . . . Few of the "coca-dollars" appear to reach the ordinary soldier, but its effects are already felt throughout much of the rest of society.[8]

One may quickly reach the conclusion that those who benefit most from the production and traffic of cocaine are the classes and groups that define and officially "fight against cocaine traffic." Many law-enforcement agents make substantial investments to gain their assignments in the jungles or narcotics squads. It may not be an exaggeration to state that the real question to ask in Peru is which members of the middle class are *not* involved in cocaine traffic. It should be underscored that the control of the international traffic in cocaine was always the domain of the national middle-class groups.

Even during "military revolutionary days," the refining and marketing of cocaine was controlled by national middle-class groups. In 1974 a young member of the Peruvian aristocracy, a close relative of the then minister of foreign relations, was caught with large amounts of cocaine in his possession. Because of his relationship to power groups, his operations continued smoothly and uninterrupted. Ten years later, this aristocrat trafficker was killed in an explosion in his "kitchen." To avoid the embarrassment of other members of the "Peruvian connection," police investigations ended at the trafficker's funeral services.[9] On January 10, 1978, a Peruvian bank executive, the niece of the last military dictator in Peru, Francisco Morales Bermudez, was caught in Los Angeles with eleven pounds of cocaine hydrochloride then worth $2 million. A report of this incident was not published in Peru.[10]

To close the argument, there are also indications that the trafficking in Peruvian cocaine may have directly involved some Hollywood movie stars and high social echelons. On September 21, 1985, American actress Margaret O'Brien's husband, a Peruvian native, was caught in the International Airport of Lima while trying to smuggle 1.1 kilos of high-quality cocaine out of Peru.[11] In another instance, allegedly, Canadian Prime Minister Pierre Trudeau issued one of the seven passports of a Peruvian cocaine trafficker in a disco in Montreal.[12]

Narco-Politics

Parallel to the cocaine boom, Sendero Luminoso ("Shining Path"), a Maoist guerrilla movement, emerged in May of 1980.[13] The initial focus of the Shining Path's terrorist acts was the southeastern city of Ayacucho, which in Quechua means "corner of the dead." It was in this south-central department where Spain's last hopes to profit from Peru were shattered. One century and a half later, a different kind of political movement emerged in Ayacucho. This time, the enemy was not any foreign power but the social, economic, and human conditions that the Indians and peasants at large were, and still are, enduring. One Peruvian official admits that the southeastern area is the poorest, most abandoned, and most forgotten region of Peru where economic and social indicators are among the worst not only of Peru and Latin America, but of the entire world. Why terrorism? The state has done nothing for these people for 400 years and now it's difficult to catch up.[14] The

Shining Path could have organized its guerrilla operations anywhere in the highlands of Peru; it was only a question of leadership. A number of sociologists and anthropologists at the University of Huamanga (Ayacucho) seem to have been ideologues who incited both young mestizos and peasants to attempt armed struggles against the government. Universities have always been the sources of rebellions and political movements. When Fidel Castro exported his revolution to Peru and Bolivia in the late sixties, historical and dialectical materialism were added as core curricular subjects in the general studies of the universities. This ideological wave brought with it bank robberies and armed assaults in support of the guerrilla movements in central Peru and Bolivia.

Peruvian leadership has always been the responsibility of a handful of middle-class and urban working-class politicians. The latter have little or no understanding of the complex problems presented by many ethnic groups in the highlands of Peru. Some maintain that existence of the Shining Path in the jungle is entirely correlated with drug production and traffic. *Executive Intelligence Review* suggests that the Shining Path's capability to move quickly and secretly as many as 2,000 terrorists in a country where transportation service is still a serious problem, indicates the degree of sophistication and availability of means of transportation (airplanes) owned by drug traffickers.[15] It is true that drug traffickers have at their disposition scores of airplanes. But the small crafts have payload capacities of less than 1,000 kilos. Would a smuggler's plane make over 300 trips required to transport 2,000 guerrilla members? Drug traffickers can smuggle some arms and ammunition to the jungle as part of their contraband goods, but they cannot afford to be at the rebels' service. The U.S. State Department and the DEA speculate about links between left-wing guerrilla organizations and the drug trade.[16]

Although many terrorist attacks may have helped drug traffickers escape from prison, the Shining Path's actions were not necessarily aimed at liberating them.[17] Drug traffickers and Shining Path guerrillas represent two totally different social movements. Drug traffickers are members of a monolithic underground social organization with purely economic interests. Cocaine lords do not have any ideological and emotional identification with national problems. The Shining Path and other political groups have their raison d'être in the ongoing abuses and social injustice against the Indians and the peasantry at large. One reason why the Shining Path and other urban guerrillas are relatively successful, since they have not disintegrated as did the political movements of the sixties, is that the working class and the peasants are slowly grappling with their own social and economic realities. That is why these political movements are dangerous and threatening to the prevailing system.

Although it is true that initial leadership comes from without, hundreds of adolescents in both the highlands and urban areas are joining the guerrillas. For these young people, there is no other way to express the frustration, poverty, misery, and abuse experienced in their country. The revolutionary ideology is already drawing first- and second-generation Andean migrants to metropolitan cities, especially those who come from the south-central Andes. During my last trip to Peru I found that three close friends, one of whom was my coworker in a textile factory in the fifties, had joined the Shining Path. Their wives informed me that their husbands were "at the front" and "they were alive and fighting for the Indian." One of the rebels had been my classmate in grade school, high school, and college. Although we were sympathetic to the Indian issue, each of us had different approaches to its solution. As his wife said, "He had the courage to face the problem, while others avoided it." She meant me.

Since the Shining Path's beginnings, thousands of people have been killed in Peru, including policemen and soldiers. At least 750 peasants have been killed.[18] However, the number of casualties from direct attacks involving the guerrillas and uniformed Peruvians may not reflect the journalists, lawyers, teachers, and children detained by government forces, whose whereabouts are unknown to date.[19]

In June 1985, only a few miles from the community where I had done my doctoral research, the Shining Path had killed several ex-landlords and government officials. In one instance in the northeast, there were vicious killings by both the Shining Path and the army in a town that served as one of the major gates to the Upper Huallaga, about five kilometers from my hometown. A group of about twenty guerrillas attacked the local police station. The three policemen did not surrender and badly wounded one of the attackers. Since the guerrillas had identified one of the policemen, they came back a few days later, seized and decapitated him, and took his head as a trophy. Subsequently, the town became a garrison. A fourteen-year-old guerrilla, an expert in assembling and dismantling arms, turned himself in. The army made him confess the Shining Path's secrets and dig out the place where the rebels had hidden stolen arms. Then they shot the boy on the spot.

The assaults of both insurgents and government forces are generally considered ruthless and brutal by the highland peasants, but they slowly are becoming more and more sympathetic to and supportive of the Shining Path. It may not be an overstatement to hypothesize that, as economic conditions stand, many young peasants find only two alternatives: either join the Shining Path or migrate to the jungles for wages. There are two main reasons why the highland Indian and peasant directly or indirectly support the rural guerrillas. First, the "revolutionaries" identify with the Andean people's immediate problems. The majority of urban guerrillas are teachers (31 percent) and college students (35 percent) who are more than familiar with the Peruvian countryside.[20] Second, the Andean people fear being "judged" and "sentenced" by the Shining Path.

It should be made clear that the myth of sudden attacks on disarmed and helpless peasants has, in many cases, been created by police and the army to discredit the Shining Path. For instance, it was reported that one night a group of guerrillas broke into many houses in a small town and robbed the peasants of their sheep, chickens, and pigs, to feed their comrades. When a peasant woman went to the police station to report the robbery, she saw her animals in the station. She called her pet sheep by its name and the animal jumped all over her. The woman went back home without her sheep, but with a knowledge of the truth about the latest "rebel" assault.

This and many other accounts of abuses by police may lead one to believe that the Indians of Huaychao killed the seven guerrillas because the peasants had on many occasions been forced to give up their crops and animals. The first assailants may not have been guerrillas, but government soldiers. On August 14, 1985, at least fifty-nine peasants, including children and women, were killed by soldiers in the highlands of Ayacucho.[21] Perhaps the only reason for the slaughter of defenseless highlanders was that the villagers protected the Shining Path, or at least collaborated with it.

The guerrilla activities made officials believe that the eastern forests had become the scene for political rebellions, cocaine production and traffic, and homicides. By 1981, the political situation of Peru was almost a carbon copy of the chaotic and corrupt government that ruled Peru from 1963 to 1968. The government in office, to distract national and international attention and civil liberty outcries, claimed that every single protest movement was intimately related to the Shining Path. There was also speculation that some terrorists were involved in the cultivation of coca or in drug trafficking. In this regard, even in Colombia, where radical armed struggle is almost part of national politics,

> there are differing views on the involvement of FARC and M-19 guerrilla groups in narcotics production and trafficking. Some officials assert that there is no hard evidence linking these groups to trafficking, other than the fact they allow production and trafficking in areas under their control to take place. Others assert that there are strong ties between the traffickers and the guerrillas.[22]

Because of the Peruvian government's inability to control the powerful underworld, the corruption of officials, or various social protest movements including the Shining Path, the state argues that all attacks and rebellions are due to the Shining Path's presence in the jungle. Data collected in the heart of the cocaine economy raise serious doubts about the Shining Path's participation. Conversations with coca planters, colochos, traffickers, and others were astonishingly revealing. The groups that produce and distribute coca and cocaine had a clear and defined attitude toward the political aspect of their work. They would talk about some "happenings," "events," and "crushes" with the agents of control and eradication. The most common explanation for their attacking police was "because the police persecute us too much" or "because they become too greedy."

On June 1, 1987, in a town about three hundred miles northeast of Lima, a band of about sixty drug mercenaries attacked the local police station. The station, now closed, was located about one mile from the town's main square. The attack came around midnight and residents reported that the skirmish lasted for six hours. The police radioed frequently to ask for help from other stations. Five officers were killed. Two escaped into the woods, and the captain was caught alive and taken into a bathroom, where he was tortured in the most brutal way. The assailants set fire to the building, took their casualties with them, and left. The fire killed four other people in the concrete building next to the police station. People in the town assert that the motive for the attack was entirely business-related. Allegedly, some local bosses had been paying the police $1,000 per pickup from flights at the local airport. The police demanded more for their cooperation. The bosses objected and decided to give them a bloody lesson.[23]

The so-called narco-terrorists should neither be confused with revolutionary movements, nor should it be assumed that the Shining Path is economically and technically supported by the cocaine underworld. Because illicit coca planters and cocaine manufacturers are entrepreneurs, they cannot afford to wage a political movement that does not report profits. Moreover, the international traffic in cocaine consists of monolithic organizations whose outside heads have control over the lower strata, as well as the local and community economies. Besides, small planters and cocaine producers are part of micro-economies, whereas the Shining Path, by now, is a nationwide political front planned and supported by the Peruvian Communist Party. Attacks in the jungles are typically mob vendettas rather than armed attacks and bombings. Most important is the fact that coca dollars are helping the ruling middle classes to survive in their political role at local and national levels.

The facts substantiate this position. First, social and economic conditions in the rain forests are not as bad as in the highlands. On the contrary, cocaine-producing areas boast the highest cost of living and a variety of occupations with cash wages that satisfy most of the population's material needs. The majority of these populations are migrants from all parts of Peru; their stay in the woods is temporary and purely for economic reasons.

Second, all so-called terrorist attacks have been directed toward

Some days as many as five bodies of "informers" who have been killed by traffickers are seen along the roads. The victims endure indescribable and vicious methods of torture. Rarely are they shot. The male pictured here was strangled to death.

agencies, offices, and personnel associated with the eradication of the coca plant and control of the production of and trafficking in cocaine. In the forests, unlike the rest of the country, no banks, schools, or power plants have been destroyed. Such terrorist acts would have affected local drug economies more than the national economy. Roadblocks do not interrupt the flow of chemicals and other supplies to the underground. Supplies used in the large-scale manufacture of coca paste come to the jungle through different routes and various means of transportation. Despite all inconveniences, supply of food and basic commodities is constant, for the jungle is the best market for many populations. The two biggest cities that provide consumer goods to drug-producing areas have not been targets of any kind of serious terrorist attacks so far, whereas other highland cities and towns whose economies are not based on cocaine have attracted the Shining Path.

Third, if the Shining Path were politically important in towns and villages producing drugs, and if the movement were supported by organized crime, there would have been more than scattered and sporadic attacks. Both the highland guerrillas and the cocaine underworld are more organized and better equipped than the national army in the area. All of these facts, as well as the struggle between the drug industry and the government, support the argument that conditions in the jungle do not invite control by the Shining Path. On the other hand, the cocaine underworld itself does not need a large army of rebels. It cares little about national, social, and economic conditions and would oppose the equitable distribution of wealth and other communist goals.

Resentful traffickers and coca planters organize themselves into bands to attack the enemy. By their definition, their enemies are not only forces of control and repression, but news reporters, journalists, and government officials who do not accept the "gifts" sent to them and who are antipathetic to their economic operations. For that matter, the enemy is any person whose presence creates an undesired imbalance in the daily life of the cocaine-producing populations. Unlike guerrilla members, the cocaine underground does not see the difference between impartial legal activities and forces that would control. Unless the suspect's behavior is obvious, as with some media representatives, executions are based on suspicion alone.

Most of the victims of the drug traffickers' attacks are police informers (*soplones*), police stations, and of course, individual policemen and members of the armed forces. They have diverse methods of "punishing" the "fools." (To them, the police are fools because they come to a land where they know they are going to lose.) They set fire to encampments and offices, torture their victims and chop their bodies into pieces, put them in plastic bags, and dump them in the woods or throw them in the river. When they get their hands on people they want very badly, they beat them up and hang them with barbed wire, putting signs on their bodies that read, "This is the way informers die." It is the job of the bodyguards, hired gunmen, and *macheteros* to kill suspects and traitors. The slayers may be newspaper boys, wage laborers, or non-uniformed policemen. The same applies to the hordes and bands that besiege official settlements and projects.

In September 1982 in a town which now is the national center of cocaine production and traffic, a young drug lord killed a journalist. The reporter, on assignment for a magazine of the Upper Huallaga region, was shot to death in the main square. The suspect was arrested and jailed in Lima, where he escaped from prison after bribing the guards with 500 million soles.[24] I was informed that in the same square in June 1985 another reporter had been gunned down by a newsboy riding on the back seat of a motorcycle. This town was the second most dangerous and lawless place to which I went during my fieldwork.

Executions of intruders, busybodies, and infiltrators are carried out based entirely on suspicion or more solid information received from other groups. The drug traffickers communicate and organize so quickly against police raids that many law-enforcement officers are more concerned with their own survival and livelihood than with law-enforcement functions. A branch of UMOPAR sent fifteen policemen to arrest some coca-paste manufacturers. By the time they reached the target hamlet, the manufacturers were already organized. Most of them hid in the woods. The police, in fact, seized approximately two hundred kilos of coca paste from deserted pits. But as they were on their way back, the villagers crowded into the dirt road, beat the police, recovered their drugs, and dumped the police pick-up truck into the river.

Several recent publications have suggested a closer connection between guerrillas and drug traffickers, failing, however, to present convincing data save for photographs of armed peasants and of communist graffiti. These publications allege that the guerrillas protect the *cocaleros*, thus co-opting and taking advantage of drug traffickers who exploit peasants and wage earners alike. Those traffickers, it is alleged, may provide the guerrillas with arms and money in exchange for their protection. It is extremely difficult, however, to demonstrate a clear relationship between the two underground groups—revolutionaries and traffickers—although recent terrorist actions in the Upper Huallaga suggest a connection.[25]

As a research consultant for *National Geographic*, I spent the first half of August 1987 in the Upper Huallaga. In a hamlet near the village where the two reporters from *Caretas* were seized and brought to a guerrilla encampment, I met Oscar, who claimed to be one of the radical communists and local underground leaders. (He happened to be

Not all terrorist actions come from guerrillas. The *cocaleros* also cut ditches in roads to stop traffic to coca fields being worked.

the son of a peasant from my birthplace.) I wanted to meet a peasant who supposedly was a successful coca farmer. When I came to the hamlet, the farmer was not at home. When Oscar saw my hiking shoes and my camera bag he thought I was a reporter and did not even invite me in to sit and wait for his father. I sat by the door. Fortunately, the father soon showed up.

The peasant remembered my mother's name as well as many other names of people we both knew. We chatted, teased each other, and told jokes in Quechua. Through other migrant peasants, he knew that my mother had a son who lived in the United States. At this point, Oscar's part in the conversation was very marginal, but because of my identification with his father's culture, Oscar became more open and friendly. Among other things, I asked him about Gonzalo Pomareda (known as President Gonzalo), one of the legendary figures in the Shining Path. The subject sparked Oscar's interest, and he became very emotional and argued his beliefs and viewpoint as if he were trying to recruit me. His poise and mental stamina were typical of a charismatic leader.

After lunch he gave me a tour around the hamlet and introduced me to other *compañeros* (comrades). Since I was very familiar with the ways of the people in the area and with their defensive attitudes, I asked no questions and showed no interest in anything other than coca. After our short walk around the hamlet we went to the nearest busy town. By then, Oscar was already introducing me to other people as his "primo" (cousin). In Tintown, Oscar and I visited restaurants, bars, street peddlers, shoemakers, food vendors, and schoolteachers. There were instances where Oscar was consulted privately and others where he would summon his compañeros and whisper in their ear. His trust in me was unusual and suspicious, for people in the jungle say that "one cannot afford to trust one's own shadow."

For example, he revealed that all of his compañeros had identities that made it difficult for the police to find them. They had code names for many key terms such as cocalero, ammunition, arms, and police that were totally different from the regional slang words used for the same things. When I left for Lima, Oscar asked me to deliver letters to two lawyers who, when I met them in their law office, made fun of me, saying, "Sanmarquino y Yanqui, que ironía" (San Marcos alumnus and Yanqui, what a contradiction).

In August 1987 the Carretera Marginal was impassable at many points, including one place where on August 19 a bridge was destroyed.[26] People who have witnessed the so-called "Sendero terrorist actions" assured me that the cocaleros and traffickers had torn up the roads.[27]

Anyone who has had actual contact with the underground would conclude that "terrorist attacks" correlate almost directly with drug law-enforcement actions such as Operation Condor and Operation Lightning. Drug traffickers keep a number of mercenaries and hire wage laborers and unemployed people to perform a specific "job." They hire ex-police officers to train their mercenaries. For instance, residents describe that, in an attack on a police station where six officers were killed in June 1987, most of the mercenary attackers were untrained *pañacos* (a pejorative term describing people from neighboring highland communities).

The argument that guerrillas are "taxing" traffickers may, on the other hand, be a counterargument concocted by corrupt officials (who usually are the sources of information for the outside world) or by the traffickers themselves. Playing intelligence is very much part of an underground war which, at times, can be a subsistence tactic. Both traffickers and law-enforcement agents benefit from coca and cocaine. Traffickers bring in dollars for the country and, considering the legal income alone, police officers receive more than $100 a month from the United States on top of their high salaries.

One thing to bear in mind is the fact that drug traffickers enjoy the help of farmers and the local population. When faced with taking sides with either the police or with traffickers, people volunteer to protect cocaine outlaws. One day, after their informant let them know of the details of police plans to arrest them, two "Colombians" decided to stay overnight in a local hotel. About two hours later, five anti-drug policemen showed up in the hotel and asked the employee for the room numbers of the two "Colombians." A hotel employee asked the policemen for an arrest warrant or for the manager's consent to break into the rooms. The employee managed both to call the manager and to alert the traffickers, who hid in the bush surrounding the hotel building. The general attitude of people who thwart police action is that they have nothing against the traffickers, "for arrests only satisfy the police's greed" and that unlike the traffickers, "the police never share their pie."

Police also use the words "terrorism" and "terrorist" to cover up their killing of innocent victims and petty traffickers, and they then present to the general public their clean, heroic image in an area infested by two kinds of outlaws. For instance, in July 1987 a local union leader was shot to death. The labor leader was a local colectivo driver who the day of his death was trying to smuggle sulfuric acid. The anticocaine police ordered the driver to stop for a routine search. The driver sped away but was stopped a few blocks away by the police and gunned down. A local radio station's newsbreak was that "the heroic police had faced a shootout against a group of guerrillas" and that, in the action, one radical had been killed. The wife of the victim and other passengers traveling with the driver were detained. The widow was in detention for almost a week, and she had to pay many hundreds of

Anti-eradication and radical political signs are everywhere in the Upper Hua-llaga, as shown here in graffiti protesting Operation Lightning.

dollars to make bail. The passengers were defenseless migrants or com-muters who were not even armed with machetes.

Politically, the power of the coca dollar is the underworld's best weapon to exert pressure on national politics. In 1984 one of the drug-core towns was designated the capital of a new province. By law, this meant that the government had to appoint one judge as well as other legal authorities appropriate to the town's political status. Besides pe-titioning for such services, the citizens complained about the excessive abuses and civil rights violations that the armed UMOPAR and the Guardia República were perpetrating against them. Because their for-mal petitions did not have the desired result, the residents decided to go on a general strike. The people's assembly demanded the following objectives:

> The UMOPAR be removed from the town and the area.
> Production, marketing, and "industrialization" of coca plants be part of free enterprise.

An electoral district for the town be created immediately.
A judge and prosecutor for the new province be appointed.
˙ A special political and military committee be established to investigate allegedly abusive and corrupt officers.

The general strike lasted for nine days. Stores closed. Farmers, laborers, and housewives organized themselves secretly as local picketers for the strike. At about three in the afternoon, the picketers took their positions. They advised the drivers either to leave the area early or not to go any farther into town. At dusk, these strikers positioned themselves along the main road to cut the tallest trees down to block traffic. For nine days the area was economically paralyzed, and notably, the shortage of U.S. dollars in the open black market in Lima coincided with the strike.

After about twenty hours of conversation between representatives of the central government and the people, the strike ended on June 14, 1985. As expected, the first condition for settlement of the strike—removal of the UMOPAR from the new province—was met. All forty UMOPAR were transported out by helicopter. Creation of the electoral district, appointment of one judge and a prosecutor, and installation of a control committee were tabled. The "coca issue" was left off the agenda, for as a national problem, it had to be included in the new government's agricultural policies. In many ways, this important political juncture resulted from cooperation between the police, drug production and traffic, and the local economy established since the cocaine boom began.

In 1979, the local parish priest and two nuns had been thrown out of that same town. One of the nuns was a public schoolteacher in the community and very active in the National Teachers Federation Union (SUTEP). Time after time, the priest and the two sisters had formally complained to the police about their routine torturing of common robbers and pickpockets. The officer in charge of the police station was constantly seen driving the car of one of the local bosses, a common practice in the cocaine underworld. Most likely, the police members' relationships with cocaine traffickers went beyond close friendship. It was obvious that the priest and the nuns were obstacles to the collaboration of the police with the underworld. The precinct captain persuaded the community authorities and local merchants to sign a petition against the Catholic missionaries. Despite the people's protest, the three clergy members were forced to go to another town three hours from their parish. The provincial bishop recommended that the Cardinal's office request the removal of the officer before the priest and the nuns returned to their own parish.[28]

To justify their presence and maintain their positions, law enforcement officers and bureaucrats alter the facts to suit their own purposes. Similarly, to gain support from the people, drug traffickers tend also to distort and exaggerate the truth. They inform the general public that police presence disrupts the cocaine trade and hurts the pocketbooks of many farmers and traffickers. Recently, in Bolivia, the alleged sexual attack of a woman by two off-duty policemen was used as a pretext for a siege.[29] The raping of women by policemen in traditional "machista" societies such as Peru and Bolivia is nothing new. However, what is peculiar to today's society is that drug traffickers, to satisfy their own interests, are using real and practical issues to fight back against the legal system. Police brutality and civil-rights violations are legitimate arguments that the underworld uses to create confrontations between the indigenous people and the forces representing the ruling classes; that is, the peasantry's subsistence economy and cultural values stand side by side with the underworld's struggle for survival.

Drug dealers, as citizens, have contributed to the rise of national political figures, exerted pressure on elected officials, and even offered alternatives for solving national debts. At the international level, cocaine countries seem to use coca as their economic "security blankets." The drug industry is turning into a political sacred cow. The United States, having incorporated the alcohol and tobacco industries into its national economy, might take the credit for this model of political economy.

A drug dealer popularly known as the "Little Rockefeller of the northeastern slopes" was probably the foremost example of the drug economy's emergence in Peru. He was the main, if not the only, benefactor of his small town. He bought a power generator that supplied enough electricity for all the townspeople, graded the streets, and sponsored soccer games and expensive bullfights. His "front" was the mayor who later was elected senator from "Little Rockefeller's" home state. The senator's campaign radio announcements were paid for by one of the dealer's companies. When elected, the senator triumphantly returned to his coastal hometown aboard Little Rockefeller's plane. The drug dealer, of course, was part of the welcoming bandwagon. In return, the senator combined his political power and his legal expertise to protect and defend his loyal friend, despite convincing criminal evidence against him.[30]

When in 1985 Alan García visited Tingo María as a presidential candidate, he was cheered by the biggest crowd that the city had ever seen. Notwithstanding the advice of local party figures to keep silent on the drug issue, he took a stand against the cocaine industry, whereupon the cheering crowd started to desert the meeting.[31] In fact, in apparently reviving the APRA party's original platform, the government announced an "all-out war on drug traffic in 1985." When the Peruvian president spoke in the United Nations, his message to cocaine-consuming countries was that drug production could not be stopped if consumption kept increasing. He used as a basis for his message a cocaine raid on the border of Colombia in the second week of August 1985.[32] It is doubtful whether in the near future this government will be successful in its struggle against its three overwhelming enemies: the desperately impoverished economy; the Shining Path; and the drug industry. Its first priority is to fight hunger and misery in the countryside. Cutting drug production and traffic at the grass roots would increase unemployment, inflation, and, obviously, guerrilla warfare.

Some lawmakers have already taken positions against the eradication of the coca leaf. A young congressman's address to his constituency emphasized his concern over the problem of coca farming, more so than drug manufacturing and trafficking. His argument was that, before any policy decision, actual sizes of coca plantations and the number of people engaged in that economy should be properly indexed. To demonstrate the magnitude of the problem, the legislator used as an example the community of Chinchao in his district, located near Tingo María and near the major Andean city of Huánuco, where at least 24,000 people depend on coca farming for their livelihood. He assured his constituency that his role in the parliament would be to propose laws to initiate production and taxation of coca agriculture, as well as to protect the peasant economy. He was against the indiscriminate program of eradication. His position on the international problem of coca was that countries interested in eradication should buy the leaves at reasonable prices and use the raw material as they will. He concluded that coca leaf should not be excluded from "United States interest in Peruvian natural resources."[33]

Similarly, Bolivia contends that coca and cocaine are the problem of the consuming countries and not the producing countries. The Bolivian vice president told the United Nations General Assembly that the sale of cocaine could be curtailed if an international economic fund were set up to purchase the coca leaves from peasants. Such an international fund would prevent the product from falling into the hands of organized crime, and it would establish a world system of control of the raw material without damaging the economy of the peasants. Bolivia cannot afford to give up its most important foreign export to join an isolated campaign against illicit drug trafficking. The official urged cocaine-consuming societies to contribute to the formation of an "anti-coca social welfare fund."[34]

To coca-producing countries, it is clear that coca and cocaine are an economic issue rather than one of drug use and abuse. This brings to mind a proverbial statement by a coca village politician who sarcastically simplified the issue by saying: "The ballgame will go on and on. The ball (political pressure) thrown to the Andes will become a snowball (cocaine) and keep bouncing back to the United States."

Uncle Sam Lost in the Jungle

On the international scene, the United States searches for peaceful and rational solutions for reducing the cultivation of coca and production of coca paste and cocaine. The American government's intention is to cut the supply of cocaine in the country by sponsoring the eradication of coca in Peru. But American involvement in controlling the production of coca and cocaine is limited to economic aid, advice, training, and political pressure, all of which fall under the umbrella of cooperation or collaboration. Treaties, policies, and vested interests in both the cocaine-producing countries and the economic powers have not resulted in reducing, let alone eradicating, the illegal production of coca and cocaine. Two United States agencies participate in the control and eradication of coca and of cocaine production and trafficking: the Agency for International Development (AID) and the U.S. Bureau of International Narcotics Matters (INM).

The Proyecto Especial del Alto Huallaga (PEAH) five-year project lasted from September 1981 to September 1985. Of PEAH's total operating budget, $18 million came from the United States, of which $3 million was a grant in aid and $15 million a loan to be repaid in twenty-five years. The interest rate was fixed at 2 percent per year for ten years and at 3 percent on the principal and accrued interest for the next fifteen years. The initial payment, applied to interest, was due no later than six months from the date set by AID (sec. 4.1 and sec. 4.3).[35]

The AID program encourages the cultivation of food and cash crops other than coca leaf. PEAH is the Peruvian instrument to carry out AID's commitments. The fundamental principles of PEAH are: 1) to conduct environmental research to determine the agricultural, social, and economic aspects of technological assistance; 2) to expand and enhance existing services; 3) to train agricultural scientists at the Universidad Nacional de la Selva (UNAS); 4) to provide short- and medium-term credit; 5) to improve agricultural activities such as establishment and organization of effective land distribution; 6) to provide maintenance of roads and highways; and 7) to supply potable water and sanitation facilities.[36]

In their effort to fulfill these ambitious goals, both the United States and Peru have allocated $26.5 million to support a five-year program to aid the peasants in the Upper Huallaga section of Peru, that is, $5.3 million per year. Salaries and expenses of a sizeable bureaucracy are also included in the global budget. PEAH headquarters is in a town where there is heavy production and traffic of cocaine. Potential creditors come day after day to apply for a loan, or to follow up bureaucratic procedures for meeting the preconditions for the loans. If they are lucky, they get the loan at an annual interest rate of 106 percent. The national lending bank is the Banco Agrario del Peru.

Signs in front of the U. S. AID–Proyecto Especial del Alto Huallaga (PEAH). PEAH has not been successful in the crop substitution program. Its contribution to urbanization, such as the construction of an auditorium (bottom) for a local university, does not dissuade peasants from planting coca.

There are four conditions of eligibility for a loan: 1) the applicant must produce a certificate or title of ownership of the land where aid will be invested; 2) for loans over $24,000, the applicant is requested to present a copy of his income tax (*declaración jurada*). In lieu of the last income tax, if aid is approved, the peasant is required to register at the regional tax bureau; 3) for applications in amounts over $24,000 farmers must be evaluated and approved by U.S. AID (although loans up to $50,000 are available for agro-industrial investments); and 4) an affidavit whereby the debtor clearly states that in no case will the proceeds of the loan be used to plant coca.

Unfortunately, while most of the loans appear to support elimination of the cocaine in the jungle, they are actually used for planting coca rather than for crop substitution. The peasants' chances of complying with their financial obligations to the lending institution cannot be met with cash returns from their crops of corn, rice, and cacao. To mask their real agricultural activities, they plant rice or oil palm trees, or they raise cattle on land included in the affidavit. Legal cash-crop farmers, as well as coca planters, have many good "commonsense" reasons for either subsidizing their economy or depending entirely on illegal coca cultivation. Peasants weigh the conditions and terms of the loans, based on their experience with the military land reform and the cost of living that makes labor more expensive, and so forth.

Most cocaleros are small farmers who cannot satisfy the prerequisites and conditions set by the institutions that allocate foreign aid. Although loans translate into millions of soles, the buying power of credit is minimal. Besides, PEAH indirectly creates and encourages an urban lifestyle. Its plans for a potable water supply, maintenance of roads, grading streets, and so forth, bring about new needs. Small farmers cannot satisfy these expectations unless they become part of the underground coca economy. In addition, the limitations of aid are valid arguments for the peasants' reluctance to accept small-scale development. Dozens of families embargoed by the Banco Agrario, who thanks to coca cultivation have recovered their subsistence economy, are now models very often cited by the peasants. More importantly, the peasant, the indigenous migrant, and the uneducated native usually do not understand the language of the terms and conditions of the loans.

An ex-priest who had always preached against the evils of drug production and use, along with his associate, an ex-uniformed policeman who had been fired because of his involvement in drug trafficking, had bought thirty-eight hectares of land and obtained from the government another forty-two hectares. On the eighty hectares of pasture land they started a dairy farm. For the first four years, the farm did not report gains to meet their repayment obligations with the Banco Agrario. On many occasions, they had asked, in person, that the bank defer their delinquent debts for another year. They had even given "good tips" to bank officers who assured them that no action would be taken against them. However, one day three bank employees and five policemen showed up at the farmhouse and drove off their cattle. The next day, the ex-priest and the ex-policeman bought coca seeds and began preparing their land to plant six hectares of coca. Just when their coca plants were in full production, the first eradication program, *Operación Verde Mar*, began. The army set fire to their plants, which quickly resprouted and yielded an even more productive harvest. Now, the six hectares, along with other "secure" plots, are among the best coca fields I have seen in Peru.

From 1981 to 1986, PEAH issued 1,028 loans for a total of more than 2 billion soles (1985 soles), or 4.3 percent of the $5 million allocated for agricultural credit. This clearly demonstrates that $15.9 million was spent for urbanization projects such as a potable water supply, community education, nursery schools, road maintenance, scholarships and fellowships granted to some faculty members in the regional university, salaries, motor vehicles, and so forth. In an informal conversation, the head of PEAH in a regional office, who did not know I was a researcher, shared with me his professional point of view about his project. He argued that, in 1984, as much as $2 billion of coca had come to Peru through the jungles. In his judgment, in order to be minimally successful, an annual investment of at least $50 million per year was needed. "It seems," he continued, "that they expect us to emulate the highlander migrant who comes to the forests with little or no money and generally makes his dreams come true." He ironically concluded by saying that PEAH's nickel-and-dime loans were at times used to purchase imported consumer goods in the boutiques and appliance stores.

The failure of PEAH is due more to its budget limitations. Dishonesty, lack of discipline, and bureaucratic corruption may eventually account in part for its defeat. This is likely unless it is better implemented, although to the general public it is made to appear as a successful alternative. Financially, it only adds more burden to an already debt-laden country. The total number of short-term loans and the amounts extended as aid to the peasants ($215,993) do not even compensate for the $300,000 of interest owed annually, 2 percent for the first ten years and 3 percent for the last fifteen years. PEAH is very costly "plastic money" for the country and may in fact support the cocaine industry.

Minimum-wage PEAH workers supplement their incomes with extra work on private farms and plantations. Teams of road-maintenance workers, usually made up of one Caterpillar operator and about five helpers, clean up or open roads along which "bosses" and "cycling traffickers" transport their coca paste and other contraband. Orders for PEAH workers come from the foremen who are close friends or acquaintances of successful farmers. This is not to say that all PEAH lower-level field laborers are corrupt; they need not be corrupt to indirectly make things easier for the unlawful industry, for they share their communities and services with the drug-production subculture. While field laborers and Caterpillar drivers may unknowingly and indirectly contribute to the enhancement of transportation infrastructures in drug villages and hamlets, others have gone a step further in taking personal advantage with the aid money. They demand fixed "commissions" for their signatures approving crop substitution and agricultural development loans.

For example, one company distributes American water pumps used for rice growing. A rice planter contacts the regional salesman and signs all the forms of both the Banco Agrario and the water-pump distributor. Unless the salesman offers a direct bribe of 2 percent of the equipment's retail price, the bank officer in charge will not approve the final credit line to cover the price of the water pump. The company passes the extra expense on to the farmer. After harvest, the peasant can sell his crop only to the state-owned marketing company, Empresa Comercializadora de Arroz (ECASA), at prices fixed by the government. This is yet another reason why peasants cling to coca cultivation.

The AID-PEAH project stated that of two hundred peasants surveyed by a consulting firm, all said they did not plant coca.[37] Perhaps the survey researchers sampled only the families living along the roadside, where few, if any, coca plantations are visible. When I asked the farmers about their small plots of coca plants, they said they were for personal use (residents of the rain forests chew very few coca leaves) or to send to relatives in the highlands.

Limited investments in crop substitution, obstacles presented by the legal system, and resistance of the peasantry at large to accepting coca-substitution development plans turn into advantages for organized crime. Bosses, coca-leaf black-market merchants, and independent coca-paste manufacturers all take part in exploiting small farmers. They offer gracious interest-free cash advances for coca leaves or coca paste. These loans, at times, may turn out to be either beneficial or unfavorable to the farmer. However, both sides generally abide by their original informal, oral contracts. Furthermore, the cocalero can get amounts higher than the loans available at PEAH. As it stands now, it is unlikely that PEAH will accomplish its intention, for it faces substantial competition from many groups whose goals are antithetical to those of PEAH.

Consequently, it is almost impossible to find any crop to substitute for coca, owing to environmental conditions in the coca-growing areas, the absence of markets for other crops, the problem of insects and diseases that affect other crops, the intensive labor needed to weed fields, and price controls on major legal cash crops such as rice.

While the AID project tries to stop the cultivation of coca by motivating the peasants to plant other cash crops, the U.S. Bureau of International Narcotics Matters (INM) finances a more radical and violent eradication approach: the actual destruction of legal and illegal plantations of coca. An INM-sponsored project, Eradication and Control of Coca Leaf Planting in the Upper Huallaga (CORAH) began in May 1983. Its central office is located in Tingo María. It is staffed with three technicians, a full clerical staff, and 780 field workers; the last uproot forty and more hectares of coca a day.[38] The pulling operation is coordinated by UMOPAR.

Those farmers who are licensed by the Peruvian Ministry of Agri-

Coca plants leach soil of nutrients, and after uprooting the plants the soil becomes unproductive for many years. A 1987 photograph of a plot that was
eradicated in 1978.

culture to plant coca are paid $300 per hectare for the loss of their coca
plants; illegal planters are not compensated at all. Although during
work hours the coca pullers are protected by the UMOPAR, organized
attacks by peasants are not unusual. Since the beginning of CORAH
more than thirty workers and one foreman have been killed.[39]

Between May 1983 and June 1985 CORAH eradicated 4,605.36 hectares of coca. This represents about 8 percent of the total estimated legal
production by the Peruvian government (60,000 hectares). To date,
CORAH has received a total of $2.9 million from the United States. In
addition, from 1978 to 1985, the INM spent $11.7 million, of which $7.7
million went to support control and $4 million was allotted to eradi-
cation. Thus, a sizeable amount of money goes to train and sustain
control procedures both in the Peruvian customs and the police force.
In addition to financing the removal of a small percentage of coca plantations, U.S. participation resulted in 16,575 arrests between 1982 and
1984, the destruction of 438 coca-paste and cocaine laboratories, and

the seizure of 23,774 kilos of coca paste and 595 kilos of cocaine hydrochloride.[40] As manual eradication has proved ineffective, some American officials have insisted that producing countries use glyphosate in aerial eradication.[41]

Data on the eradication and control of coca and cocaine are collected by the national police, who are corrupt at every level. As one INM official in Lima stated, the figures and statistics cannot be taken as indications of the effectiveness of control and eradication. Most if not all arrests involve petty dealers and wage laborers who participate in drug dealings. In contrast, the bosses and their transporters travel back and forth to the United States with tourist and diplomatic visas.

A perfect example of misleading statistics in reference to control and eradication is the highly acclaimed "destruction of 438 coca-paste and cocaine laboratories" by the police. What they dynamited were hundreds of concrete coca-leaf drying houses used by both legal and illegal coca planters. The destruction of the two-floor coca driers was not a major loss to coca-paste entrepreneurs. Now many macerate their leaves immediately after collection (see chapter 4). As for coca-paste pits, the "laboratory" consists only of a large plastic sheet and a few sticks. Dynamiting cement coca-paste pools should not be considered a remarkably effective drive against the underworld.

Before the creation of CORAH, the army set fire to coca plantations. This was actually the greatest favor that the army could have done for the planters. Coca stalks grew back healthier and in greater numbers. The plantations that were "renovated" by the army yield as many as 60 arrobas of good quality leaves per hectare every three months, yielding enough leaves to manufacture 24 kilos of coca paste—about 6.5 kilos of export-quality cocaine hydrochloride. At that time, anti-coca operations were isolated campaigns in response to political pressure from the United States.

When a coca plant is pulled, the soil around it becomes totally unproductive for a period of at least eight to ten years. Realizing the ineffectiveness of cutting and setting fire to coca plantations, Peruvian officials resolved to uproot the plants. The farms and plots that were affected by the "Operación Verde Mar" in 1978 were still barren in 1987. The equivalent of $300 per hectare given as compensation to the legal coca planter can barely pay for clearing a new hectare of land or compensate for the loss of productive land. So the peasant becomes an illegal coca farmer deep in the forests, at many hours' walking distance from the nearest town, where his chances of being discovered are minimal.

The Riddle of the
Cocaine Sphinx

Es mejor gozar bien un día que vivir cien años con hambre.
(It is better enjoying a short life than being poor forever.)

A Colombian drug dealer

Most South American peasants live along the Andes running from
Chile to Colombia. Before the Spanish conquest, Inca territory included what is now Ecuador, Bolivia, Peru, parts of northern Chile,
and Colombia. During the reign of the Incas, the cultivation of coca in
the eastern foothills of the Andes, the *Hatun Yunca*, was probably limited to a few patches cultivated for religious purposes and dedicated to
the Andean emperor. However, there is archaeological evidence that
coca was cultivated and used thousands of years before the Incas. This
may suggest that after the Incas overpowered the rest of the Andean
tribes, they made exclusive use of coca, banning its consumption by
their subjects. A coca-leaf black market may therefore have existed as
early as the fifteenth century.[1]

After the overthrow of the Incas by 1525, the ten million Indians who
survived the Spanish conquest developed their coca-chewing habit. It
was in the interest of the invading society to ignore the vice, which
gradually became a traditional pastime. Some Spaniards also embraced
Indian culture and tradition. As a new social stock, the mestizo,
emerged, coca chewing became a common daily practice.[2]

The Catholic Church disapproved of coca-chewing by the Spanish, mestizos, and Indians, claiming that the divine status given the coca plant was contrary to the postulates of Christianity.³ But the moral goals of the Church conflicted with the political and economic ambitions of the Spanish kingdom. The objective of the Spanish settlers who used the coca leaf was to exploit the Indian population in two ways, by controlling the production and the marketing of coca, and by encouraging coca chewing in Catholic rituals and during forced labor. Coca chewing and the consumption of alcohol were and still are tolerated in religious festivities. Fulfillment of religious obligations and payment of taxes may have been more important than questioning the Indian's immersion in coca.⁴

Andean culture incorporates Catholic religious celebrations and social practices resulting from the fusion of two cultures that took place in Latin America. Coca leaf is one major element that distinguishes Andeans from other traditional cultures. It is present in almost all religious celebrations and popular practices. The coca-chewing Indian has been the foundation of the Peruvian feudal system: the Spanish lord, the mestizo tenant farmer, and national and international agribusiness alike exploited coca-chewing Indians. From the earliest days, coca leaf conditioned the Indian's allegiance to the fief. Besides his payment of rent to his direct master, the feudal subject's coca-chewing habit was taxed by the central government dominated by the national landed classes and connected to international corporations. The coca economy helped ease only the psychological lot of the Andean peoples.

The romantic ideological, social, political, and cultural movement of *Indigenismo* was an attempt to rationalize the problem of the Andean Indian as part of the Western world. The Indian's social and economic concerns were perceived as issues that could be settled by applying models that had been implemented in other societies and settings with totally different problems. Land reform was a significant political movement by the Peruvian middle classes to protect the dispossessed inhabitants in the countryside. Its failure may be held partly responsible for the present indiscriminate, irrational use of land in the rain forests.

Aside from the abolition of rent on land, the peasants of Peru have benefited very little from the land reform dictated by the military government in 1969. The promise to redistribute land so that every family would have at least five hectares did not go any farther than talk. The breach between the landed and the landless was not closed. On the contrary, the reform frustrated the peasants' dreams of becoming individual, legal landowners.[5] The real objective of the reform may have been to make the poor and the landless dependent upon state-controlled collective organizations. This attempt to develop state capitalism in the countryside, imposed from above rather than demanded from below, was likely one of the causes for the rise of political insurgent organizations like the Shining Path.

During the last thirty years, the development of roads between the remote highlands and the coast has had a great impact on traditional society. The Andean Indian did not need the use of mass transportation, for his economy was restricted to subsistence. Neither his culture nor his technology was geared to the manufacture of goods to satisfy material needs. In most villages and communities in the early 1950s, there were very few outside goods besides salt and pepper. People who went to the coast had to walk for many days before reaching roads. Children made their own toys of clay and other substances available in the physical environment. Riding a truck and seeing electricity in modern towns were marvelous experiences and tremendous culture shocks as well.

The dream of owning land drove peasants to desert their native lands. Migration of the poor and the landless to metropolitan areas was the first option. Then population movement shifted to many untouched lands in the Amazon basin. Here the settlers found other exploiters in addition to their national, provincial, and local authorities and leaders: the international cocaine industry. This change affected small urban sections and remote villages more than it did large metropolitan cities.

The most important influence of the international underworld on the marginal peasant is the development of a new economic dependency. The present exigencies of the ever-expanding market economy require a cash flow that can be supplied only through participation in some aspect of the underground economy. Now hundreds of elementary and high-school students go to work in the cities and towns in the rain forests. Many drop out of school to extend their stay. Because of their knowledge and training, Andean youngsters are more employable in coca agriculture than their metropolitan counterparts.

The jungles are also scenes of human heroism and family dedication. Single mothers, widows, and ambitious young boys and girls seek an economic security that is impossible to achieve by other means. The employability of cheap and unskilled labor in the jungles is similar, if not identical, to that which took place in the late fifties and early sixties, when domestic and menial jobs were plentiful in Peru. Adolescent migrants were hired for a monthly wage of as little as $4.80. Today, the average monthly salary for a migrant boy doing the same type of work is just under $41.00. The minimum wage in coca fields is about three times as much, with all the added advantages of gaining extra income after completion of regular working hours or after finishing piecework assignments. The migrant peasant finds it is difficult to break ties with this illegal white gold mine.

The bureaucratic solution to the problem of Andean backwardness is to help poor populations by offering food relief and supplying the indigenous people with modern conveniences available in large metropolises. The worst consequence of such development, however, is its negative psychological effect. Pessimism and feelings of dependence contribute directly to failure to develop the countryside. The intention, of course, is to pacify the poor, abused for the last four centuries. To some extent, these approaches make the Indians believe that they are making progress and that something is being done to integrate them into national life. Whether such pacification is their ultimate goal, the developers and funding agencies have only made the peasants and Indians hungrier than they were before their arrival.

However, if the intention is to make the Andean people efficient producers and active participants in the national and international economy, other policies to help the peasant forge his own economic future should be implemented. Otherwise, the Andean peasantry will resort to armed rebellion as in other parts of Latin America. The drive to appease individual and collective hunger is more powerful than the alliance to the cause of freedom and democracy in the international arena. The two most dramatic expressions of this general discontent are drug production and the emergence of the Shining Path and the Movimiento Revolucionario Tupac Amaru (MRTA).

The peasants' sympathy with the rural and urban guerrillas, as well as their support for the cocaine industry, is probably not censurable; their participation in both is inevitable. Both the Maoist ideologues and the new coca trade are closely intertwined with the larger Indian question in which the peasantry's fate is at stake. While the increasing contact between peasants and cocaine dealers brings about changes in indigenous behavior, the presence of the Shining Path sows an ideology which the Andean may not be ready to harvest.

The story of the guerrilla-dealer alliance is perhaps inaccurate. The Fuerza Armada Revolucionaria de Colombia (FARC), the Movimiento 19 de Abril (M-19) in Colombia, and the Shining Path and the MRTA in Peru are movements whose political ideologies have been developing for the last thirty years. The mere fact that traffickers and guerrillas operate in areas that are inaccessible to law-enforcement and government forces is not a valid argument to assess a drug-guerrilla alliance. If the alleged alliance between a powerful economy and a fanatic political ideology were true, the extremists would have already taken the government over. The myth of the alliance of the two undergrounds is a justification invented by law-enforcement agents to explain away the difficulty of actually conducting raids.[6] In many areas, peasants feel that traffickers create better economies, however inflationary, and that the guerrillas are fighting for a legitimate cause. Some peasants, traffickers, and guerrillas consider the war against drugs to be only in the interest of the United States. The implicit anti-American feeling in Latin America, especially in Peru, is another obstacle that drug-law enforcers must overcome.

In the production, distribution, and marketing of coca paste and cocaine there is a clear division of labor at the local, national, and international levels. As in any industry, those who contribute most to the creation of a product—in this case cocaine—are less economically rewarded than those who market the end product in the underground. The commercial network and the traffic in cocaine are controlled by the local and national middle class and international crime networks. The latter groups get the biggest bite of pie in the booming industry.

Some researchers suggest that the number of U.S. dollar bills that reach the peasants' pockets almost correlate with the number of coca leaves cropped. Information on the economic effects of cocaine trafficking in Peru are exaggerated and unrealistic. For instance, James Inciardi claims that, in Tingo María, Chevette compact cars sell for $25,000, Cadillacs and Lincolns for $100,000, and Mercedes-Benz sedans for as high as $350,000.[7] Neither in Tingo María nor in middle-class sections of Lima is a Chevette, let alone a Cadillac or a Mercedes, often seen. In Peru, a Japanese compact car equivalent to a Chevette sells for about $10,000. All four car dealers in Tingo María sell and service Japanese-manufactured vehicles only, and never has the demand for vehicles been greater than the supply.[8]

The dynamics of the underground economy go far beyond merely making a living. Power groups and impoverished middle-class segments uphold or regain their status because of their control of cocaine traffic. Thus, the main motivation for the production of coca and cocaine is the purchasing power of illegal earnings.

The cocaine industry operates like any legitimate business; it has a defined social organization, employs many people, operates on a credit system reinforced by rules and regulations, has policies of protection and, most important, has as its ultimate goal the accumulation of wealth. The personnel in charge include an international boss, the middle man, the national local bosses, collectors, transporters, legal and illegal coca farmers, and their work forces. The organization is fragmented to the degree that employees have very limited information on details of time and place of transactions or locations of the airfields. Key members are in contact with relatively few persons.

Consignment of coca or cocaine and the provision of credit to small farmers and new settlers bind producers and lower-level traffickers to rigid and unyielding organizations. The creditor expects the debtor to be loyal and to trust him to market his merchandise. Disloyalty is condemned and often viciously punished; betrayers, informers, and others who interfere with it are the sworn enemies of the drug economy. Seven people were brutally murdered within a 100-kilometer distance during a single twenty-day period in the summer of 1986. The bodies of the victims were found along the roadside blindfolded, their hands tied behind their backs. One of the victims was the wife of a coca-eradication worker.

A coca-paste runner had allegedly been raided by the police and twenty kilos of paste seized from him. His boss soon found out that the runner had in fact sold the coca paste to a colocho who had come to the hamlet. The boss went to the runner's house and took him for a few drinks in a nearby town. The next day, the runner's body was found tied to a tree trunk with a sign reading, "He who dares to pick him up will go the same way." Lamenting that her husband had not listened to her, his widow packed and left for another village. After two weeks, all that was left of the runner was a carcass wrapped in rags.

As in every lucrative industry, the cocaine business also rewards and protects those who are loyal to its organization by helping an employee out in difficult times or defending coca growers from the police. International traffickers and big bosses are frequently eager to help the poor with their collective needs. They can afford to supply immediate provisions that otherwise are out of the villagers' reach. A European colocho gathered an entire village to discuss its needs. The villagers asked for school supplies and furniture and a small power plant. Their requests were granted in less than a week. In exchange for the aid, the villagers became illegal coca farmers.

The police normally learn of coca fields when the plants are already in full production. Many bosses, especially Peruvian nationals, sustain a permanent intelligence service to warn them of eradication schedules. Coca farmers who are constant suppliers of leaves or paste seldom lose their crops. As they say, "Money is power."[9]

At the international level, Peru as a coca- and cocaine-producing country is on the verge of serious social, economic, and political troubles. While the national government intends to protect the social habit of the Andean coca chewers and blames consumer societies for the existence of the Peruvian cocaine industry, it accepts the imposition of new policies of coca production from the United States. This bilateral agreement between a country with limited economic resources and an international power makes Peru dependent on foreign investment for the solution to its social problems—that is, the eradication of coca and the preservation of coca chewing. Because of the need for coca dollars, the Peruvian government's action against the cocaine economy is largely limited to newspaper headlines.

The present Peruvian government cannot allow foreign military intervention in restraining production and trafficking of cocaine, as did Bolivia. The same may be true for Colombia, the third world's largest coca producer. Because of the existing guerrilla movements in Colombia and Peru, international superpowers refrain from using the military to repress the cocaine trade. Sending another military task force to Colombia or Peru would likely lead to a revolution in the Andes, including Chile. On the other hand, the coca-belt governments are not seriously concerned with the cocaine problem or their guerrilla threat. Current political conditions in Colombia and Peru may hamper American interventionism, but they may also encourage terrorism abetted by its rival superpower, the Soviet Union. The international demand for cocaine and the rise of political sects—FARC and M-19 in Colombia, Shining Path in Peru—have made the outside world aware of the Latin American dilemma.

Investment in programs to eradicate coca and to substitute other crops for it has been minimal, and what little of it there has been has not reached the poor and unemployed masses—although the burden of repaying the principal and interest on foreign loans falls directly on their shoulders. For how could a crop-substitution investment of $5.3 million per annum conquer an economy that brings Peru some $2 billion each year? Why would a peasant choose to pay 106 percent interest on a legal loan when he could borrow without interest from cocaine traffickers?

When compared to cash yields from cocaine, to money spent on establishing drug policies and on the immense political and bureaucratic interests in consuming countries, investment in coca-crop substitution and eradication has been minimal and has not relieved the poor and unemployed masses who depend on the coca and cocaine economy. That is, such control efforts by way of crop substitution are not realistically designed to meet the expectations of coca growers and entire populations enmeshed in the illicit economy. The payments and interest on foreign loans are great to impoverished peasants. Crop substitution faces imminent defeat because of insufficient funds, resistance from the peasants, and the unwillingness of the Peruvian government to alter land-distribution patterns. For the Peruvian government a total anti-coca and cocaine policy would mean social disaster. And so PEAH workers now clean the culverts of the Carretera Marginal; Caterpillar tractors grade the streets of some towns; and anti-drug funds are being used to build an auditorium on the campus of the Universidad Nacional Agraria de la Selva in Tingo María.[10] Eradicating the coca economy in Peru is not a realistic goal.

If Peru did not have the rain forests, the Andean people would literally starve.[11] The pressure to migrate from the highlands does not leave room for a directed or planned colonization of the rain forests. As word of land distribution spreads throughout the country, people constantly migrate to the green mines. The Ministry of Agriculture continues parceling and distributing individual plots to migrant families, who, because of inflationary prices, limited capital investment and high wages paid by illicit dealers, either shift totally to coca growing or subsidize their legal agriculture with illegal, secret coca patches.

The question then becomes how to promote a self-sufficient agricultural economy. The best solutions benefit the poor of Peru, but they conflict with American economic and political interests. The possible alternatives in fighting the cocaine industry are: 1) reduction of demand in the United States; 2) stricter law enforcement and political pressure from the United States on cocaine producers and gateway nations; 3) eradication campaigns, including the effective destruction of coca fields; 4) rational and authentic economic development in coca-belt countries. As one U.S. official puts it:

In the end it simply boils down to supply and demand. The bottom line is to get Peru and Bolivia to get rid of their coca plants. You can kick ass and do all sorts of raids. But as long as you have that supply, they are going to be in business. If you don't stop the supply of raw materials, you don't turn the water off.[12]

But supply is dictated by demand. Rather than cut off the water supply, would it not be more practical to teach people, especially Americans, how more effectively to quench their thirst?

In another instance, Eric Rosenquist of the U.S. Department of State said in the *New York Times* (June 1988): "If you are saying that coca farmers won't be able to make a living after spray, that's right. That is the point of the exercise." This statement reflects the superficial understanding that exists among politicians who legislate and maintain anti-cocaine policies in the United States. The Reagan administration and like-minded politicians fail to understand that those who profit the most from cocaine production and trafficking, such as bankers, investors, and developers, are the very people who endorse and financially support American drug-war policies. The politicians, in the end, are manipulated and exploited as much as the small coca farmers. The difference is that politicians do the bidding of their supporters to maintain power, while peasants work within the cocaine economy to survive.

Drug production and trafficking will continue as long as there is demand in the United States. As Bruce Bagley has remarked,

> It simply cannot be eradicated nor can any other commodity be substituted for it. We can accept it as a fundamental fact of life. The U.S. government has resisted accepting this fact because we have a bureaucracy and a group of drug-enforcement people which have a vested interest in preserving or even expanding their programs. This phenomenon is not unknown in bureaucracies. In fact, the Reagan administration has railed against this process in a number of areas in our society. The resistance of people who make their living and whose careers and futures are tied to claiming victory from time to time with one or another bust [such as Caqueta-Tranquilandia and Operación Condor] and telling us how much they have been able to confiscate, and so on, is a similar phenomenon.[13]

Executive orders alone will not suppress the economic forces of supply and demand. In 1986, the Reagan administration broadcast its intention of "beefing up law enforcement activities along the southern border of the United States" with $500 million.[14] However, in January 1987, the Reagan administration announced cuts in funds proposed for local law-enforcement and drug-education efforts.[15] This American attitude results from underestimating the problem of cocaine production and economic development in the supplying countries, and it will continue to prove negative and costly to the American taxpayer. As one anonymous dignitary at the American Embassy in Mexico has made clear, the "United States cannot be too critical of Latin Americans if it won't take responsibility for the problems of consumption back home."[16]

Another law-enforcement operation is the campaign for eradication. In exchange for the destruction of their coca plants, legal growers receive a nominal amount of money equal to the cash yield of about 3 arrobas or the equivalent of 2.4 percent of the annual yield of one hectare of coca. The Bureau of International Narcotic Matters of the U.S. Department of State funds the national eradication police, UMOPAR, in Bolivia and Peru. The UMOPAR works in cooperation with the CORAH (see chapter 6). Most of the 4,605.36 hectares of coca that had been destroyed by 1985 were from illegal plantations.[17] Even if the total lands ravaged were in legal production, the amount paid to the farmers does not surpass $1,381,608, or 11 percent of the INM's 1978–84 funds ($11.7 million) for Peru.

In light of the failure of the eradication program, the simplest and cheapest way to combat drugs, according to some Latin Americans, is to buy the coca crops and dispose of the leaves however they choose.[18] This approach may be the most economical and practical solution in the long run. If America were mainly a tobacco- and liquor-exporting country, and if we were to face drastic cuts in demand, our congressmen would likely take the same political position.[19] This new policy would certainly be less embarrassing and destructive than the failure of our drug policies and the continuing corrosion of our society through cocaine addiction. For the taxpayer, the amount spent would be half of what is currently allocated to law-enforcement programs.

To purchase coca-leaf harvests would be a complex process. Although the new export economy would obviously benefit Peru, Bolivia, and Colombia (in that order), certain technicalities would need to be addressed. Since this would be a new policy, recommendations to protect the potential buyer or buyers would need to be considered. Annual production limits, quality control, prices, and the roles of national governments as intermediaries would have to be firmly established, carefully defined, and rationally planned.

Every coca-belt government should be responsible for recording its total annual production and detailing the number of growers, the age of plants at the time of registration, and the estimated life span of those plants. Why are these statistics important? The American buyer should not accept any increase in coca farms. If, for example, a given percentage of plants are thirty years old, and we know that coca plants can last as long as thirty-five years, that percentage of production should yield no crops in five years. We should also bear in mind that the coca plant erodes the soil totally and no other plant can be grown on the same land for at least ten years. A more sensible method of eradication and necessary soil-rehabilitation procedures should be implemented.

Another important aspect is quality control. It should be underscored that the good leaf is the one which is picked between sixty-five and seventy days after the last harvest. In the best of cases, a plant can yield at most five crops per year. In some areas, the leaves take as many as ninety days to mature. Today, many growers who sell their crops to coca-paste manufacturers pick the leaves before they reach maturity.

To the growers, prices and the intermediary role of national governments may be the most critical considerations. In 1985, the black market was paying about $90 per arroba while the ENACO rates were about $20 per arroba or about 22 percent of the black-market prices. ENACO buys coca leaves only from duly registered growers, while the black market buys from both legal and illicit coca farmers. Ironically, enforcing ENACO prices would benefit the cocaine industry, because the cost of production of cocaine would decrease significantly.

Finally, the intermediary function of the Peruvian coca monopoly (ENACO) could either comply with the established purchasing policies or simply be out of the picture. This would minimize corruption. If ENACO or another Peruvian agency takes part in the purchasing process, it would not be surprising to find corrupt officials mixing fresh leaves with the ones that have already been processed to obtain coca paste. There have been cases in the Andes where some chewers have had mouth and throat infections from chewing coca that "had no taste at all." (In the process of making coca paste, coca leaves are not destroyed, merely soaked.) The United States would buy only coca leaves of optimum quality. Private companies or international organizations, closely overseen by the United States, could be used to monitor this.

If 240,000 hectares yield an average of 140 arrobas per hectare per year, the total production of coca in the international coca belt would be 33,600,000 arrobas (318,818 metric tons); at $90 per arroba, the cost would be about $3 billion, a sum the United States can afford to pay.

Once purchased, the leaves could have industrial use in the manufacture of chewing gum (Weil 1977), as well as scientific and medical applications.[20] The various alkaloids and other chemicals found in the leaves could be substituted for synthetic anesthetics, for example. The $3 billion spent to prevent cocaine manufacture, in other words, would be an investment. Direct and indirect tax revenues from coca leaf-related industries would undoubtedly surpass the $3 billion outlay.

One major drawback to buying coca crops would be the persistent migration from the countryside to the jungles, which would promote coca farming for the black market. If other effective sources of income are not developed, the migration of peasants in search of coca dollars will be inevitable. There is tremendous need to create local economies based on agriculture and geared to cutting dependence on foreign food. Such rational and authentic economic development would obviously reduce migration drastically. All development programs, such as education, transportation, and health infrastructures, would then contribute to substantive changes. Today, such development programs hinder real economic growth because they are only cosmetic. Rather than raising the standard of living among the indigenous people, the artificial demand created for modern conveniences is alien to their traditional way of life.

A status quo in controlling the production and trafficking of cocaine will certainly demand much more expensive drug-program budgets than would a comprehensive regional economic development program in coca-belt regions. Faced with the impossibility of cutting supply, proposed preventive measures will also have negative results; the use of newspapers, flyers, posters, and television programs as educational tactics to make our youth avoid the use of cocaine simply does not coincide with the values of the young. Will an additional $500 million toward law enforcement stop supply and make America drug-free? My guess is that this approach to fighting drugs will not go any farther than occasional sloganeering.[21]

However, intelligent solutions that would benefit coca-belt societies may not coincide with the political interests of the international powers. Healthy economic development in the coca belt would, in the long run, make these countries less dependent upon foreign aid. As consumer power increased, industrial output would grow considerably. While the first world would still be the source of technology and continue to control the international political economy, gains would not be the same as from the now-established avenues of dependency.

Political pressure exerted on governments in poor countries may be an indication of the perception in the United States that the world ends in its borders, that civilization is all but a creation of American society, and that the rest of the world should conform to its ethnocentric standards and conditions.[22] This blind attitude hinders the formulation of a reasonable drug policy. The failure of the present, capricious drug-control policy should make America aware of the fact that Uncle Sam's hat may be running out of tricks to solve global problems.

So long as the Indian and the peasant coca planters' legitimate needs are confused with the rapacious traffickers' greed, and until a rational economic development is implemented, the escalation of law enforcement despite other social and economic factors may shift dangerously to declared anti-drug war operations. The underlying reason given for this step, although unfounded, may be the existence of guerrillas such as the Shining Path and MRTA in Peru and the M-19 and FARC in Colombia. This may lead to the build-up of an escalated military anti-cocaine war. The inaccurate speculation that guerrillas are supported by the cocaine industry may create the foreign war of the 1990s. This alternative of masking foreign interventionism as drug hostility may serve two key purposes: the immediate and effective destruction of coca fields and the beginning of an international battlefield.

With much clandestine coca cultivation already in full production in other tropical areas, and with demand remaining the same, none of the currently proposed U.S. policies will make cocaine disappear—that is, unless some other drug is discovered or synthetically manufactured. The alternatives lie with the leaders of the world: to ignore the hunger of the peasants, to continue policies that have been ineffective, to maintain an army of methadone users, to escalate military intervention, or finally to open their eyes and recognize the true problem and try new solutions.

Current programs do not address the fundamental problem: What economic force will replace coca? Without a plan for alternative economic development, coca will continue to thrive, and the forces of both government authority and the criminal underworld will exploit the farmers and cocaine dealers for their own gain. Band-aid economic and enforcement programs will not cure the epidemic in the Andes.

The Colombian government decided in 1987 to invest more than $1 billion to develop the depressed regions that cover a third of Colombia's territory and are home to 10 percent of its 27 million inhabitants. This approach is a clear indication of the search for economic alternatives to minimize both guerrilla movements and the dependence of the country upon the cocaine economy.[23] To be successful, ambitious economic development programs need not be all-inclusive and unattainable agendas, especially if they are dependent upon foreign assistance, for, in the words of Lester Pearson,

> aid is no fairy godmother touching everything with her magic wand so that, presto, the little mice and pumpkins of local effort are turned into large luxury carriages. Development is a long, slogging, grinding effort by the people themselves of each country. If they don't make that effort, there will be no development. For example, aid has encouraged some countries to neglect changes in agricultural policy for too long. But aid for genuine economic development not only helps ease critical shortages, but should help to build a base for independent and self-reliant growth.[24]

Irrigation networks and application of technology appropriate to the social and cultural conditions of the Andean people would be good places to start in the move toward independence, which should be the ultimate aim of foreign assistance. Then the Andean people could slowly channel their traditional life toward modern systems of agricultural production and progressively make changes in their social ideas and values. Irrigation would help satisfy the need for food. There is no question that the economic development spurred by anti-cocaine investments would boost national economies. Nevertheless, by no means would drug abuse be totally displaced. Coca and cocaine traffic would be confined, however, to some unscrupulous officials and authorities at both ends of the market. Cocaine might then revert to being a hedonistic status symbol among the upper classes, rather than pose a major threat to the physical and mental health of the entire society.

Unquestionably, drug production and traffic in Peru have addicted thousands of people to illegal sources of hard cash. By doing so, it has helped people compare their situation with other standards of living, spurred the irrational use of land, encouraged migration and brought to the foreground poverty, exploitation, and many other social issues. Today, even in most remote villages in the Andes, people who, in one way or another, have been exposed to the underground economy speak of better wages, modern goods and entertainments, and the state of their lives vis à vis other groups and societies. Thus, the coca farmer's primitive rebel behavior against law enforcement, to use Hobsbawn's words, may be isolated political retaliations against the dominant classes. Because of Peru's unhealthy economy, this incipient movement may contribute to the emergence of a popular ideology. If to this incipient or primitive political consciousness we add the role of the radical ideology in many highland areas, then we may conclude that coca- and cocaine-supplying countries may soon face even more serious and profound changes. The indigenous Andean, the migrant urban wage laborer who go to the jungle to "make it" or to satisfy primary needs, and instead see their dreams fade away because of law-enforcement actions, may have their own legitimate right to participate actively in or collaborate with the defense of their livelihood.

In Latin America, drug production and traffic and radical political movements have social and economic roots. It is these roots that the world should address, rather than try to uproot the tree by destroying its branches. If only the billions of dollars invested in unsuccessful eradication and law-enforcement programs were used more rationally, the riddle of the cocaine sphinx could be solved.

Appendix:
Researching Peasants and
Drug Producers

During a visit to my hometown in the spring of 1980, I decided to do what a professor in college had advised me: "Go back home and look into the changes in the community." Neither during my childhood nor in numerous visits back had I ventured outside the boundaries of my native community, Llamellín. In my youth, I was part of the indigenous culture and, as an adult visitor, I lacked the skills to make sense of the obvious. Becoming an ethnographer of the Andes, native though I was, was a long process, for learning from or observing other people whose culture and society is the same as one's own roots I found very difficult and possible only when a disciplined approach was incorporated into my everyday routine.

On my exploratory trip in 1980, the first thing I did when I arrived in the district capital of Llamellín was to look for a companion who was familiar with the route and the area. A local photographer volunteered for the trip. The next step was to rent a horse or a mule for transportation, and prepare a *fiambre*, provision consisting of two guinea pigs, toasted maize, and some homemade bread for at least two days' travel. My companion and I left town and headed for Paras, the community of my first fieldwork.

After thirteen hours of tedious horseback riding, we followed the recommendation of a teacher we had met on our way and stopped in one of the five villages of Paras. At the church of San Martín, we washed our hands and watered our horses. Directly across from the church was a house with Coca-Cola posters on the door. We knocked on the door but there was no answer. Through the next door of the same house we heard voices. Someone noticed us and came out to ask what we wanted. He was drunk. We told him that we only wanted a bottle of Coca-Cola, to which he answered that all he had was alcohol and alcohol was as good as cold water. We had run out of boiled drinking water and had to try to find something to satisfy our thirst. He asked our names and we asked his. We found out that he was the lieutenant governor (*teniente gobernador*) for the five villages of Paras. Assuming that he would use his influence, we asked him to recommend someone in the community to give us shelter for at least one night. He went into the room where the rest of his friends were discussing their plans. Shortly thereafter six drunken peasants stood before us.

They introduced themselves by their titles. They were the members of the central committee of the community. Each of them asked us questions about our identity, profession, and especially the purpose of our visit to Paras. They wanted me to show them some kind of letter of introduction or at least a personal identification card bearing my picture and my name, or even a calling card from any provincial authority introducing me to the community. I had nothing, not even my school identification card. I explained my presence and purposes to them over and over and begged them to believe me. They would not accept the excuse that I had left all my documents in Llamellín, nor would they believe that I had been born and raised in the province.

Since I could not provide identification, they asked us "kindly and immediately" to leave the village. It was getting dark and we had nowhere to go. Suddenly the president of the Administrative Council addressed my companion and said, "I think I know you." My companion presented his identification as a photographer, but I remained a problem. They invited us to have a drink before leaving the village and we accepted. My companion and I drank the alcohol, smiling and looking at the Coca-Cola poster. At this point I asked the peasants to let me take their picture. They liked the idea of posing as members of the central committee. Almost in unison they said, "Yes, my engineer." Then they wanted me to pose with them for another frame. Right after my assistant snapped the camera, I suggested we have another drink and offered to pay for it. "Correct, my engineer," they answered. By the time we had emptied the bottle we all were friends, and the same person who had asked us to leave the village offered us his humble home for as long as we wanted to stay in Paras. He hoped it would be a long stay.

The Solís family gave us the best room they had, which apparently had been unoccupied for some time. We used the only steel bedstead they had. Our bed linen consisted of four sheepskins and two wool quilts infested with fleas and lice that made our nights interminable. One day before we left the village the Solís family killed a pig to give us a farewell lunch. They assigned us their best mules for our transportation back to Llamellín and one of them even walked for about one hour with us up to the point where the broad trail began that would make our return easier.

Aside from the first day of difficulty, I had no problem at all as a visitor in Paras. There was some hesitation when I presented myself as a sociology graduate student from New York and spoke to them in Quechua. However, as they listened to me speaking to them in terms that only a native could understand, telling them jokes and fairy tales, they gave broad smiles as a sign of accepting their visitor. From then on, they acted friendly and were responsive and cooperative. I entered their lives and functioned almost as one of them. Good humor, patience, and the bottle of alcohol spent on the first day produced excellent returns.

I had not decided until my initial visit to Paras to concentrate my research efforts there. As I now reflect upon the evolution of my decision, I feel I have learned a great deal about the field to which I am devoting my time as a sociologist. Long before leaving New York for Peru, I had held the idea of doing research that would deal with social and economic problems of the whole province of Antonio Raimondi, where I was born and raised. Three main factors influenced me to change the subject: my own determination to concentrate on a specific area; the fact that the five villages in question did not follow the pattern dictated by the government after land reform; and the election of President Fernando Belaúnde, leader of Acción Popular Party, in May 1980. The ideology of the party, "Cooperación Popular," was based upon community development, particularly in rural areas where conditions were already unstable and showing signs of rapid change. The new democratic Peruvian government planned to intervene in community life, using Cooperación Popular to hasten the process of change in the peasantry. It seemed clear that I would have the opportunity to observe whether the ideology of the party reached the remote villages of Paras and, if it did, how effective its plans and programs were.

The project was to be carried out during the second half of 1981, since these were the seasons—winter and spring in Peru—when almost everyone was in the area for the harvest season and therefore available for interview.

Initial Steps and Experiences

In the spring of 1981, about one month before my trip from New York, I asked the chairperson of my committee to sign a letter in Spanish addressed to the head of the police, the subprefecto, the mayor, the judge of First Instance, and the director of education of the Province. In Lima, I obtained a letter of introduction from the American Embassy wherein the cultural attaché stated the purpose of my stay in Peru; this letter opened the doors of public libraries (there are not many of them), universities, museums, and so forth.

Once in the capital town of the province to which Paras belongs, I paid formal visits to the authorities to whom the letter from my mentor had been directed. The authorities, in turn, had already sent a transcription of the letter to their representatives in other towns announcing my presence and asking them for cooperation in the research.

When I arrived in Illauro, the village of my residence during fieldwork, the local teacher whom I had met a year before was expecting me. He had already rented a one-room house for me near the school building where he lived. He had my room cleaned by his students and borrowed a bedstead, sheepskins, quilts, and a table from various families. I had taken my own sleeping bag. Despite my experience the year before with lice and fleas, I failed to bring with me any insecticides, so pediculosis was inevitable.

The next morning I was having breakfast when a delegation of authorities from the village of San Martín came to welcome me and, at the same time, invite me once again to live in their village. I explained to them that I had not come exclusively to spend my time in Illauro or any of the five villages. I said I would be visiting every family I could, and that the only reason I had settled in Illauro was that the local teacher had rented a house for me there. When they knew the location of my house, which lay about twenty-five steps from a young, attractive widow's house, they smiled, wished me luck, and left.

The first person I had planned to visit was the village leader who, during my previous visit, had offered me full cooperation and whom I thought would be my key informant. He had changed his mind and refused to cooperate, offering the excuse that the documents he held were in Lima in his sons' possession. He advised me to pick another community to avoid problems with the local people. He had secretly started warning his co-villagers of the danger of my presence in Paras owing to my "identification with the other party." He also urged them to expel me from the community, for I had no official authorization to stay in Paras. He did not know that I had been authorized by the provincial authorities to do research, and he was surprised when he learned that I had been cleared in every respect. My research project became more and more challenging.

It had first been my plan to collect historical and political data, but as a result of the visit to the leader I decided to start immediately interviewing and observing the people. No one resisted. Fortunately, when I went back to Llamellín after staying two weeks in Paras, I met an Aprista congressman visiting the province who had already been informed of my project. The congressman asked me to join him at a lunch where he was to be a guest of the notables of Llamellín. After lunch, while we were still talking, the leader who had tried to create difficulties for me knocked on the door. He came to urge the congressman to visit Paras. The lawmaker took the opportunity to ask him his reasons for refusing to cooperate with my endeavor and pleaded with him to change his attitude.

The Fieldwork

So many activities go on in a community every day that a great deal of organization and planning are required prior to the field research. However, the research should not be limited to the "script" designed before the onset of the data-collection process because other interesting findings may arise while in the field, as happened in my research.

An initial goodwill visit to the community and villages involved in a project or the hamlets around the rural towns is a good practice. This does not require a house-to-house visit, only a walk around the setting to let the population know that one is there and that, at any time, a formal visit may occur. This is what I call a "familiarization walk," and it is extremely helpful for two reasons: Peasants become resentful very easily when they are ignored or a supposed preference is given to others, and if visits for the interviews are carried out without the first *imallata vida* ("what's up?") drop-in visit, total or partial resistance from the respondents is inevitable. Another strategic visit to local schools is a key factor in spreading the word of the researcher's presence in the area. Teachers are good, if not the best, sources of information on most of what happens in the research setting. They are usually a reliable source about life in a community.

In any direct contact with the observed population, the researcher perhaps enters the field under the aegis of an official agency or as a social scientist directly identifying himself as such. In the present research, to avoid the problem of role performance in the community, I took the second alternative. Any official sponsorship could have created serious difficulties because of the conflict existing among the members of the community, as well as their hostile attitude towards the government.

During the process of data gathering as a participant-observer, I became a temporary member of the community without identifying with any of the political groups, thus avoiding a dual identity. I structured my grounds for research by direct observation rather than testing a priori hypotheses. I informally interviewed and observed a total of 101 Paras households, from the 125 planned. I visited three to five families per day; I spent the rest of the day talking with shepherds and workers in the fields or taking notes. I conducted the interviews in Quechua in order to make the people feel comfortable and to facilitate a better and more precise expression of their feelings, opinions, attitudes, and ideas. I would always start conversations with flattering statements to elicit a discussion or a friendly argument. For example, I would approach a shepherd girl or a woman on her land by saying "you have such a large herd," or "you look beautiful on your plot," to which they would always answer by telling stories of their past or by comparing their land possession to that of some families whom they thought had more land than they needed.

Sometimes people would avoid the question and ask the reason for my stay in the area. I would tell women that I was in "search of a girl to marry," and this led to questions of their marital status, number of children, size of land, and so forth. Male peasants like conversations involving women, so I would approach them by asking whether there was any "available girl in the community, for everyone says that they are all yours; why do you not leave one for a poor guy like myself?" Some would name the single women or just smile at me. Others would bounce the question and say, "Why would you want another woman when you already have your blonde widow?" This approach worked much better than just knocking on doors with a long questionnaire in hand and saying: "Hi, I am doing research on peasant economy and would like you to answer some questions." Some may contend that too much personal involvement jeopardizes a good scientific approach. But objectivity, whatever it may mean, should not be conceived prior to data gathering. Rather, it should take place in the final analysis.

The purpose of the research had been to study the effects of land reform and modernization in the peasant community of Paras *(Comunidad Campesina de Paras)*. A basic questionnaire designed to obtain data on the demographic, social, and economic aspects of the community was taken to the field. In the process of my visits and interviews I discovered that, right after the harvest, some peasants started making preparations for a long trip. Thus, my plan had to be changed. It needed to fit what was going on in the field, which was different from what I had expected. After discovering the new research material, I centered my efforts on the *montañero* peasants and some informants in small towns in the area. The reason informal conversations with indirect questions were formulated was that peasants are very sensitive to direct questions about themselves.

After defending my dissertation, I spent most of the summer of 1983 in Peru. The purposes of the trip were to study more closely the peasants of Paras who were connected to the underground economy, to make some exploratory visits to coca- and cocaine-producing communities, and to try to meet and become acquainted with experts in the industry. I completed most of the data on the economics of coca and cocaine in the traditional society during this trip.

My trip to the drug-plagued communities made many people think that I was a *pichicatero* (drug trafficker). On more than one occasion they offered me certain amounts of the "best stuff," but I cautiously avoided both too much information and direct or indirect involvement in drug trafficking. My cautious attitude owed to my suspicion that a trap had been set by local drug lords, many of whom had been my grade-school friends, high-school classmates, and fellow factory workers in Lima. Although to the people in the Andes I was continuing to do research on the changes in traditional communities, some suspected I was interested in something else. However, to them, that "something else" was not research but "white business."

My aluminum camera case was always the first thing to be searched at every police checkpoint. In many communities people thought that I was a foreigner. They whispered to each other in Quechua saying, "God knows what this *Colombiano* carries in that shiny case." Situations like this were opportunities to start conversations about drug production and traffic. Socializing with people at every level was my basic method of research. The disadvantage of this strategy is that it is time-consuming and limited to researchers with a deep knowledge of native language and culture.

I carried out the decisive and crowning phase of the project in the summer of 1985. Two forces hampered my research plans. The pressure from my family to give up the idea was based on the concern that, allegedly, guerrillas of the Shining Path were present in my hometown. The second obstacle was bureaucratic red tape in New York.

In Lima, a friend who had worked in the Upper Huallaga for many years suggested I visit the setting to get acquainted with some of the professionals in the area. This trip coincided with a general strike in a section of the Upper Huallaga. We rented a van to travel along the striking communities. The strikers blocked the road at some points with trees and branches. People were tense and suspicious, but the psychologist whom they called "doctor"—he held a B.A. in psychology—was the best person to vouch for me. However, the real purpose of this short exploratory trip was not always revealed when I was introduced.

After securing indirect help from local residents, I went back to Lima and from there to the highland community for a few days. I wanted to make sure that some of my peasant friends had made arrangements with their *patrones* for me to visit their plantations and pits. Fortunately, on the bus I met two migrant workers from a village near my hometown who were coming back from the Upper Huallaga. They supplied the first details I had obtained on the preparation of coca paste. Three peasants from Paras not only provided the names and exact locations of research settings but also were willing to go with me to the jungles. A local teacher from a highland village who was taking a leave of absence to work on the coca plantations also became part of my direct connections to the underworld. Sitting in the airport of Lima waiting for my flight to Tingo María, I made friends with an agronomist working in the jungles. He introduced me to high authorities, members of local middle classes, civil servants, and coca-paste retailers.

I continued my trip north to the hamlet where my friend the teacher was working. All I had were the names of the teacher's relatives, the nearby village, and a piece of paper giving vague directions. Despite the fact that I had asked the driver and his helper to drop me at the place where I had been told to get off, I missed my stop by about two kilometers. I got off at a place where about ten people were picking coca leaves, and I walked back until I found the right house. Neither my friend the teacher nor his relatives were home. The man in charge of the small hardware store was very apathetic toward me. When I asked him about the owner of the house, he brusquely answered, "He is not in."

My hosts introduced me to the area residents as one of their relatives from Lima visiting them for a few weeks. I spent the first days of fieldwork socializing. As days passed, I got deeper and deeper into the underground economy and subculture, avoiding direct questions regarding formulas, proportions, procedures, and prices. I participated in every routine or special event I could and observed others. For example, after a volleyball game among local residents, I sat and had refreshments with the neighbors who usually asked about my plans for the next day. I was always open to suggestions and invitations to visit their plantations or their farmhouses deep in the forests. Often, the trips involved hours of hiking, especially when the visits were to secret airfields.

Following a successful stay, I would move to other sites. The strategy was always to produce networks of friendship. But I never went anywhere without actually knowing the setting and the host families. This meant many hours of traveling by car, bus, truck, or on foot. My peasant friends from Paras helped me cross passes and mountain ranges to reach areas that did not have road service. They always made jokes about my limited physical endurance. For the longer hikes, my traveling equipment consisted of my worn-out sleeping bag, a small tin pot in which to boil water, some matches, basic medicines, my 35mm camera, and many rolls of film. Hunger and thirst made us drop in on communities or isolated houses during the treks across the mountain ranges. Under the pretext of having the peasant women cook our meals, we stopped overnight in houses and huts where friends or acquaintances of my peasant hiking experts lived. Questions such as, "What brings you here?" and "Where are you from?" were constantly addressed to me. To them, I was from Llamellín, my hometown. Some peasants, especially males, tested me with their questions. My responses never failed to reassure them about my identity.

The actual recording of data varied according to the conditions in the settings, types of subjects, and kinds of information needed. Days in the highlands are short and the majority of people do not have electricity. Wax candles, kerosene lanterns, and flashlights are used by those who can afford them. I therefore made field notes immediately following interviews and conversations during the day. Evenings and nights were usually spent chatting with neighbors in my village of residence. Thus, the apparent physical disadvantage of the setting turned into an advantage. Evening and night conversations and discussions were ways to double-check information I had collected.

I gathered data on coca-leaf economy, costs and process of manufacturing, and national and international trafficking of coca paste and cocaine at different places in the country. Knowledge of every aspect of the underground hustle and bustle came from direct observation and participation.[1] As I had good rapport with the people, some days I would ask them to let me drop into their work settings. Then I would show up with a couple of bottles of beer, Coca-Cola, or anything that would season my visit. During the first visits, I tried not to be too inquisitive, for I perceived tension in some individuals, especially the full-time cocaine entrepreneurs. As had happened in the highlands in 1980, patience and good humor paid good returns.

A professional chemist, who also is an independent cocaine refiner and international trafficker, introduced me to other people who were in the same business. In order to observe and interview independent cocaine refiners, long hours of traveling were required. On one particular occasion, I was in the same plane with a person who was going to connect me to a "cook." Later, I found out that this same person was the "cook" in his own "kitchen." Screening procedures were much more strict in the urban cocaine laboratories than they were in coca-paste manufacturing centers in the jungles.

In addition to the 101 families in Paras, 73 coca-paste smokers and about 150 persons from every part of the coca and cocaine industry participated either directly or indirectly in the study. While I avoided asking questions during actual on-site observation, I collected details on illegal activities at other times. This tactic made the research more effective and objective, for in any serious research, confidence in both the researcher and the informant is essential. Had

I not withheld my role from people performing illegal functions, my efforts would have been thwarted.

The study, besides being an intellectual and an academic endeavor, was an opportunity for photographic expression. If my two native tongues, Quechua and Spanish, were extremely valuable during data collection, my photographic skills were equally important. Since my first visits to my hometown in the mid-seventies, I have been photographing the people and the culture of the Andes. Hundreds of exposures of color slides document my presence and knowledge of the Andean countries at large. The visual side of the research in and of itself represents a whole new dimension of social research. However, a camera hanging on the researcher's neck can be potentially dangerous when people do not want to be photographed and sometimes brought rejection, disappointment, and setbacks.

Audiovisual Research Tools

During data collection, taking field notes is sometimes difficult or impossible because of the setting or the time at which the interviews take place. Here cameras and tape recorders aid the process of data collection and make it more effective. However, care in the use of these tools must be observed to avoid suspicion and to prevent discontent among the people observed. Photographing and taping subjects raise the ethical question of whether or not the participants in the research should be made aware of the use of audiovisual devices during research contact. Many Andean populations are sensitive to having their voices taped or their images recorded on film.

In 1975, during my first visit to my hometown from New York, I wanted to photograph the people from a nearby village. I found two peasant shepherd boys who seemed to make an interesting picture. I aimed my camera mounted with a long telephoto lens. One of the children realized that I was snapping the camera. The boys started screaming and throwing stones at me. A few minutes later, parents and neighbors came out with their dogs, sticks, and more stones. They thought that I had been trying to shoot the children with a gun. On another occasion during fieldwork in 1981, a peasant asked me to use my camera to see whether there was underground water in the mountains surrounding the community. My experience and knowledge of these subtleties made me more cautious in the taping and photographing I did afterwards.

If in the Andes my nightly research companion was a cassette recorder, during the day my camera was the research associate always hanging on my shoulder, ready to freeze segments and instants of what was happening in the community. Now and then, to break the monotony of visiting households every day, I dedicated some days to taking pictures or movies. I exposed ninety minutes of super 8 sound film and many rolls of still film. Because of favorable weather conditions in the highlands, low- and medium-speed films satisfied the conditions for good exposures.

Strangers carrying cameras are not yet seen in the cocaine towns and villages, because there is no such thing as tourists or visitors taking snapshots of farms and landscapes or posing with natives for a souvenir photo. Tingo María, for example, used to be a good tourist city. Drug production and traffic have frightened away Peruvian and foreign tourists alike. Reporters who are assigned to cover the drug-infested jungles are, at best, either thrown out or threatened; murders are common.

In the underground world, nobody wants to be photographed regardless of his status. Obviously, not everyone toting a camera is a journalist. On the other hand, there is no way for the illegal world to know whether an occasional visitor is a drug spy or an undercover law-enforcement agent. They suspect that anyone taking pictures of them working is an enemy. This may be one of the reasons why photographs or films that reach our attention have almost always been taken under police protection or as part of a crackdown or a drug bust. These kinds of photographs and films are more sensational and biased. Lack of respect and consideration for the subject breaks the interrelationship between the photographer and his subject. Furthermore, the police seem to be oriented toward showing how excellent the control and eradication programs are or publicizing widespread drug abuse.

On the last day of my stay in the green mines, I decided to take some pictures of a busy Sunday in one of the cocaine centers. When a peasant friend and I were walking around the main square taking candid shots of migrant workers, three men approached us. They pointed at me and said, "You are an outsider, aren't you?" Then they asked whether my cameras were for sale. I replied no. They all deliberated briefly. They asked me at which hotel I was staying. I gave the name of a low-class hotel. Their advice was that I should leave town immediately. They showed me the park bench where two reporters had been shot to death a few feet from where I was standing and emphasized their advice by saying, "If you don't pack and leave the town immediately you'll be another statistic; so if you want to live longer than twenty-four hours, get the hell out of here."

I thanked them for their advice and expressed my gratitude for their concern. I accepted the glass of beer they invited me to drink. Isn't life full of hellos and good-byes? What had happened to me in the highlands in 1980 was repeated at the other end of my research. This time, however, rather than trying to make friends as I had done in the highlands, I put my gear away, walked around the square, and left the town. The same evening, as I had planned, I packed my tote bag and left for Tingo María, where I stayed overnight, for the flight to Lima was at 3:00 P.M. the next day. In Tingo María, I spent the night with a grade-school companion in the highlands. We chatted and remembered events of the 1950s.

Following my friend's advice, I packed my film, lenses, camera, local newspaper clippings, and my field notebook in my suitcase. In Lima, I found out that my suitcase containing months of hard work was missing. I thought that I had been followed and that my followers, whoever they were, had seized my baggage. I made plans to delay my return to New York and go back to the jungles to take the pictures that I had lost. Fortunately, the next day my canvas bag arrived with its contents intact.

The Ethics of Covert Research

The four problems that the participant observer has to contemplate in ethnographic research are the questions of entry in the field, the truthfulness of data, communicating research plans to the subjects being studied, and the confidentiality of the subjects interviewed.

Collection of ethnographic data on both traditional groups and the drug economy requires a special methodological approach. The individuals representing local networks of the international drug subculture have their own social characteristics. Open to some researchers is the indigenous peasant who supports the underground through his legal participation in the coca economy. But petty peasant traffickers, illegal coca farmers, and national and international coca-paste and cocaine entrepreneurs are difficult to socialize with, let alone persuade to participate in any research.

Traditionally, although not exclusively, anthropologists and sociologists enter their settings through the sponsorship of organizations that are directly or indirectly connected to the groups to be studied. The organizations sponsoring or connecting the researcher to the setting may be the Red Cross, CARE, the Peace Corps, religious denominations, AID, the Fulbright Foundation, or other internationally recognized entities.

> From [this] point on, interaction with those who control entry into the field are primarily manipulative, involving figuring out how to gain entry while preserving the integrity of the study and the investigator's [re-

search] interests. The degree of manipulation varies depending on the purpose of the fieldwork and the expected or real degree of resistance to the study. Where the field researcher expects cooperation, gaining entry may be largely a matter of establishing trust and rapport. At the other end of the continuum are those research settings where considerable resistance, hostility, [or even threat] is expected.[2]

Where resistance to the fieldworker threatens not only the project but also the physical well-being of the researcher, clearance from organizations whose functions are relevant to the subjects of study may compound the already existing danger. Thus, for example, if a sociologist wants to collect empirical data on the peasants' attitudes toward AID crop-substitution programs in the Upper Huallaga section of Peru he may get better results by not going to the field under the aegis of the AID or its Peruvian equivalent. Anti-American feeling in the area and the sensitivity of the issue may hinder any research attempt. The student then may end up doing indirect and conjectural analysis of the crop-substitution program. The original research plan may be feasible only by infiltrating the setting and taking a covert role.[3]

The fieldworker's process of infiltration may take different routes and names. To illustrate this infiltration process, perhaps one analogous type of human migration could be described. Thousands of illegal aliens come to the United States each year. In order to enter the country, Europeans, Asians, Africans, and Latin Americans first attempt to obtain a visitor's visa (B-2). Even before the expiration of their legal stay, those who had been successful in entering the country legally become illegal aliens by engaging in gainful activities. Those whose petitions to "visit" the United States were denied cross the borders with the help of "Mexican coyotes," "Caribbean pirates," and many other "professional passers." Once in the country, both those who entered the country "through the front door" with a B-2 visa and those who came in "through the back door" function smoothly in the American society. Those whose nationalities are identical to the ethnic origin of the majority become part of the mainstream culture, while others whose foreign identity is obvious join their corresponding subcultures.[4] Similarly, students, researchers, and scholars who make their living by writing on other cultures and societies find their ways of crossing social and cultural borders to satisfy their thirst for knowledge. Some fieldworkers whose physical traits conceal their research interests fulfill their intellectual endeavor with relative ease.

Once the scientist enters the setting, the question of mutual trust comes to the foreground. How could the social investigator reassure his informants that he is not a tax collector, a police informer, or a missionary? Does the observed group have control over the data and the final report? Even if the research was successfully disclosed, manipulation of data would be under the total control of the ethnographer, one of the principals in the research relationship, or, in the case of survey research, the principal investigator. On the other hand, how does the investigator coming from an advanced technological society communicate effectively with a peasant who believes that airplanes are big steel birds that enter a giant gate in the sky? As with any human endeavor, all social sciences are subject to human errors and deceptions.[5] However, a social scientist is expected to be an objective reporter. Thus the issue of mutual trust among subjects and researchers is a serious one for the ethnographer.

Confidentiality of the participants in the study may be the least of the methodological problems that the participant-observer has to confront. In the United States, human subjects are protected by the investigator's certificate of confidentiality. This method of protecting the participants is potentially effective only as long as both the researcher and the subjects are bound by the same civil and criminal laws. Otherwise institutional measures taken to protect the informant may be useless bureaucratic procedures.

Confidentiality can be a problem if the number of participants is relatively small and the descriptions of individual characters, or their direct quotations, disclose the subjects' criminal roles.[6] The subjects in this book who participate in the coca and cocaine industry have been given fictitious names, as have cities and towns.

Regardless of methodological orientation and the nature of individual studies, "the goal of social research is to discover, understand and communicate about human beings in society."[7] Social investigators, especially anthropologists, political scientists, and sociologists strive to discover the truth using their own techniques and approaches. In drug research, primarily two methods of data collection dominate the field: the ethnographic approach and the American mainstream sociological research approach. The former tries to analyze what people say or think, while the latter relies on meticulously designed questionnaires. Often, those who consider survey research to be the method of research par excellence question the validity of ethnographic research and raise the ethical issues discussed above.

The so-called quantitative method of drug research also faces its own ethical problems. Human feelings and ideas recorded in the answers are arbitrarily coded to construct variables and indicators. Answers to open-ended questions are translated into categories that may be far from showing the message of the original answer. Furthermore, just as television producers and reporters pay the drug addicts to appear on TV or to be photographed, drug-survey researchers recruit their subjects by advertising in local newspapers, giving out cards showing dollar signs, and paying for interviews, money that often ends up being spent on drugs around the corner. The answer to the question of which method faces more serious ethical issues is entirely up to the reader.

Notes

Introduction

1. U.S. Senate, Subcommittee on Alcoholism and Drug Abuse, Committee on Labor and Human Resources, *Drugs and Terrorism 1984* (Washington, D.C.: US Printing Office, 1984), p. 8.

2. Deustua (*El Narcotráfico y el Interés Nacional*, Lima, Peru: CEPEI, 1987, p. 25) says that Peru produces as much as 180,000 hectares and that production of 10,000 hectares satisfies the traditional chewing practices.

3. For extensive and detailed discussion of the use of the coca leaf, see Allen 1981; Barrantes 1984; Bolton 1978 and 1979; Burchard 1974; Fuchs 1978; Demic 1980; Hanna 1974; Henman 1978; Dobkin de Rios 1984; and Plowman 1980 and 1986.

4. See, for example, Edward P. Lanning, *Peru before the Incas* (Prentice Hall, 1967), p. 77; and Marlene Dobkin de Rios, *Hallucinogens: Cross-Cultural Perspectives* (Albuquerque: University of New Mexico Press, 1984), p. 151.

5. For coca chewing during the colonial era, see Pedro Cieza de Leon, *The Incas* (Norman: University of Oklahoma Press, 1959), pp. 259–60.

6. The term "coca belt" refers to the ecological conditions favorable for the production of coca, rather than the universal and exclusive production of it.

7. Instituto Nacional de Estadística (INE), *Censos Nacionales VIII de Poblacion III de Vivienda 1981* (Lima, Peru: INE, 1984), p. xxvi.

8. The term "Colombia" is a vague one, for the coca paste could be delivered in refining labs set deep in the Peruvian lowland jungles, or transported directly to the Caribbean or the United States. "Colombia" actually means international organized crime rather than the country itself.

9. For a discussion of infiltration in the setting and covert research see Jack D. Douglas, *Investigative Social Research* (Beverly Hills: Sage Publications,

1976), p. 167, and Patricia Adler, *Wheeling and Dealing* (New York: Columbia University Press, 1985), p. 17.

Chapter One

1. Eric R. Wolf, *Peasants* (Englewood Cliffs: Prentice Hall, 1966), p. 4.

2. George Kubler, *The Indian Caste of Peru, 1795–1940* (Washington D.C.: Smithsonian Institution, Institute of Social Anthropology Publication No. 14, 1950), p. 36.

3. Luis A. Guevara, *Granjas Comunales Indígenas* (Lima, Peru: By the Author, n. d.), p. 3.

4. In the Quechua language spoken in many areas, "marca" means village, community, town, territory, and the word "topo" denotes the existence of contracted work performed for wages or payment in kind.

5. F. Bonilla, *Estatuto de Comunidades Campesinas* (Lima, Peru: Editorial Mercurio, 1974), p. 7.

6. Hildebrando Castro Pozo, *Nuestra Comunidad Indígena* (Lima, Peru: Perugraph Editores, 1979), p. 15.

7. Ibid., p. 57.

8. José María Caballero, *Economía Agraria de la Sierra Peruana* (Lima, Peru: IEP, 1981), p. 63.

9. José Matos Mar, *Yanaconaje y Reforma Agraria en el Peru* (Lima, Peru: IEP, 1976), pp. 15–60.

10. In one ex-hacienda community, the subtenant had to labor sixteen days during fallow time, eight days in plowing, eight days during weeding, and as many days as were required to finish collecting the crops. The subtenant's labor obligations ended with the transportation of eight sacks (576 kilos) of grain, mostly wheat, from the threshing floors in the field to the warehouses in the hacienda quarters. For a detailed narrative of feudal subjects during the sixties see Samuel Cavero, *Un Rincón para los Muertos* (Lima, Peru: Editores Asociados, 1987), especially pp. 12–62.

11. By 1957, in some *haciendas*, labor obligations were reduced to three days of work (Edmundo Morales, "Land Reform, Social Change, and Modernization in the National Periphery: A Study of Five Villages in the Northeastern Andes of Peru," Ph.D. diss., City University of New York, 1983), p. 55.

12. Garcilaso de la Vega, *Comentarios Reales de los Incas* (Mexico: Editorial José M. Cajica, n.d.), p. 276.

13. Alden Mason, *The Ancient Civilizations of Peru* (Switzerland: Plata Publishing, 1975), p. 181.

14. Billie Jean Isbell, "Parentesco Andino y Reciprocidad Kuyaq: Los Que Nos Aman," in *Reciprocidad e Intercambio en los Andes Peruanos,* ed. Giorgio Alberti and Enrique Mayer (Lima, Peru: IEP, 1974), pp. 110–51. Also cf. Samuel Cavero, *Un Rincón para los Muertos* (Lima, Peru: Editores Asociados, 1987), pp. 43–49.

15. The labor performed for one week by an ox pays for its keep as well as for forage consumed by cows, sheep, and other domestic animals.

16. See also Paul L. Doughty, "Peace, Food and Equity in Peru" in Jack R. Rollwagen, ed., *Directions in the Anthropological Study of Latin America: A Reassessment* (Brockport, New York: Department of Anthropology, State University of New York, 1986), p. 56.

17. Guillermo Bonfil, *Campesinado e Indigenismo en América Latina* (Lima, Peru: Centro Latinoamericano de Trabajo Social, 1978), p. 134.

18. Among many others, anthropologists and even some Latin Americans use the term *piksha* with the exclusive connotation of "coca bag." In Quechua, the word *piksha* can be translated into English as "bag." Thus, they have *cachi piksha* (bag to keep salt), *escuela piksha* (school bag), *cori piksha* (jewelry or valuables bag), and so forth.

19. Again, *puru* means "container" without reference to its size or what it contains. It is the use or the contents of *puru* (gourd) that determine the meaning of the term.

20. Some researchers who have done fieldwork in the Andes claim that they understand the real meaning of coca chewing because they have chewed the leaves along with the Andeans. Placing a few leaves in the mouth and keeping them for hours does not make one a coca chewer.

21. Catherine J. Allen, "To be Quechua: the symbolism of coca chewing in highland Peru," *American Ethnologist* 8 (1981): 165.

22. Santiago Marquez Zorrilla, *Huari y Conchucos* (Lima, Peru: Imprenta El Condor, 1965), p. 67.

23. Nancy Lois Richards, "Erythroxylon Coca in the Peruvian Highlands: Practices and Beliefs," Ph.D. diss. (University of California at Irvine, 1980), p. 18. Compare this to the idea that coca chewing was invented by the Virgin Mary who, when she lost her son, chewed coca to allay her grief (Allen 1986:36).

24. Pedro Cieza de León, *The Incas* (Norman: University of Oklahoma Press, 1959), pp. 259–60.

25. Every local parish had the right to receive one tenth (*diezmo*) of the crop. *Primicia* was the local parish's privilege of tasting the first yields of the crop.

26. Because of my successful participation in this and many other circumstances in some villages, they expected from me more than just a "miracle pill." My conversations about birth control methods, for example, made some married men ask me to perform a vasectomy or to provide them with intrauterine rings.

27. In some sections of the Andes these forms of offerings, although not under the same name, are exclusively religious rites. On All Souls' Day, in addition to following the mandates of the Catholic church, some families cook their dead relatives' favorite dish and leave it overnight on the table or in an empty room. They believe that if the soul did not find its favorite food or drink it would be hungry or thirsty and the living would be blamed.

28. In Quechua it is not correct to use the plural "leaves" when referring to coca.

29. Before removing the spell, the witch visits the client's house or the client goes to the witch for consultation. These visits take place as many times as required for the witch to steal something personal from the client, especially clothing. The witch makes a bundle with the client's belongings, and he or his assistant places it where the client later discovers it.

Chapter Two

1. George Andrews and David Solomon, eds., *The Coca Leaf and Cocaine Papers* (New York: Harcourt Brace Jovanovich, 1975), p. 107.

2. The Inca Empire (Tahuantinsuyo) ran from the Maule River in Chile to Pasto in Colombia. It included what is now Bolivia, Ecuador, Peru, and parts of Argentina, Colombia, and Chile.

3. Instituto Nacional de Estadística, *Censos Nacionales VIII de Población III de Vivienda* (Lima, Peru: Instituto Nacional de Estadística, 1985), p. xiv.

4. José María Arguedas, *Formación de una Cultura Nacional Indoamericana* (Mexico, Siglo Veintíuno Editores, 1981), p. 22.

5. Garcilaso de la Vega, *Comentarios Reales de los Incas* (Puebla, Mexico: Publicaciones de la Universidad de Puebla, 1953), pp. 37–39. In the province of Marañón, near the rain forests, there is a town called Huacaybamba; they say that the name of this town derives from *huacay* (to weep or to cry). Inca wept over the defeat of his army in this place, which is along the banks of the Marañón River.

6. Pedro Cieza de León, *The Incas* (Norman: University of Oklahoma Press, 1960), p. 260.

7. Alain Gheerbrant, *The Incas: The Royal Commentaries of Garcilaso de la Vega 1539–1616* (New York: The Orion Press, 1961), p. 101.

8. Antonio E. Alvarado, "Diagnóstico Socio-Económico del Cultivo y la Comercialización de la Coca en la Provincia de Leoncio Prado, Huánuco," B.A. thesis, Universidad Nacional Agraria de la Selva (Tingo María, Peru, 1974), p. 85.

9. Fernando Belaúnde Terry, *Peru's Own Conquest* (Lima, Peru: American Studies Press, 1965), p. 218.

10. *Mitimaes* were families from other conquered tribes who were uprooted to different points in the Tahuantinsuyo.

11. George Kubler, *The Indian Caste of Peru 1795–1940* (Washington, D.C.: Smithsonian Institution, Institute of Social Anthropology Publication No. 14, 1950), p. 34.

12. "Monstruosa macrocefalia es la ciudad de Lima," *El Comercio* (Lima, Peru, 3 July 1984), p. A8.

13. Fernando Belaúnde Terry, p. 215.

14. To date, the Peruvian census bureau (Instituto Nacional de Estadística) does not have any available data breaking down information on the origins of the immigrants or the destinations of emigrants. It is difficult to establish who migrates where. Of eight departments on the coast, only Piura increased its rate of newcomers by 1.2 percent.

15. Ciro Alegría, *La Serpiente de Oro* (Lima, Peru: Editorial Universo, 1967), p. 47.

16. According to Garcilaso de la Vega, the Antis, Chunchos ("uncivilized people"), and Aucas were Arawak tribes who lived in the forests of the eastern Andes. In Ecuador (Vickers 1984, p. 9) the Amazon tribes are stereotyped as Aucas.

17. For further discussion of civilization, conquest, and extermination policies in eastern Peru see Anthony Stocks, "Indian Policy in Eastern Peru," in Marianne Schmink and Charles Wood, eds., *Frontier Expansion in Amazonia* (Gainesville: University of Florida Press, 1984), pp. 33–59.

18. Cleber Flores, "Problemática del Colono Inmigrante y su Adaptación a la Zona del Alto Huallaga," unpublished paper (Lima, Peru, 1985), p. 4.

19. Carlos E. Aramburú, "Expansion of the Frontier in the Peruvian Selva," in Marianne Schmink and Charles Wood, eds., *Frontier Expansion in Amazonia,* (Gainesville: University of Florida Press, 1984), p. 164.

20. Anthony Stocks, "Indian Policy in Eastern Peru," in Marianne Schmink and Charles H. Wood, eds., *Frontier Expansion in Amazonia* (Gainesville: Uni-

versity of Florida Press, 1984), p. 35, formulates four approaches to develop the Amazon basins in Peru: "civilization," conquest, advocacy (reservation-type), and extermination or removal, which, he argues, "has rarely been a goal in Peru though it has been in other countries in South America."

21. Alvaro Salazar Pereira, "Situación Actual de los Proyectos Especiales de Selva," in *Población y Colonización en la Alta Amazonía Peruana* (Lima, Peru: Consejo Nacional de Población [CNP] and Centro de Investigación y Promoción Amazónica [CIPA], 1984), p. 245.

22. For a general discussion of the breakdown of the budget for the development of the Peruvian Amazon see Alvaro Salazar Pereira, "Situación Actual de los Proyectos Especiales de Selva" in *Población y Colonización en la Amazonía Peruana* (Lima, Peru: CIPA and CNP, 1984), pp. 245–74.

23. As has been true throughout the history of Peru, upper and middle groups have been costly to the peasant and the Indian. For instance, when the present Aprista government took over office it was discovered that money to pay the high salaries (in U.S. dollars) of the management of Petroperu came from foreign loans.

24. Robin Shoemaker, *The Peasants of El Dorado* (Ithaca: Cornell University Press, 1981), p. 232.

25. Instituto Nacional de Estadística (INE), p. 17.

26. José Matos Mar, *Reforma Agraria: Logros y Contradicciones 1969–1979* (Lima, Peru: IEP, 1980), p. 36.

27. Fernando Belaúnde Terry, *Peru's Own Conquest* (Lima, Peru: American Studies Press, 1965), p. 197.

28. Edmundo Morales, "Coca and cocaine economy and social change in the Andes of Peru," *Economic Development and Cultural Change* 35(1), 1986, p. 151.

29. "Hacen análisis sobre migración a la selva alta," *El Comercio* (Lima, Peru, 16 June 1985), p. 12.

30. James Shields, *La Educación en el Desarrollo de la Comunidad* (Buenos Aires: Editorial Paidos, 1967), p. 36.

31. Ministerio de Agricultura, Unidad de Estadística Agrícola, Lima, Peru.

32. U.S. Congress, *Latin American Study Missions Concerning International Narcotics Problems*, Select Committee on Narcotics Abuse and Control (Washington, D.C.: Government Printing Office, 1986), p. 56.

33. Roger Barrantes Campos, "Implicancias Farmacológicas en el Uso de las Hojas de Coca en el Peru," *Boletín de Lima* (Lima, Peru), vol. 34, no. 6 (July 1984): 68.

34. The U.S. Congress Select Committee on Narcotics Abuse and Control reports that 8,300,000 plants (equivalent to about 830 hectares) were destroyed in Brazil and that 114 hectares of coca were eradicated in Ecuador.

35. Coca paste, also called cocaine basic paste or cocaine sulfate, is a whitish semi-solid substance that contains cocaine sulfate acid, methanol, kerosene, alkaline compounds, sulfuric acid, and other impurities.

36. These estimates are based on my observation of three major areas in coca production in the Peruvian rain forests.

37. This estimate applies only to small-scale cocaine refining operations set near coca and coca-paste-producing sites or in other parts of the country. If cocaine is refined in large-scale processing centers where concentration of coca paste requires many days, refinement may take as long as 120 days.

38. The President's Commission on Organized Crime, *Organized Crime and Cocaine Trafficking*, Record of Hearing IV. (Washington, D.C.: Government Printing Office, November 27–29, 1984), p. 4, estimates that "drug trafficking is an $80-billion-a-year industry." The commission calculates that "over 40 metric tons [of cocaine] enter our borders every year." Taking as a base figure the average price of $100 per each gram of pure cocaine hydrochloride, the 40 metric tons of cocaine may translate into at least U.S. $40 billion, 50 percent of the estimated amounts of profit from illicit drugs.

Chapter Three

1. For an excellent historical documentation of the cultivation of coca in eastern Peru, see Daniel Gade, "Inca and colonial settlement, coca cultivation and endemic disease in the tropical forest," *Journal of Historical Geography*, 5(3), 1979: 263–79.

2. For more details of the excellent description of the botanical characteristics of coca leaf see Timothy Plowman, "Coca Chewing and the Botanical Origins of Coca (*Erythroxylum* spp.) in South America" in Pacini and Franquemont, *Coca and Cocaine in South America* (Cambridge, MA: Cultural Survival Report No. 23, 1986), pp. 5–35.

3. Margaret Towle, *The Ethnobotany of Pre-Colombian Peru* (Chicago, Ill.: Aldine Publishing, 1961), p. 58.

4. Timothy Plowman, pp. 12–21.

5. Craig Van Dyck and Robert Byck, "Cocaine," *American Scientific* 246 (1982), pp. 128–41.

6. According to the Peruvian government, legal production of coca is about

60,000 hectares. The 160,000 metric tons estimated here comes from a total production of about 100,000 hectares.

7. Mathea Falco, "The Big Business of Illicit Drugs," *New York Times Magazine*, 11 December 1983, pp. 109–12.

8. Nancy Lois Richards, "Erythroxylon Coca in the Peruvian Highlands: Practices and Beliefs," Ph.D. diss. (University of California at Irvine, 1980), pp. 40–43.

9. Literally, the term *llanqui* means "sandals." In the social and economic context, it implies the idea of "putting sandals on a relationship to secure service or a contract." Thus, they have words such as "llanquitsida" meaning "contracting process."

10. In the Andes the metric system of measurement has been adopted in almost every respect. However, measurement of coca leaves is still in ounces, pounds, and arrobas.

11. The Peruvian government estimates that there are one million coca growers cultivating 135 hectares of coca (Committee on Foreign Affairs, U.S. House of Representatives, February 22, 1985; *U.S. Narcotics Control Programs Overseas: An Assessment*, Washington, D.C.: U.S. Printing Office, 1985); see also 99th Congress, Second Session, House of Representatives, *Latin American Study Mission Concerning International Narcotics Problems* (Washington, D.C.: Government Printing Office, 1986), p. 56, and Hearing Before The Committee on Foreign Affairs House of Representatives, 99 Congress, November 12, 1985, *Development in Latin American Narcotics Control, November 1985* (U.S. Government Printing Office, Washington, D.C., 1986), p. 66.

12. 99th Congress, Second Session, House of Representatives, *Latin American Study Mission Concerning International Narcotics Problems* (Washington, D.C.: U.S. Government Printing Office, 1986), p. 47.

13. Roger Barrantes Campos, p. 68.

Chapter Four

1. In Peru, tipping (bribing) the police is a normal practice and almost institutionalized. Night highway patrols stop any commercial or passenger vehicle and, at the end of the "routine check," they ask for "something for their coffee." This is a practice not only along the roads leading toward the jungle, but throughout the country.

2. The term "Colombia" is ambiguous, for not all refining centers are in Colombia. They may be set up in bordering areas or somewhere in the Peruvian Amazon lowlands.

3. Compare this with the DEA's estimated prices for cocaine hydrochloride of $8,000 in Bolivia and of $8,000 to $10,000 in Colombia (U.S. Department of Justice, Drug Enforcement Agency, *Special Report, Worldwide Cocaine Trafficking Trends*, Washington, D.C.: DEA, 1985), p. 9.

4. Henkel (1986:8) claims that there is an established technical assistance from Colombia to Bolivian and Peruvian cocaine refiners. I have not found cases to prove this claim. What is true though is that some "colochos" who come to establish their refining centers bring their own "cook" with them. Those Peruvians who come to "Colombia" learn the trade not because they "train" but because they are exposed to actual operations.

5. I observed the loading in both instances. To confirm the traffickers' "visit" to the United States, I asked them please to call two friends collect and give them a message. The telephone bill registering the two calls with reversed charges verified their short stay in the country. In both cases, the calls were made from different area codes, not from cities they claimed to have visited.

6. Each organization has its own method of sending radio information. Some are too obvious, others impossible to intersect. My responsibility to protect my informants and observed situations prohibits my discussing details and codes of communication.

7. I observed two airfields of this type. In both cases, the settings presented the same features. During winter, the small planes also land on the dry river shores.

8. By their Spanish accents, nationality coincided with their claims. However, it was not my interest to prove their origins.

Chapter Five

1. There are no American or European cars. Heavy taxes imposed on imported cars even make some semi-compact American cars status symbols.

2. During the Inca empire, and probably during the colonial period, the *ayllu* was a community also connected by blood relations. Community, then, was a bio-social and economic entity bound together by land, tradition, and blood relations.

3. For detailed discussion of land reform in Peru see José Matos Mar and José Manuel Mejía, *La Reforma Agraria en el Peru* (Lima, Peru: IEP, 1980); C. Amat y León et al., *Realidad del Campo Peruano Despues de la Reforma Agraria* (Lima, Peru: Centro de Investigaciones y Capacitación, 1980); and Manuel Román, *De Campesino a Obrero* (Lima, Peru: Centro de Investigación de la Universidad del Pacífico, 1981).

4. For more detailed discussions see José María Caballero 1980 and Diego García Sayán 1980.

5. Peruvian *obreros* (factory and fieldworkers) are paid for Sunday (*dominical*), even though they do not work on that day. In order to get this benefit the *obrero* must work six consecutive days, that is, from Monday to Saturday.

6. For instance, one day I met a young peasant woman who was herding sheep along with her two nieces. I said (in Quechua), "Your nieces are beautiful." The peasant woman's reply was "You could have any of them if you treat us to three bottles of Coca Cola."

7. From "Diario Ojo," Lima, Peru, July 31, 1985, p. 2.

8. In Colombia, to keep the currency there, the national banks accept deposits in U.S. dollars without asking where the money comes from (Bruce Bagley, "The Colombian Connection: The Impact of Drug Traffic on Colombia," in Deborah Pacini and Christine Franquemont, eds., *Coca and Cocaine: Effects on People and Policy in Latin America* (Cambridge, MA: Cultural Survival, 1986), p. 92. For a discussion of the economic and political impact of cocaine in Bolivia, see Ray Henkel, "The Bolivian Cocaine Industry," *Studies in Third World Societies*, no. 37 (Williamsburg: College of William and Mary, 1988), pp. 53–82.

9. U.S. House of Representatives, Committee on Foreign Affairs, February 22, 1985, *U.S. Narcotics Control Programs: An Assessment* (Washington, D.C.: U.S. Government Printing Office, 1985), p. 13.

10. Yonel Ramirez and Pedro Ruiz, "El Tráfico Ilícito y el Uso Indebido de Coca y Cocaina Detectados en el Peru en 1978," in Raul Jeri, ed., *Cocaina 1980* (Lima, Peru: Pacific Press, 1980), p. 231.

11. Corporación Departamental de Desarrollo de Huánuco, Huánuco, Peru, 1985.

12. Taken from an anti-drug leaflet prepared by Corporación Departmental de Desarrollo de Huánuco, Divulgación No. 04–85, "Cupizo y el infierno blanco," Huánuco, Peru, 1985.

Chapter Six

1. Committee of Foreign Affairs, House of Representatives, February 22, 1985, *U.S. Narcotics Control Programs: An Assessment* (Washington, D.C.: U.S. Government Printing Office, 1985), p. 20.

2. This incident appeared in a newspaper ("Policias matan a cuatro narcos, les sacan visceras y fondean en el río, *La República*, 23 July 1985) almost two weeks later.

3. For instance, on August 2, 1987, during the Operation Lightning (*Operativo Relámpago*) directed by DEA advisors, a law-enforcement helicopter pilot sold a radio-cassette-recorder (National Panasonic, model RX 1270W, serial scratched) he had grabbed from a *cocalero* to a local hotel housekeeper for about $50. The excuse to take away things is lack of proof of purchase or illegal coca farming.

4. "La peste de la pasta," *Caretas* (Lima, Peru), 6 July 1978, p. 47.

5. For more details see "cocaina de alto vuelo," *Caretas* (Lima, Peru), 17 March 1980, pp. 10–14.

6. I had a chance to follow and observe this matter, for then I was a clerk at the cargo terminal of one of the carriers in question.

7. One dissatisfied passenger, who allegedly had been deceived by the trafficker, publicly declared that he had actually seen how cocaine was smuggled inside *kingkongs*, a popular Peruvian traditional pastry (*Diario La República*, 12 August 1985).

8. Edward Schumacher, "Bolivian Leaders Tied to Lucrative Cocaine Trade," *New York Times*, 31 August 1981, p. A1.

9. "Estos Son Los Socios," *Equis* (Lima, Peru), 25 June 1984, p. 5.

10. "Peru President's Niece Arrested," *New York Times,* 22 January 1978, p. 6.

11. The trafficker in question is a former television model who, according to the newspaper, is known for his drug addiction.

12. "Príncipe peruano de la cocaina deslumbró a la alta sociedad del Canadá," *Oiga* (Lima, Peru) 24 February 1986, pp. 40–43.

13. For a detailed description of the social causes for the emergence of the Shining Path see, for example, Samuel Cavero, *Un Rincón para los Muertos* (Lima, Peru: Editores Asociados, 1987) and for a description of the evolution of this movement and its political significance see David Scott Palmer, "Rebellion in Rural Peru: The Origins and Evolution of Sendero Luminoso," *Comparative Politics* 18 (2), January 1986:127–46.

14. Alan Riding, "In the Incas' Land, a War for the People's Hearts," *New York Times* 18 November 1986, p. A4.

15. Executive Intelligence Review, *Narcotráfico, S.A., La Nueva Guerra del Opio,* updated Spanish version of Dope, Inc., (Lima, Peru: Coalición Nacional Antidrogas, 1985), p. 313.

16. For a detailed discussion of the alleged "guerrilla-cocaine" alliance in Colombia see Bruce Bagley, "The Colombian Connection: The Impact of Drug Traffic on Colombia," in Deborah Pacini and Christine Franquemont, eds., *Coca and Cocaine: Effects on People and Policy in Latin America* (Cambridge, MA: Cultural Survival, 1986), p. 96.

17. Executive Intelligence Review, p. 320.

18. Mario Vargas Llosa, "Inquest in the Andes," *New York Times Magazine*, 31 July 1983, p. 56.

19. Amnesty International, *Peru* (January, 1985) lists 1,005 people who disappeared after detention by government forces between January 1983 and October 1984.

20. "La mayoría de guerrilleros urbanos son profesores," *El Comercio* (Lima, Peru), 4 April 1985, p. A–8.

21. "Peruvian Peasants Say Soldiers Killed 59," *New York Times*, 24 October 1985, p. A5.

22. Committee on Foreign Affairs, US House of Representatives, February 22, 1985, *US Narcotics Control Programs: An Assessment* (Washington, D.C.: U.S. Government Printing Office, 1985), p. 23. See also Hearing Before the Committee on Foreign Affairs, House of Representatives, November 12, 1985, *Development in Latin American Narcotics Control* (Washington, D.C.: U.S. Government Printing Office, 1985), p. 68.

23. This information was gathered in August 1987. I visited the town while I was doing a consulting trip to Peru for *National Geographic* (January 1989). For published information, see "Peru Drug Dealers Kill 6 Officers," *New York Times*, 3 June 1987, p. A11.

24. "Responso en Uchiza," *Caretas* (Lima, Peru), 27 September 1982, p. 16.

25. See for example Raul Gonzalez, "Coca y Subversion en el Alto Huallaga," *Quehacer 48* (Lima, Peru: Desco, September 1987), pp. 59–72; Abilio Arroyo, "Sendero en el Alto Huallaga: Encuentro," *Caretas* (Lima, Peru) vol. 971, September 7, 1987, pp. 31–38; and Monte Hayes, "Peruvian rebels use drug trade to finance fight against regime," *Miami Herald*, 21 December 1987, p. 8A. A third position, not publicized at all, is assaults—robberies and murders committed by common criminals and police disguised as guerrillas.

26. For details on the alleged "pact" between drug traffic and the guerrilla movements, and specifically the destruction of the Pendencia Bridge, see Abilio Arroyo, "Sendero en el Alto Huallaga: Encuentro," *Caretas* (Lima, Peru), vol. 971, September 1987, pp. 31–38.

27. Personal communication with people acting as middlemen in the sales of arms and ammunitions. A detailed description of the case would lead to the identification of confidential informants, thus exposing them to the risk of facing criminal charges.

28. "Policias y Narcotraficantes se apoderan de Tocache," *Marka* (Lima, Peru), 23 August 1979, p. 32.

29. "Bolivia Farmers Lay Siege to 245 Drug Police," *New York Times*, 11 January 1986, p. A1.

30. "Mosca Loca y el Senador," *Caretas* (Lima, Peru) 6 Octubre 1980, pp. 20–25.

31. Reliable political experts give the assurance that as many as one-third of the crowd may have left immediately after his short, politically harmful statement.

32. When the cocaine complex was raided, I was in the area getting information on the refining process from an independent entrepreneur.

33. "Hay que parar la erradicación indiscriminada de la coca," *Pura Selva* (Tingo María, Peru), June 1985, pp. 8–10.

34. Esther B. Fein, "Bolivia Offers Plan on Drugs," *New York Times*, 9 October 1985, p. A14.

35. Proyecto Especial Alto Huallaga, Convenio de Proyecto entre el Peru y los Estados Unidos de América para Desarrollo Regional del Alto Huallaga, September 15, 1981, p. 3.

36. Convenio de Proyecto entre el Peru y los Estados Unidos de América para el Desarrollo Regional del Alto Huallaga: 1, section 2.1.

37. Peru, AID-Proyecto Especial del Alto Huallaga, Aucayacu, personal communication, July 1985.

38. Peru, CORAH headquarters, Tingo María, personal communication, July 1985.

39. I had made arrangements with CORAH officers to photograph the pulling operation, but after this incident CORAH suspended its activities for three weeks. The victim was a migrant worker. His body was transported to his hometown.

40. Peru, U.S. Embassy, International Narcotics Matters Office, personal communication, August 1985.

41. U.S. House of Representatives, Committee on Foreign Affairs, February 22, 1985, *U.S. Narcotics Control Programs Overseas: An Assessment*, (Washington, D.C.: US Government Printing Office, 1985), p. 12.

Chapter Seven

1. Manco Capac, founder of the Inca Empire (*Tahuantinsuyo*), reigned in Cuzco circa 1200 A.D. (Federico Kauffman-Doig, *Los Incas y el Tahuantinsuyo*, [Lima, Peru: Instituto de Estudios Peruanos, 1963], p. 9).

2. An example of Spanish assimilation to the Indian culture and society is

the Morochucos Indians of Ayacucho, whose ancestors were Spanish soldiers and whose families, after their defeat in the civil war between the rebel conquerors and the army representing the Spanish crown, fled to the Pampas of Ayacucho and thus became Morochuco Indian communities without descending from Indian blood.

3. See Pablo José Arriaga, *The Extirpation of Idolatry in Peru,* translated by L. Clark Keating (Kentucky: University of Kentucky Press, 1968), p. 43.

4. The *diezmo* (one-tenth of the Indian's crop) and *primicia* (the first fruits of land) were taxes imposed on the Indian population to support local clergies. This same taxing method is being used now by the new emerging religious sects.

5. For instance, 32 percent of the peasants from a community that sustains constant economic exchange with cocaine-producing populations have more land than the minimum established by law, while 57 percent are below the theoretical minimum size.

6. See House of Representatives, Hearing Before the Committee on Foreign Affairs, November 12, 1985, *Development in Latin American Narcotics Control* (Washington, D.C.: U.S. Government Printing Office, 1986), p. 68.

7. James A. Inciardi, *The War on Drugs* (Palo Alto, CA: Mayfield Publishing Company, 1986), p. 183.

8. Inciardi (p. 183) gives the impression that Tingo María is a town full of imported cars. He writes, "When a vehicle breaks down it is simply abandoned in the jungle and replaced with a new one."

9. On some occasions when the bosses take long business trips to "Colombia," Bolivia, or the United States, coca planters have been affected by the eradication squads.

10. PEAH also paid for the paint of the main building of the *Universidad Nacional Agraria de la Selva.*

11. Barbara d'Achille, "Selva Alta: Problemas y soluciones," *El Comercio* (Lima, Peru), 12 July 1986, p. 24.

12. Richard T. Pienciak, "Tracking the 'sacred leaf,'" *Daily News,* 15 December 1986, p. 5.14.6.

13. Bruce Bagley, "The Colombian Connection: The Impact of Drug Traffic on Colombia," in Deborah Pacini and Christine Franquemont, eds., *Coca and Cocaine. Effect on People and Policy in Latin America* (Cambridge, MA.: Cultural Survival, 1986), p. 99.

14. Myron S. Waldman, "Reagan Orders Testing, Urges $894M Drug Plan," *Newsday* (New York), 16 September, 1986, p. 4.

15. Bernard Weinraub, "Reagan Call for Cut in Drug Fight Ignites the Anger of Both Parties," *New York Times*, 8 January 1987, p. A1.

16. William Stockton, "New Envoy to Push U.S. Role in Mexico Drug Fight," *New York Times*, 26 January 1987, p. A15.

17. The CORAH officers in Tingo María provided information only on the total eradication. They were reluctant to give details on how much legal and illicit coca had been destroyed.

18. Richard M. Firestone, "An Even Simpler Way To Fight Drugs," *New York Times*, 18 September 1986, p. A30. Although Mr. Firestone's prices and estimations are wrong, his American pragmatic idea is shared by some Latin American politicians.

19. For instance, the power of the tobacco industry in American politics may be reflected in the fact that the American Bar Association rejected the proposal that it join efforts to seek Federal laws barring all advertising of tobacco products (E.R. Shipp, "A.B.A. Rejects Plan on Tobacco Ad Ban," *New York Times*, 17 February 1987, p. A14).

20. Coca-leaf tea exported by the Empresa Nacional de la Coca, a Peruvian agency, is already sold in some stores in the United States (Ronald K. Siegel, "Cocaine in Herbal Tea," *Journal of American Medical Association*, 255 [1], 1986:40).

21. Myron S. Waldman, "Reagan Orders Testing, Urges $894M Drug Plan," *Newsday* (New York), 16 September 1986, p. 4.

22. Often, when Americans come back from other countries they say, "Finally, we are back to civilization," an ethnocentric conception of the world.

23. Alan Riding, "Colombia Wages a Cooler Peace Effort on Rebels," *New York Times*, 26 January 1987, p. A14.

24. Lester B. Pearson, *The Crisis of Development* (New York: Praeger Publishers, 1970), p. 49.

Appendix

1. Here "participation" does not suggest actual involvement in the manufacture and trafficking of cocaine. It means an active socialization with subjects whose livelihoods were tied directly to some of the facets of the coca and cocaine industry.

2. Michael Quinn Patton, *Qualitative Evaluation Methods* (Beverly Hills: Sage Publications, 1980), p. 170.

3. See Jack D. Douglas, *Investigative Social Research* (Beverly Hills: Sage

Publications, 1976), p. 169, and Patricia Adler, *Wheeling and Dealing* (New York: Columbia University Press, 1985), p. 17.

4. To cite two examples, one of my graduate school friends, a European, earned his Ph.D. as an illegal alien. Another, an anthropologist, received his Ph.D. from a major private school and was hired for a tenure-track teaching position in a New York college.

5. See also Gideon Sjoberg and Roger Nett, *A Methodology for Social Research* (New York: Harper & Row Publishers, 1968), p. 177.

6. See Michael Quinn Patton, p. 107.

7. Jack D. Douglas, p. 1.

Bibliography

Adler, Patricia A. *Wheeling and Dealing*. New York: Columbia University Press, 1985.

Agar, Michael H. *Speaking of Ethnography*. Beverly Hills, CA: Sage Publications, 1986.

Agarwala, A., and S. P. Singh. *The Economics of Underdevelopment*. New York: Oxford University Press, 1964.

Alberti, Giorgio, and Enrique Mayer, eds. *Reciprocidad e intercambio en los Andes peruanos*. Lima, Peru: Instituto de Estudios Peruanos (IEP), 1974.

Alegría, Ciro. *La Serpiente de Oro*. Lima, Peru: Editorial Universo, 1967.

Alexander, Herbert E., and Gerald E. Caiden. *The Politics and Economics of Organized Crime*. Lexington, Mass.: Lexington Books, 1986.

Allen, Catherine J. "To be Quechua: the symbolism of coca chewing in highland Peru." *American Ethnologist* 8 (1981): 157–68.

———. "Coca and Cultural Identity in Andean Communities." In Deborah Pacini and Christine Franquemont, eds. *Coca and Cocaine: Effects on People and Policy in Latin America*. Cambridge, Mass.: Cultural Survival, 1986.

Alvarado, Antonio. "Diagnóstico Socio-Económico del Cultivo y la Comercialización de la Coca en la Provincia de Leoncio Prado, Huánuco." B.A. thesis, Universidad Nacional Agraria de la Selva, Tingo María, Peru, 1974.

Ander-Egg, Ezequiel. *Introducción a las Técnicas de Investigación Social*. Buenos Aires, [Argentina]: Editorial Humanitas, 1978.

Andrews, George, and David Solomon, eds. *The Coca Leaf and Cocaine Papers*. New York: Harcourt Brace Jovanovich, 1975.

Aramburú, Carlos E. "Expansion of the Agrarian and Demographic Frontier in the Peruvian Selva." In Marianne Schmink and Charles H. Wood, eds. *Frontier Expansion in Amazonia*. Gainesville: University of Florida Press, 1984, pp. 153–79.

"Archivos de las Comunidades Campesinas del Departamento de Ancash." Oficina de Reforma Agraria y Asentamiento Rural. Huaraz, Peru.

Arguedas, José María. *Formación de una Cultura Nacional Indoamericana.* Mexico: Siglo Veintiuno Editores, 1981.

Arriaga, Pablo José. *The Extirpation of Idolatry in Peru.* Translated by Keating, L. Clark. Kentucky: University of Kentucky Press, 1968.

Arroyo, Abilio. "Sendero en el Alto Huallaga: Encuentro." *Caretas* (Lima, Peru), 971, September 7, 1987, pp. 30–38.

Bagley, Bruce. "The Colombian Connection: The Impact of Drug Traffic on Colombia." In Deborah Pacini and Christine Franquemont, eds. *Coca and Cocaine: Effects on People and Policy in Latin America.* Cambridge, MA: Cultural Survival, 1986.

Barrantes Campos, Roger. "Implicaciones Farmacológicas en el Uso de las Hojas de Coca en el Peru." *Boletín de Lima*, vol. 34, no. 6 (July 1984): 67–72.

Belaúnde Terry, Fernando. *Peru's Own Conquest.* Lima, Peru: American Studies Press, 1965.

Bennett, Wendell. *Andean Culture History.* New York: Handbook Series No. 15, 1949.

"Bolivia Farmers Lay Siege to 245 Drug Police." *New York Times*, 11 January 1986, p. 1.

Bolton, Ralph. "Andean Coca Chewing: A Metabolic Perspective." *American Anthropologist*, vol. 78, no. 3 (September 1976): 630–33.

———. "On Coca Chewing and High-Altitude Stress." *Current Anthropology*, vol. 20, no. 2 (June 1979): 418–30.

———. "Guinea Pigs, Protein, and Ritual." *Ethnology*, vol. 18, no. 3 (July 1979): 229–52.

Bonfil, Guillermo. *Campesinado e Indigenismo en Latinoamérica.* Lima, Peru: Centro Latinoamericano de Trabajo Social, 1978.

Bonilla, F. *Estatuto de Comunidades Campesinas.* Lima, Peru: Editorial Mercurio, 1974.

Brecher, Edward M. *Licit and Illicit Drugs.* Boston: Little, Brown & Co., 1972.

Brinkley, Joel. "4-Year Fight in Florida Just Cannot Stop Drugs." *New York Times*, 4 September 1986, p. A-1.

Buitrón, Aníbal. *Como Llegó el Progreso a Huagrapampa.* Mexico: Instituto Indigenista Interamericano, 1966.

Burchard, Roderick E. "Coca y trueque de alimentos." In Giorgio Alberti and Enrique Mayer, eds., *Reciprocidad e intercambio en los Andes peruanos.* Lima, Peru: Instituto de Estudios Peruanos, 1974, p. 209–51.

Caballero, José María. *Agricultura, Reforma Agraria y Pobreza Campesina*. Lima, Peru: IEP, 1980.

———. *Economía Agraria de la Sierra Peruana*. Lima, Peru: IEP, 1981.

Cagliotti, Carlos Norberto. "La economía de la coca en Bolivia." *Revista de la Sanidad de las Fuerzas Policiales*, vol. 42, no. 2 (1981):161–65.

"Caso Coca." *Caretas* (Lima, Peru), 863, August 12, 1985, pp. 10–18.

Castro Morales, Jorge. "Farmacodependencia en el Peru." *Psicoactiva*. Lima, Peru: Centro de Información para la Prevención del Abuso de Drogas, vol. 1, no. 1, 1987, pp. 15–53.

Castro Pozo, Hildebrando. *Nuestra Comunidad Indígena*. Lima, Peru: Perugraph Editores, 1979.

Cavero G., Samuel. *Un Rincón para los Muertos*. Lima, Peru: Editores Associados, 1987.

Christian, Shirley. "Bolivia is Hoping U.S. Drug Forces Will Extend Stay." *New York Times*, 22 August 1986, p. B4.

Cieza de León, Pedro. *The Incas*. Norman, Okla.: University of Oklahoma Press, 1959.

Collier, John, Jr. *Visual Anthropology: Photography as a Research Method*. New York: Holt, Rinehart & Winston, 1967.

"Cupizo y el Infierno Blanco." Corporación Departamental de Desarrollo de Huánuco. Huánuco, Peru, 1985.

Cussianovich, Alejandro. *Amazonía, Un Paraíso Imaginario*. Lima, Peru: Instituto de Publicaciones Educación y Comunicación, 1985.

D'Achille, Barbara. "Selva Alta: Problemas y soluciones." *El Comercio* (Lima, Peru), 12 July 1986, p. 24.

de Castro, Josué. *The Geography of Hunger*. Boston: Little, Brown & Co., 1952.

de las Casas, Bartolomé. *Tratados*. Mexico: Fondo de Cultura Económica, 1974.

Demic, Zorca. "Revisión, Crítica Bibliográfica y Consideraciones Generales Acerca del Masticado de Coca." In Raul Jeri, ed. *Cocaina 1980*. Lima, Peru: Pacific Press, 1980, pp. 201–05.

de Soto, Hernando. *El Otro Sendero*. Lima, Peru: Instituto Libertad y Democracia, 1987.

Deustua, Alejandro. *El Narcotráfico y el Interés Nacional*. Lima, Peru: Centro Peruano de Estudios Internacionales, 1987.

Dobkin de Rios, Marlene. *Hallucinogens: Cross-Cultural Perspectives*. Albuquerque: University of New Mexico Press, 1984.

Douglas, Jack. *Investigative Social Research*. Beverly Hills, CA: Sage Publications, 1976.

———. *Creative Interviewing*. Beverly Hills, CA: Sage Publications, 1985.

Echevarría, Máximo. "Dominación y Diferenciación Campesina en la Comunidad de Astobamba (Cajatambo)." Unpublished B.A. thesis, Universidad Nacional Mayor de San Marcos, Lima, Peru, 1975.

"Estos Son Los Socios." *Equis* (Lima, Peru), 25 June 1984, p. 5.

Executive Intelligence Review. *Narcotráfico, S.A. La Nueva Guerra del Opio.* Lima, Peru: Coalición Nacional Antidrogas, 1985.

Falco, Mathea. "The Big Business of Illicit Drugs." *New York Times Magazine,* 11 December 1983, pp. 109–12.

Fein, Esther B. "Bolivia Offers Plan on Drugs." *New York Times,* 9 October 1985, p. A14.

Firestone, Richard M. "An Even Simpler Way To Fight Drugs." *New York Times,* 18 September 1986, p. A30.

Flores, Cleber. "Problemática del Colono Inmigrante y su Adaptación a la Zona del Alto Huallaga." Unpublished paper, Lima, Peru, 1985.

Frank, Andre Gunder. *Lumpen-Bourgeoisie Lumpen-Development.* New York: Monthly Review, 1974.

Franklin Pease, G.Y. *Del Tawantinsuyo a la Historia del Peru.* Lima, Peru: IEP, 1978.

Fuchs, Andrew. "Coca Chewing and High-Altitude Stress: Possible Effects of Coca Alkaloids on Erythropoiesis." *Current Anthropology,* vol. 19, no. 2 (June 1978): 277–91.

Gade, Daniel. *Plants, Man and the Land in the Vilcanota Valley of Peru.* The Hague: Junk, 1975.

———. "Inca and colonial settlement, coca cultivation and endemic disease in the tropical forest." *Journal of Historical Geography,* vol. 5, no. 3 (1979): 263–79.

García, Diego. *Estado y Política Agraria.* Lima, Peru: Desco, 1980.

Garcilaso de la Vega. *Comentarios Reales de los Incas.* México: Editorial José M. Cajica, n.d.

———. *Comentarios Reales de los Incas.* Puebla, Mexico: Publicaciones de la Universidad de Puebla, 1953.

Gheerbrant. *The Incas: The Royal Commentaries of Garcilaso de la Vega 1539–1616.* New York: The Orion Press, 1961.

Gillespie-Woltemade, Nellice. "Issues in Teaching Visual Sociology: Power, Politics, and Photography." *International Journal of Visual Sociology* 1 (1985): 23–29.

Gonzales, Raúl. "Sendero Vs. MRTA: La Pelea por Lima." *Quehacer* 46 (Lima, Peru: Desco, 1987): 47–55.

Gorriti, Gustavo. "Responso en Uchiza." *Caretas* 716, 27 September 1982, p. 16–20.

Gott, Richard. *Guerrilla Movements in Latin America*. London: Thomas Nelson and Sons, 1970.

Guevara, Luis A. *Granjas Comunales Indígenas*. Lima, Peru: n.d.

"Hacen análisis sobre migración a la Selva Alta." *El Comercio* 16 (June 1985): 12.

Hanke, Lewis. *Aristotle and the American Indians: A Study in Race Prejudism in the Modern World*. London: Hollis and Carter, 1959.

Hanna, Joel. "Coca Leaf Use in Southern Peru: Some Biosocial Aspects." *American Anthropologist*, vol. 76, no. 2 (June 1974): 282–96.

"Hay que parar la erradicación indiscriminada de la coca." *Pura Selva* (Tingo María, Peru), June 1985, p. 9.

Henkel, Ray. "Regional Analysis of the Latin American Cocaine Industry." Paper presented at the Conference of Applied Geographers, West Point, New York, October 1986.

Henman, Anthony. *Mama Coca*. Bogota, Colombia: El Anacora Editores, 1981.

Herbert, David L., and Howard Tritt. *Corporations of Corruption*. Springfield, Ill.: Charles C. Thomas, 1984.

Hirshchman, Albert. *The Strategy of Economic Development*. New Haven: Yale University Press, 1961.

Hopkins, Raul. *Desarrollo Desigual y Crisis en la Agricultura Peruana 1944–1969*. Lima, Peru: IEP, 1981.

Howard, Mary D. "Jacob A. Riis and Lewis W. Hine: Art Imitates Life." *International Journal of Visual Sociology* 2 (1985): 21–34.

Iguinez, Javier. *La cuestión rural en el Peru*. Lima, Peru: Pontificia Universidad Catolica del Peru, 1986.

Inciardi, James A. *The War on Drugs*. Palo Alto, CA: Mayfield Publishing Company, 1986.

Instituto Indigenista Interamericano. *América Indígena*, vol. 38, no. 4, October-December, 1978, Mexico.

Instituto Nacional de Estadística (INE). *Censos Nacionales VIII de Población III de Vivienda*. Lima, Peru: INE, 1981.

Instituto Nacional de Estadística (INE). *Censos Nacionales VIII de Población III de Vivienda*. Lima, Peru: INE, 1984.

Isbell, Billie Jean. "Parentesco Andino y Reciprocidad Kuyaq: Los Que Nos Aman," in *Reciprocidad e intercambio en los Andes peruanos*. Giorgio Alberti and Enrique Mayer, eds. Lima, Peru: IEP, 1984.

Jeri, Raul F. "The Syndrome of Coca Paste." *Journal of Psychedelic Drugs*, vol. 10, no. 4, Oct.–Dec., 1978: 361–70.

————. "Coca-paste smoking in some Latin American countries: a severe and unabated form of addiction." *Bulletin on Narcotics*, vol. 36, no. 2 (1984).

Johnson, Bruce D. *Taking Care of Business*. Lexington, Mass.: Lexington Books, 1985.

Karsten, Rafael. *A Totalitarian State of the Past: The Civilization of the Inca Empire in Ancient Peru*. Helsinki: Helsingsfors, 1973.

Kaufman Doig, Federico. *Los Incas y el Tahuantinsuyo*. Lima, Peru: Peruanística, 1973.

Khan, Qaiser M. "Poverty and Household Responses in Rural Bangladesh." *Studies in Third World Societies*, Number 29, September 1984.

Kubler, George. *The Indian Caste of Peru, 1795–1940*. Washington, D.C.: U.S. Government Printing Office, 1950.

"La peste de la pasta." *Caretas* (542), July 1978, p. 47.

Lanning, Edward P. *Peru Before the Incas*. Englewood Cliffs, N.J.: Prentice-Hall, 1967.

Lazarsfeld, Paul F., and Morris Rosenberg. *The Language of Social Research*. New York: The Free Press, 1955.

Leary, Timothy, Ralph Metzner, and Richard Alpert. *The Psychedelic Experience*. Secaucus, N.J.: The Citadel Press, 1983.

Leung, Woot-Tsuen Wu. *Food Composition Table for Use in Latin America*. Washington, D.C.: U.S. Interdepartmental Committee on Nutrition and National Defense, 1961.

Lobo, Susan. *A House of My Own*. Tucson: The University of Arizona Press, 1982.

Lockhart, James. *Spanish Peru 1532–1560, A Colonial Society*. Madison, Wisc.: University of Wisconsin Press, 1968.

————. *The Men of Cajamarca. A Social and Biographical Study of the First Conquerors of Peru*. Austin: University of Texas Press, 1972.

Lumbreras, Luis. *Arqueología de la América Andina*. Lima, Peru: Editorial Milla Batres, 1981.

Lund, Alan Mark. "Identifying, Developing, and Adopting Technologies Appropriate for Rural Development with Applications to Huari Province in Peru." Unpublished Ph.D. dissertation, Iowa State University, 1975.

McClintock, Cynthia. *Peasant Cooperatives and Political Change in Peru*. Princeton: Princeton University Press, 1981.

Machado, Edgardo. "Determinación de Variedades y Cultivares en Cocas Peruanas." In F.R. Jeri, ed. *Cocaina 1980*. Lima, Peru: Pacific Press, 1980, pp. 275–81.

Malpica, Carlos. *El Mito de la Ayuda Externa*. Lima, Peru: Francisco Moncloa Editores, 1970.

Mariategui, José Carlos. *Siete Ensayos de Interpretación de la Realidad Peruana*. Santiago de Chile: Editorial Universitaria, 1955.

Marquez Zorrilla, Santiago. *Huari y Conchucos, Monografía*. Lima, Peru: Imprenta El Cóndor, 1965.

Marzal, Manuel. *Historia de la Antropología Indigenista: México y Peru*. Lima, Peru: Pontificia Universidad Católica del Peru, 1981.

"Mas Sangre Ofrece Sendero." *Caretas* (Lima, Peru), 837, Febrero 11, 1985, pp. 22–24.

Mason, Alden. *The Ancient Civilizations of Peru*. Switzerland: Plata Publishing, 1975.

Matos Mar, José. *Yanaconaje y Reforma Agraria en la Peru*. Lima, Peru: IEP, 1976.

Matos Mar, José, and José M. Mejía. *Reforma Agraria: Logros y Contradicciones 1969–1979*. Lima, Peru: IEP, 1978.

———. *La Reforma Agraria en el Peru*. Lima, Peru: IEP, 1980.

May, Clifford D. "U.S. Secretly Grows Coca to Find Way to Destroy Cocaine's Source." *New York Times*, 12 June 1988, p. A1.

"Mayoría de guerrilleros urbanos son profesores." *El Comercio*, 4 April 1985, p. A8.

Miller, Solomon, Charles Erasmus, and Louis Faron. *Contemporary Change in Traditional Communities of Mexico and Peru*. Urbana, Ill.: University of Illinois Press, 1978.

Ministerio de Guerra de Peru. *Catálogo de Nombres Geográficos del Peru*. Lima, Peru: Instituto Geográfico Militar, 1979.

"Monstruosa macrocefalia es la ciudad de Lima." *El Comercio* (Lima, Peru), 3 July 1984, p. A8.

Morales, Edmundo. "Coca and Cocaine Economy and Social Change in the Andes of Peru." *Economic Development and Cultural Change*, vol. 35, no. 1 (Fall 1986): 143–61.

———. "Coca Culture. The White Cities of Peru." Thesis, *CUNY Graduate School Magazine*, vol. 1 (1), Fall 1986: 4–11.

———. "Land Reform, Social Change, and Modernization in the National Periphery: A Study of Five Villages in the Northeastern Andes of Peru." Dissertation. New York: City University of New York, 1983.

Morner, Magnus. *Race Mixture in the History of Latin America*. Boston: Little, Brown & Co., 1967.

"Mosca Loca y el Senador." *Caretas* (Lima, Peru), 618, 1980, pp. 20–25.

Murra, John. *The Economic Organization of the Inca State.* Greenwich, Conn.: Jai Press, 1980.

Musto, David M. *The American Disease.* New York: Oxford University Press, 1987.

Nicholl, Charles. *The Fruit Palace.* New York: St. Martin's Press, 1986.

"Ofensiva de Sendero." *Equis* (Lima, Peru) 306, June 26, 1984, p. 13.

"Las Palmas del Espino." *Pura Selva* (Tingo María, Peru), June 1985, p. 29.

Palmer, David Scott. "Rebellion in Rural Peru: The Origins and Evolution of Sendero Luminoso." *Comparative Politics,* vol. 18, no. 2 (January 1986): 127–46.

Parker, Gary, and Amancio Chavez. *Diccionario Quechua Ancash-Huailas.* Lima, Peru: IEP, 1976.

Patton, Michael Quinn. *Qualitative Evaluation Methods.* Beverly Hills: Sage Publications, 1980.

Pearson, Lester B. *The Crisis of Development.* New York: Praeger Publishers, 1970.

Pease, Henry, Diego García-Sayán, Fernando Eguren Lopez, and Marcial Rubio Correa. *Estado y Política Agraria.* Lima, Peru: Desco, 1977.

"Peru President's Niece Arrested." *New York Times,* 22 January 1978, p. 6.

"Peruvian Peasants Say Soldiers Killed 59." *New York Times,* 24 October 1985, p. A5.

"La Peste de la pasta." *Caretas* (Lima, Peru), 6 July, 1978, p. 47.

Petras, James, and Robert LaPorte, Jr. *Cultivating Revolution.* New York: Random House, 1971.

Pienciak, Richard T. "Tracking the sacred leaf." *Daily News,* 15 December 1986, p.6.

Plowman, Timothy. "Aspectos Botánicos de la Coca." In F.R. Jeri, ed. *Cocaina 1980.* Lima, Peru: Pacific Press, 1980, pp. 100–117.

———. "Coca Chewing and the Botanical Origins of Coca *(Erythroxylum spp.)* in South America." In Deborah Pacini and Christine Franquemont, eds. *Coca and Cocaine: Effects on People and Policy in Latin America.* Cambridge, MA.: Cultural Survival, 1986, pp. 5–33.

"Policias matan a cuatro narcos, les sacan vísceras y fondean en el río." *La República,* 23 July 1985, p. 5.

"Policias y Narcotraficantes se apoderan de Tocache." *Marka* (Lima, Peru), 23 August 1979, pp. 32–33.

Pompa, Gerónimo. *Medicamentos Indígenas.* Panama: Editorial América, 1980.

Portugal Vizcarra, José. *Crísis y Política Agraria en el Peru, Problema y Solución.* Lima, Peru: Consultora de Proyectos Agro-Industriales, 1981.

"Prensa y drogas." *Caretas* (Lima, Peru), 771, October 23, 1983, pp. 15–16.

The President's Commission on Organized Crime. *Organized Crime and Cocaine Trafficking*. Washington, D.C.: U.S. Government Printing Office, 1984.

"Príncipe peruano de la cocaina deslumbró a la alta sociedad del Canadá." *Oiga* (Lima, Peru) 24 February 1986, p. 40.

Punch, Maurice. *The Politics and Ethics of Fieldwork*. Beverly Hills, CA.: Sage Publications, 1986.

Quijano, Aníbal. *Problema Agrario y Movimientos Campesinos*. Lima, Peru: Mosca Azul, 1979.

Ramírez, Yonel, and Pedro Ruiz. "El Tráfico Ilícito y el Uso Indebido de Coca y Cocaina Detectados en el Peru en 1978." In F.R. Jeri, ed. *Cocaina 1980*. Lima, Peru: Pacific Press, 1980, pp. 228–33.

Richards, Nancy Lois. "Erythroxylon Coca in the Peruvian Highlands: Practices and Beliefs." Ph.D. diss., University of California at Irvine, 1980.

Riding, Alan. "In the Incas' Land: A War for the People's Hearts." *New York Times*, 18 November 1986, p. A4.

Roel, Virgilio. *Historia Social y Económica de la Colonia*. Lima, Peru: Editorial Grafica Labor, 1970.

Salazar Pereira, Alvaro. "Situación Actual de los Proyectos Especiales de Selva." In Centro de Investigación y Promoción Amazónica (CIPA) and Concejo Nacional de Población (CNP) *Población y Colonización en la Amazonía Peruana*. Lima, Peru: CIPA and CNP, 1984, pp. 245–74.

Schneider, Peter, Jane Schneider, and Edward Hansen. "Modernization and Development: The Role of Regional Elites and Noncorporate Groups in an European Mediterranean." *Comparative Studies in Society and History*, vol. 14, no. 3 (June 1972): 328–50.

Schumacher, E. F. *Small is Beautiful*. New York: Harper & Row Publishers, 1973.

Schumacher, Edward. "Bolivian Leaders Tied to Lucrative Cocaine Trade." *New York Times*, 31 August 1981, p. A1.

Select Committee on Narcotics Abuse Control. *Latin American Study Mission Concerning International Narcotics Problem*. Washington, D.C.: U.S. Government Printing Office, 1986.

Shields, James. *La Educación en el Desarrollo de la Comunidad*. Buenos Aires: Editorial Paidos, 1967.

Shoemaker, Robin. *The Peasants of El Dorado*. Ithaca, New York: Cornell University Press, 1981.

Siegel, Ronald K. "Cocaine in Herbal Tea." *Journal of American Medical Association*, vol. 255, no. 1 (Jan. 3, 1986): 40.

Sigmund, Paul E., ed. *Models of Political Changes in Latin America.* New York: Praeger Publishers, 1970.

"Sigue el Carnaval de la Policía." *Oiga* (Lima, Peru), 268, February 24, 1986, pp. 11–12.

Silva Sarnaque, Alfonso, and Esterlinda Pardavé Trujillo. *Legislación del Tráfico Ilícito de Drogas.* Lima, Peru: Ediciones Achky, 1981.

Sjoberg, Gideon, and Roger Nett. *A Methodology for Social Research.* New York: Harper & Row Publishers, 1968.

Smart, Richard. *The Snow Papers.* New York: Atlantic Monthly Review, 1985.

Stein, William. *Hualcán: Life in Highland Peru.* Ithaca: Cornell University Press, 1961.

Stocks, Anthony. "Indian Policy in Eastern Peru." In Marianne Schmink and Charles H. Wood, eds. *Frontier Expansion in Amazonia.* Gainesville: University of Florida Press, 1984, pp. 33–61.

Stockton, William. "New Envoy to Push U.S. Role in Mexico Drug Fight." *New York Times,* 26 January 1987, p. A15.

Stonequist, Everett V. *The Marginal Man: A Study of Personality and Culture Conflict.* New York: Russell and Russell, 1961.

Taswell, Ruth. "Marijuana/Hashish." *Cultural Survival,* vol. 9, no. 4 (1985): 7–11.

Taxa Cuadros, Manuel. *Cocaina y Narcotráfico.* Lima, Peru: Ediciones Diselpesa, 1987.

Terán, Mario, and Armando Sandagorda. "La Producción de Coca in Bolivia." In F.R. Jeri, ed. *Cocaina 1980.* Lima, Peru: Pacific Press, 1980, pp. 196–200.

Towle, Margaret. *The Ethnobotany of Pre-Columbian Peru.* Chicago, Ill.: Aldine Publishing, 1961.

Trebach, Arnold S. *The Great Drug War.* New York: Macmillan Publishing Co., 1987.

U.S. Drug Enforcement Agency (DEA). *Drug Enforcement.* Washington, D.C., vol. 12, no. 1 (Summer 1985).

U.S. House of Representatives, Committee on Foreign Affairs. *Narcotics Control Programs: An Assessment.* Washington, D.C.: U.S. Government Printing Office, February 22, 1985.

U.S. House of Representatives, Select Committee on Narcotics Abuse and Control. *Latin American Study Missions Concerning Narcotics Problems* (August 3–19, 1985). Washington, D.C.: U.S. Government Printing Office, 1986.

U.S. Senate, Subcommittee on Alcoholism and Drug Abuse, Committee on Labor and Human Resources. *Drugs and Terrorism 1984.* Washington, D.C.: U.S. Government Printing Office, 1984.

Valdivia Ponce, Oscar. *Hampicamayoc: Medicina Folklórica y su Substrato Aborigen en el Peru.* Lima, Peru: Universidad Nacional Mayor de San Marcos, 1975.

Valencia, Enrique. *Campesinado e Indigenismo en América Latina.* Lima, Peru: CELATS, 1978.

Van Dyck, Craig, and Robert Byck. "Cocaine." *Scientific American,* 246 (1982): 128–41.

Vargas-Llosa, Mario. "Inquest in the Andes." *New York Times Magazine,* 31 July 1983, p. 18.

Vickers, William T. "Indian Policy in Amazonian Ecuador." In Schmink, Marianne, and Charles H. Wood, eds. *Frontier Expansion in Amazonia.* Gainesville: University of Florida Press, 1984, pp. 8–32.

Waldman, Myron S. "Reagan Orders Testing, Urges $894M Drug Plan." *Newsday,* 16 September 1986, p. 4.

Warner, Roger. *Invisible Hand: The Marijuana Business.* New York: Beechtree Books, 1986.

Weil, Andrew. "Observations on Consciousness Alteration." *Journal of Psychedelic Drugs,* vol. 9, no. 1 (Jan.–Mar. 1977): 75–78.

Weinraub, Bernard. "Reagan Call for Cut in Drug Fight Ignites the Anger of Both Parties." *New York Times,* 8 January 1987, p. A1.

Whyte, William F. *Learning from the Field.* Beverly Hills: Sage Publications, 1985.

Whyte, William, and Allan Holmberg. "From Paternalism to Democracy: The Cornell-Peru Project." *Human Organization,* vol. 15, no. 3 (Fall 1956): 15–20.

Wolf, Eric R. *Peasants.* Englewood Cliffs, N.J.: Prentice-Hall, 1966.

———. *Peasant Wars of the Twentieth Century.* New York: Harper & Row Publishers, 1968.

"¿Y la Coca?" *Caretas* (Lima, Peru), 971, September 7, 1987, pp. 39–40.

Zimmermann Zavala, Augusto. *El Plan Inca. Objetivo: Revolución Peruana.* Lima, Peru: Editorial del Diario Oficial "El Peruano," n.d.

Index

Silver, 25, 48
Sinchis, xix, 122, 123
Singer sewing machine, 38–39
Sirvinacuy, 39
Sistema Nacional de Cooperación Popular
   (SNCP), 45
Slang words, 143
Slash and burn, 52
Slavery, 30
Slums, 83
"Smelling" money, 123
Smoking galleries, 83
Smuggling, 48, 61, 91, 100, 125; chemicals,
   69, 70; coca paste, 82–83; illegal aliens,
   130, 132; methods for, 67, 130, 132
Snake, 27
"Snowball" prostitution, 106
Social bonds, 77
Social control, 122, 140
Social effects of cocaine economy, 93, 98,
   103–8, 119–20, 162. *See also* Addiction to
   coca paste
Sodium carbonate, 68–69, 70–71, 76, 77,
   92
Soplones, 140
Soviet Union, 166
Spanish assimilation, 203n. 2
Spanish in Peru, xvii, 1–2, 25, 160. *See also*
   Colonial period; Inca empire
Spontaneous migration, 34
Sports, 103–4
Steered migration, 34
Stereo components, 100
Strikes, 145, 146
Students, 91, 126, 136
"Stuff," 79, 82, 84
Subtenant, 5–6, 192n. 10
Sugar, 38
Sulfuric acid, 68–69, 70, 71, 75, 76, 77, 92
Supply and demand, 38, 61–62, 80, 81, 167,
   168
Survival vs. subsistence, 122–26

Tahuantinsuyo (Peru of Incas), 2, 4
Tangana, 113
Tangay, 113
Tar, 76, 80

Tax collectors, 58, 59
Taxes, 18–19, 27, 116; from coca trade, 47,
   58, 59
Tea, 38, 57
Teachers, 91, 126, 135, 136
Technology, 12, 39
Telecommunication system, 100
Television sets, 100
Terrorism, 122, 166, 133–34, 138–39
Theft, 46, 118
Tingo María, xvii, 95–101, 103
Tinlado, 53
Tipleo, 54
Tobacco, 38, 147
Toril, 18
Torture, 138, 140, 146
Trabajo-alimento, 11
Trading, 82, 115–16
Trading goods, 60
Traditional communities, 2, 3–4
Traitors, 90, 140, 164
Transplanting, 52, 53–54
Transportation, 45, 171; in cocaine indus-
   try, 69–70, 81–82, 87, 88–89; infrastruc-
   ture, 37, 97, 154
Truck drivers, 91
Trudeau, Pierre, 133
Trujillo coca. *See* Erythroxylon Truxillense
Tullpa, 43
Turkey (bird), 64
"Two-footed jackasses," 83

UMOPAR (Unidad Movil de Patrullaje Rural), xxi, 122, 124; abuses by, 145, 146;
   role of, 155, 156, 169
Ucayli department, 32
Uman caldo, 9
Underground cocaine economy, 47, 163;
   beginnings of, 67–71; capital and materials, 71–75; coca paste, 75–79; distribution and marketing in, 79–84; effects
   of, 48, 50, 163–64; kitchens and cooks,
   84–86; methods of fighting legal system, 147–48; solutions to, 167–74;
   structure and division of labor, 86–93.
   See also Politics and cocaine; Social effects of cocaine economy

About the Author

Edmundo Morales, a native of Peru, has since 1987 been project director with Narcotic and Drug Research, Inc., in New York City. For one year before that he was a research scientist with the New York State Division of Substance Abuse Services. He is a freelance photographer and his photographs have appeared in *National Geographic,* as well as other publications. He is a frequent speaker both nationally and internationally on cocaine production and trafficking, and his major interest continues to be economic development and social change in Latin America.